In Defence of Objectivity
Other Essays

This volume addresses the interlocking themes of realism, objectivity, existentialism and (eco-socialist) politics, based on critical realism. However, it moves beyond the purely scientific orientation of earlier contributions to this philosophy, to further develop the themes.

The title essay defends objectivity in science, everyday knowledge and ethics, and examines both subjective idealism and existentialist critiques of objectivity. The other essays examine some of the same themes but from different angles, keeping the politics of the issues at the forefront.

Andrew Collier is a member of the Department of Philosophy at the University of Southampton. His previous publications addressed socialist thought or critical realism or both: most recently *Being and Worth* extends realism to ethics and *Christianity and Marxism* aims to reconcile these two world views.

Routledge Studies in Critical Realism
Edited by Margaret Archer, Roy Bhaskar, Andrew Collier, Tony Lawson and Alan Norrie

Critical realism is one of the most influential new developments in the philosophy of science and in the social sciences, providing a powerful alternative to positivism and postmodernism. This series will explore the critical realist position in philosophy and across the social sciences.

Also published by Routledge:

Critical Realism: Interventions
Edited by Margaret Archer, Roy Bhaskar, Andrew Collier, Tony Lawson and Alan Norrie

In Defence of Objectivity and Other Essays

On realism, existentialism and politics

Andrew Collier

Routledge
Taylor & Francis Group

LONDON AND NEW YORK

First published 2003
by Routledge
2 Park Square, Milton Park, Abingdon, Oxon, OX14 4RN

Simultaneously published in the USA and Canada
by Routledge
270 Madison Ave, New York NY 10016

Routledge is an imprint of the Taylor & Francis Group

Transferred to Digital Printing 2007

© 2003 Andrew Collier

Typeset in Garamond 3 by
Florence Production Ltd, Stoodleigh, Devon

British Library Cataloguing in Publication Data
A catalogue record for this book is available from the British Library

Library of Congress Cataloging in Publication Data
A catalog record for this book has been requested

ISBN10: 0–415–30599–3 (hbk)
ISBN10: 0–415–43669–9 (pbk)

ISBN13: 978–0–415–30599–0 (hbk)
ISBN13: 978–0–415–43669–4 (pbk)

Contents

Existentialist images of objectivity

Instances of objectivity

Acknowledgements

I am grateful to the journal *Radical Philosophy* for permission to reprint the first three essays in this book, which were originally published as follows:

'The Inorganic Body and the Ambiguity of Freedom', in *Radical Philosophy*, no. 57, 1991, pp. 3–9.
'Value, Rationality and the Environment', in *Radical Philosophy*, no. 66, 1994, pp. 3–9.
'Unhewn Demonstrations', in *Radical Philosophy*, no. 81, 1997, pp. 22–26.

Parts of the section on ethics in the final essay are expansions of a paper read at a Centre for Critical Realism seminar at the University of London Union on 19 November 1999 and transcribed as 'Objective Values and the Relativity of Morals' in *Alethia*, vol. 3, no. 1, 2000, pp. 6–9.

Abbreviations

BE   Berdyaev, Nicholas, *The Beginning and the End*, Geoffrey Bles, London, 1952.

BN   Sartre, Jean-Paul, *Being and Nothingness*, Methuen, London, 1957.

BT   Heidegger, Martin, *Being and Time*, Blackwell, Oxford, 1967.

BW   Heidegger, Martin, *Basic Writings*, Routledge, London, 1978.

CUP   Kierkegaard, Soren, *Concluding Unscientific Postscript*, Princeton University Press, Princeton, 1941.

CW   Blake, William, *Complete Writings*, Oxford University Press, London, 1966.

DR   Berdyaev, Nicholas, *Dream and Reality: An Essay in Autobiography*, Geoffrey Bles, London, 1950.

FU   Bultmann, Rudolf, *Faith and Understanding*, SCM, London, 1969.

ORC   Berdyaev, Nicholas, *The Origin of Russian Communism*, Geoffrey Bles, London, 1937.

PA   Kierkegaard, Soren, *The Present Age*, Oxford University Press, London, 1940.

PR   Macmurray, John, *Persons in Relation*, Faber & Faber, London, 1961.

TE   Sartre, Jean-Paul, *The Transcendence of the Ego*, Noonday, New York, 1957.

VE   Laing, R.D., *The Voice of Experience,* Penguin, Harmondsworth, 1983.

Introduction

These essays develop and defend critical realism, but they also engage critically with existentialist philosophy in a number of ways. My motive for writing about existentialism is partly autobiographical – I was an existentialist as a student and read voraciously every available text by Kierkegaard, Berdyaev, Macmurray, R.D. Laing, Heidegger, Bultmann and Sartre; I have also taught at least Sartre in most of my thirty years as a lecturer; but I have hitherto written rather little about these thinkers, apart from Laing. Although my position is critical of existentialism, I am not dismissive of it: what I think can be learnt from the existentialists emerges most clearly in the essay on Heidegger and the section on Macmurray in Part II.

In Part I, the first three essays have already been published in *Radical Philosophy*; they set the scene for the environmentalism that is one of the themes of this book. The fourth and fifth are essays in the history of ideas, and the next four are all on existentialist thinkers, although in three cases mainly from a political (socialist) standpoint. Part II, entitled 'In Defence of Objectivity', also engages with a number of existentialist thinkers in its middle section.

The essays have been written separately over a period of twelve years, during which time my ideas have been developing. This has left two marks on the book: some of the essays may contradict others on specific points, although there is a general coherence of outlook and themes; and there is some repetition, particularly on Heidegger and on the Greek and Hebrew origins of European thought, which, however, I have let stand as the material is in each case necessary to its context. In one instance this involves actual repetition of a few sentences almost verbatim.

The essays complement my book *Being and Worth*, and the last two sections argue in a different way for the same conclusions as that book.

Now I would like to say something about the interweaving of three themes in these essays: the themes of objectivity, existentialism and eco-left politics.

Existentialism and the defence of objectivity may seem to fit badly together. Does not existentialism start with Kierkegaard's statement 'truth is subjectivity' and is not Berdyaev's whole work a polemic for subjectivity against objectivity? Does not Sartre write against the 'spirit of seriousness' which asserts the primacy of the object? Some of these points will be answered in detail in the essays, and indeed there will be kinds of existentialist subjectivism which I will argue against. But in the first place it should be said in advance that existentialist subjectivism is never subjective idealism in the theory of knowledge. It has nothing to do either with Berkeley or with Feyerabend, and while it sometimes (for example in Berdyaev) has something to do with Kant, it is a version of neo-Kantianism that agrees with Kant that there are things-in-themselves (noumena) but disagrees with him in claiming that we can have access to them in certain kinds of experience. Second, several existentialists are very object-centred in their account of human existence. For Heidegger and Macmurray in particular, we know a person only when we know the objects in terms of which they define themselves, and in another way this is true of Sartre as well. This object-centredness is connected with the chief way in which the existentialists break with the Enlightenment, and it is the right sort of break with the Enlightenment, not the wrong sort as exemplified by postmodernism. It is a rejection of the whole 'way of ideas' that Descartes and Locke introduced into European philosophy: the notion that sees ideas not so much as our access to things, but as a layer between us and the things themselves, which easily comes to be seen as a barrier. As against this, it must be asserted that we experience things, we do not experience experiences (of things). Existentialists are able to recognise this because for them the focus of our access to things is in practice rather than in contemplation. And for the existentialists, the primacy of practice is a way of not becoming entrapped in the 'way of ideas', not, as for pragmatism, a response to being entrapped in the 'way of ideas'.

Existentialism, in other words, shows how to avoid those errors of the Enlightenment that led European thought away from objectivity into anthropocentrism. This does not mean that all the values of the Enlightenment should be rejected. The Enlightenment aims of the emancipation and unity of humankind through unfettered reason should be taken up and carried further. I devote an essay here to retrieving the Enlightenment heritage without its atomism or its epistemic fallacy – that is, the tendency to reduce questions about what is to questions about what can be known.

The political themes of these essays tie up with existentialism in a more straightforward way. All existentialists have been anti-capitalist, whether in an unambiguously socialist way (Macmurray, Berdyaev, Sartre) or in a partly reactionary one (Kierkegaard, Heidegger). Even the reactionary way can be seen as 'the right rebellion in the wrong cause', as I shall argue. Less obvious is the relation of existentialism to eco-politics; eco-politics became an issue later than when the existentialists were writing. But they prefigure ecological concerns, precisely because their object-centredness implies that humankind can be emancipated only if the environment is emancipated too. It is, perhaps, for this reason that, despite the individualism with which they are often credited (or discredited), no existentialist has been tempted by liberalism in politics or economics. Perhaps too this should warn us that words like 'individualism' have too many meanings to be usable in political discourse.

Finally, a word about the relation of these essays to other work in the critical realist movement. Critical realism started in the philosophy of science with Roy Bhaskar's book *A Realist Theory of Science*. But it could equally well have been developed from an analysis of everyday knowledge and is incomplete without an account of the latter. However, there are important differences between science and everyday knowledge – for instance, that in science thought precedes knowledge which arises from testing thought; whereas in everyday knowledge, knowledge derived from practice, and often not spelt out discursively, precedes and is presupposed by thought, as Macmurray points out.

It is a consequence of the scientific starting point of most critical realism that critical realism is often seen as a representational kind of realism rather than a direct one. In some of the present essays I argue for a direct realism in the theory of knowledge, in the sense that experience is a transitive verb, not a noun: we experience things, we do not 'have experiences' (although it is possible, at a high level of abstraction, to abstract from the things we experience and talk about ideas). This is, I think, the most distinctive feature of the present book within critical realist literature.

Of the first essay in the book, I can say that the seeds of everything that I have written since are contained in it, just as the seeds of everything I had written before were contained in my first published essay 'Truth and Practice'. It draws on both Heidegger and Spinoza to defend an ontocentric view of human existence (as against an anthropocentric view of being), and uses this to criticise liberal conceptions of freedom and defend a conception of freedom that is more congenial to eco-socialism.

In the second essay, I make some general applications of Marx's version of the use-value/exchange-value distinction, and argue that what economies need in order to become environmentally sensitive is a use-value-driven kind of rationality instead of the exchange-value-driven one that is characteristic of capitalism.

In the third essay, I broach the question of everyday practice-derived knowledge and its relation to scientific knowledge, and defend the view that scientific knowledge is unfinished and unusable for practice until it has issued in a 'concrete analysis of a concrete conjuncture'.

The fourth essay is my critical defence of the Enlightenment heritage, already referred to.

In the fifth essay I engage with Nietzsche, a philosopher who has been deeply influential on twentieth-century existentialism and who is often, though inaccurately, classified as an existentialist. From a partial acceptance of his critique of slave morality, I defend both the Judaeo-Christian tradition and modern socialism from the charge of being slave rebellions in morals.

In this connection I also broach the question of 'Athens and Jerusalem', the Greek and Hebrew roots of European culture, which will come up again with reference to Heidegger and Macmurray.

In the sixth essay, I attempt a critical appropriation of Heidegger to the critique of capitalism by arguing that the evils that he attributes to technology can more consistently (both with history and with his own best work) be attributed to commercialism.

In the seventh essay I raise the issue of what Sartre means by authenticity in *Being and Nothingness* – a concept that is, in a sense, the absent centre of that book since, while he discusses its opposite – bad faith – at length and with great insight, he only gestures towards authenticity.

In the eighth essay I briefly look at Sartre's relation to Marxism, arguing that the shift of ground needed from *Being and Nothingness* to encompass Marxism is different from the shift of ground that Sartre actually made.

In the last and longest of the shorter essays, I discuss the politics of the Russian Christian existentialist Nicholas Berdyaev. Later, in the long essay, I criticise the metaphysical core of Berdyaev's thought, but he is one of those philosophers whose wisdom about practical matters on the periphery of his thought – on politics, morality and religion – is greater than his standing as a metaphysician. In particular, Berdyaev's espousal of socialism as a way of organizing the economy while rejecting 'integral socialism' – that is, socialism conceived as a complete attitude to life in all its aspects – has always seemed to me exemplary.

In Part II, which gives the book its title, I try to make clear what the ideal of objectivity is and is not, and to defend it against epistemic and moral subjectivism, and against the criticisms of the existentialists (who are not, however, epistemic subjectivists and not in every case moral subjectivists either).

Part I

1   The inorganic body and the ambiguity of freedom*

> The universality of man manifests itself in practice in that universality which makes the whole of nature his *inorganic body*, (1) as a direct means of life and (2) as the matter, the object and the tool of his life activity. Nature is man's *inorganic body*, that is to say nature in so far as it is not the human body. Man *lives* from nature, i.e. nature is his *body*, and he must maintain a continuing dialogue with it if he is not to die. To say that man's physical and mental life is linked to nature simply means that nature is linked to itself, for man is a part of nature.
>
> (Marx, *Early Writings*, p. 328)

If we place this notion in the foreground of Marx's early thought, that thought immediately becomes more fertile and suggestive of important insights than if it is interpreted with 'humanism' in the foreground. We can once again learn from it, even if we entirely accept Althusser's critique of that humanism.

No doubt the 'inorganic body' thesis was not in the foreground for Marx himself. It is an aside, and he never works out its implications. But there are a few things to be said about what is implied by Marx, in context, before I go on to draw on other sources to elaborate this notion.

In the first place, it means that we interact causally with the rest of nature, and are dependent for our existence, and for *what* we are, on that interaction. That we are dependent on nature is obvious enough, but Marx is drawing attention to the special nature of that dependence: on the one hand, that it is not dependence on something *external*, in that we are constituted as the beings that we are by the way we live out that dependence; and on the other hand, that we 'live from' nature *actively*, and thereby transform it, so that nature (at least on this planet) is always shot through with human history. For instance, the New Forest, in which I walk at every opportunity, and in which I conceived many of the ideas in this paper, is no gift of nature – except in the sense that everything is; it is a monument to the Norman

* 'The Inorganic Body and the Ambiguity of Freedom', in *Radical Philosophy*, no. 57, 1991, pp. 3–9.

tyrants' lust for blood-sports. Taking these two points together, our transformation of nature is also the transformation of ourselves, and the primary
way in which we, as a species, do transform ourselves. (This last clause is
another way of formulating the materialist conception of history.)

While this position is as far as could be from any 'Luddite' hostility to
our cumulative productive powers, it does highlight their peculiarly destructive *potential* – a potential actualised by capitalism. It does so in three ways:

(1) if the world 'outside' us is essential to our being, then the propertyless-
ness of the proletarians is not a deprivation of something 'external', leaving
them in free possession of their essential being. Our advantage over the
animals is transformed into a disadvantage, in that our inorganic body is
taken away from us, as Marx comments on the page following the above
quote. When he goes on to say that 'estranged labour' estranges us from our
own body, from nature outside us, from our spiritual essence and from our
human essence, he may be read as saying the same thing in four ways, rather
than four things.[1]

(2) While we must *use* nature if we are to live, the idea that it is our inorganic
body suggests that this is essentially more like the way that we 'use' our
own bodies-actual,[2] our own limbs and organs, than it is like any means–
end relationship. Treating nature as a means to individual existence is
specially mentioned as part of estrangement, in the passage just referred to
(*Early Writings*, p. 329). This distinction between two kinds of use of nature
is taken up later in Marx's manuscripts (*Early Writings*, pp. 352–53): under
communism 'nature has lost its mere *utility* in the sense that its use has
become *human* use' – while 'the dealer in minerals sees only the commercial
value, and not the beauty and peculiar nature of the minerals; he lacks a
mineralogical sense'.

(3) The manuscript on money (pp. 375–79) can be read as spelling out two
ways of living our inorganic bodies. The omnipotence of money in the market economy does not, of course, make us any less dependent on our interaction with nature, but it takes away the personal, situated, integrated manner
of exercising our physical, emotional and intellectual powers upon the natural and human world about us, each from their historical and geographical
perspective, with its specific links to others and to one's habitat. Instead, our
powers are subsumed under a single, infinitely divisible and amassable power,
indifferent to its agent and the content of its exercise: money:

> He who can buy courage is brave, even if he is a coward. Money is not
> exchanged for a particular quality, a particular thing, or for any partic-
> ular one of the essential powers of man, but for the whole objective world
> of man and nature.
>
> (ibid., p. 379)

In the next two sections, I shall try to work out a fuller conception of what is involved in thinking of ourselves as bodies-cosmic rather than bodies-actual, drawing on the work of Heidegger and of Spinoza; in the final section, I shall spell out the political implications.

Body as world: the Heideggerian approach

One way of following up the ideas that our material being is more exten-sive than the space enclosed in our skins is Heidegger's concept of Being-in-the-world as definitive of human existence, and his analysis of what it means to be in the world. Heidegger makes a sharp break with all accounts which locate our minds inside our bodies; we *are* our worlds – and whatever it is that gives unity to ourselves (and Heidegger has two alternative accounts of what it is, according to whether we exist authentically or inauthentically), it is *not* that either body or mind is a substance.

One way in to this idea is by contrasting a metaphor of Heidegger's with two of Popper's: Popper refers to bucket-theories of the mind, and search-light-theories. Heidegger's metaphor is of a clearing in the forest. Only by virtue of the clearing are the trees visible, yet the clearing is nothing except the trees and the relations between them. We are not *in* the clearing, we *are* the clearing. And this indicates that this conception is no longer on the Cartesian ground of a theory of 'mind' at all; rather, we have extended the boundaries we assign to our bodily beings; we have exosomatic parts.

Our way of being is 'Being-in-the-world', but the 'in' does not signify spatial containment; we *are* our worlds. It is not difficult to find everyday examples to make such an extended definition of our bodies plausible; we habitually regard our clothes, tools we are using, bicycles we are riding etc. as part of us. We feel the road with the wheels of the bike; the motorist refers to 'my wing' getting scratched; the victim of a burglary feels violated, even if nothing has been taken and no damage done. Also, distant objects may be existentially closer to us than spatially nearer ones; the scene I look at through the window is more 'part of me' than the window; this is a sort of 'intentional inexistence',[3] i.e. the scene exists in me in that I comport myself towards it; what I am being cannot be understood without reference to the scene, yet it can be fairly well understood without reference to the window, or indeed to my toenails or my appendix.

The unifying force which organises my world is my practical concern. 'My world' in this sense is unique to me; 'your world' is organised around your particular concerns, which may be quite different. Yet 'my world' is not composed of appearances, of 'things for me'. It is the real bicycle, the real road, the real sunlight that go to make up my world – and of course they may go to make up your world too. We need to clarify this point, since Heidegger's phenomenological heritage places him under suspicion of subjec-tivism, and at times perhaps the suspicion is well founded. But he certainly thinks that he has shown the error of idealism, in that attempts to prove the existence of the 'external world', so far from being necessary and unsuccessful, are unnecessary and foolish, since the 'external world' is not external – and not because it is 'in our minds', but because we are 'out there' in it.

However, granted (as Heidegger grants) that we are always partly in error about the world, do not 'our worlds' come apart from 'the world' as practically determined appearances of it? May not the way things are organised in my world be unlike the way they are organised in *the* world?

Here a few remarks are in order about all those existentialist polemics against 'objectivity'. In the empiricist culture of the Anglophone world, we are accustomed to understand 'objectivity' and 'subjectivity' primarily in an epistemic sense. When we hear objectivity decried, we assume that some sort of epistemological subjectivism such as Feyerabend's is being defended. I think that there is in fact scarcely a trace of such subjectivism in the works of Kierkegaard or Macmurray or Heidegger or Sartre. Rather, 'subjectivity' is taken in an ontological sense, as referring to (epistemically quite objective) realities such as emotions, beliefs, encounters, reasonings etc. Thus when R.D. Laing, for instance, under the influence of these thinkers, says 'objectively there are no intentions',[4] he is not saying that intentions are in the mind of the beholder, but that intentions belong to the world of 'subjectivity' that a certain kind of beholder – one in the grip of a reductive metaphysics – might miss. At this point it might look as if their anti-objectivism is no more than anti-reductivism. It does include anti-reductivism, but I think it also includes something less acceptable; resistance to a certain kind of knowledge, contrasted with the knowledge inherent in practice, and variously labelled 'objective', 'contemplative' or 'intellectual'. I shall not consider here whether there really is some dirty bathwater to be thrown out under these headings, but I do think that the existentialists have thrown out a baby in the process. That baby is *counter-phenomenal knowledge*. For the capacity of knowledge to contradict appearances is essential if knowledge is to have a *liberating* function: it is, as Marx and Freud have indicated, precisely because appearances can be false and enslaving that knowledge can be liberating.

Before discussing this matter with reference to Heidegger, it may help to clarify what is at issue if I quote and comment briefly on a passage from Macmurray's book *Interpreting the Universe*:

> That immediate knowledge of the world which is the effortless result of living in it and working with it and struggling against it has a much higher claim to be taken as the type of human knowledge than anything science either has or can make possible. For the scientist takes this immediate knowledge of the world for granted and bases himself squarely upon it by his continuous appeal to facts. His particular business is simply to interpret it, to express it in such a way that we understand what we already knew in a quite different and immediate fashion.
>
> (pp. 16–17)

The first two sentences, rightly interpreted, may be accepted; but it does not follow that the scientist 'simply' interprets pre-scientific knowledge; he or she may produce radically new knowledge, and therewith new practices; and this new knowledge may contradict the 'immediate' knowledge which preceded and gave rise to it.

In Heidegger's account of phenomenology in the introduction to *Being and Time* he distinguishes 'phenomenon' in the sense used in his version of phenomenology – 'that which shows itself' – from 'appearance' in senses in which there is a contrast with something that does not appear, i.e. firstly, from *semblance*; secondly from senses this word has in contexts where something that does not appear 'announces itself' in something that does (e.g. disease in a symptom); and thirdly from the Kantian sense, in which an appearance is of something that can never appear (the thing-in-itself). Yet 'phenomenon' does contrast with something:

> 'Behind' the phenomena of phenomenology there is essentially nothing else; on the other hand, what is to become a phenomenon can be hidden. And just because the phenomena are proximally and for the most part *not* given, there is a need for phenomenology. Covered-up-ness is the counter-concept to 'phenomenon'.
>
> (p. 60)

Phenomenology then has the task of making things show themselves, which were previously covered up. That looks like counter-phenomenal knowledge – the sort of knowledge that can liberate. Yet Heidegger is reluctant to allow *science* its appearance/reality distinction. Indeed, he tends to *invert* the relation between scientific and pre-scientific knowledge, treating scientific results, despite – or perhaps because of – the fact that they are the product of a laborious work of uncovering, as merely subjective, and as tending to cover up Being, to which the knowledge implicit in everyday practice gives us genuine access.

Heidegger, in fact, sees his analysis of Being-in-the-world as, despite analysing what is closest to us, running against the difficulty that our world has been pre-interpreted to us in terms of something that is existentially further from us – i.e. the world of mechanically related objects. In the world that is closest to us – the work-world which we inhabit prior to theoretical explanations – the hammer is encountered as that with which we fix the shutter, which in turn is that with which we make a dwelling weatherproof. This world as a whole is composed of the gear that we use, and structured by its reference back to some projected being of ours. Only when the head flies off the hammer are we forced to consider it as an entity with properties other than being hammerable with. So begins objective inquiry. And we habitually misread our lived world as like the objective reality thus discovered. As so often with Heidegger, a good and a bad point are mixed up together here. There really is a Cartesian or empiricist picture of the world as composed of mutually external and independent entities, related only mechanically. Consider such ideas as: sense data, the knowledge of other minds as inferential, action as intentional muscular contraction, etc. I believe that Heidegger gives a more thorough and less obscurantist antidote to these errors than, for example, Wittgenstein. But one does not have to be an empiricist or a Cartesian in order to recognise that objective inquiry may yield deeper knowledge of what is there than that vouchsafed by the knowledge implicit in unexamined practice; that it may contradict, correct and explain that knowledge. Indeed, since the function of objective inquiry according to Heidegger (and also to Macmurray) is to put to rights some upset which has occurred in the everyday work-world, it must be able to produce more adequate ideas than were already implicit in the understanding of that work-world, or fail in its function.

At this point, I begin the transition from Heidegger to Spinoza: implicit in *our* worlds, the worlds of our practical concern, is a set of assumptions about how *the* world is causally ordered; the elements of my body-cosmic are linked by relations of causality and dependence which I must assume in my concernful dealings with them. I may be mistaken about these relations, and the project of rectifying these mistakes is always implicit in those dealings. All this is often at an entirely unreflective level: I grasp a branch to swing across a muddy stream on; I give it a little tug before trusting my weight to it, and then swing across.

If then we distinguish the practical relations of 'in order to' and 'towards which' which organise my world as analysed by Heidegger, and the objective relations of causality and dependence which organise *the* world, we may say that the former presuppose and imply the latter, and tend to rectify themselves towards correspondence with the latter.

World as body: the Spinozan approach

When Spinoza writes about the human body, what does he mean? The idea that he means the body-actual has been held up to question, though finally defended, by Odegard, who considers the possibility that only the brain might be intended, since it is supposedly this that corresponds under the attribute of extension to the mind under the attribute of thought.[5]

However, the following points require consideration: (1) Complex bodies, for Spinoza, are relatively stable equilibriating systems composed of less complex bodies. Our bodies-actual are of course such bodies, as are some of their parts. But our bodies-actual also interact causally in relatively stable ways with the world about them, and can go on being so only so long as they do. The world in its causal interaction with my body-actual, insofar as that interaction forms a relatively stable system, constitutes a composite body: my body-cosmic, considered in its objective being. To a degree, however tiny, I interact with the whole of nature. There are degrees of causal closeness of entities with me, as they are more or less essential to the equilibrium that makes me be. But 'closeness' here does not mean proximity to my body-actual – it means necessity to my body-cosmic thus constituted; I am not my body-actual, I am my body-cosmic. I may very well do without my tooth or my tonsils, but not without a roof over my head, or the sun to warm my planet.[6] (2) Granted that my body-cosmic is a composite body in Spinoza's terms, is it *that* composite body to which, under the attribute of extension, there corresponds my mind under the attribute of thought? Well, I certainly think more about my house and my bike and my path to work across Southampton Common than I do about my spleen or my lymph nodes. The usual reading of Spinoza is that the mind is the idea of the body-actual, entities outside of which are known only indirectly, through their effects on the body-actual; to greater clarity and knowledge there corresponds, under the attribute of extension, greater causal interaction between body-actual and world. On this reading, Spinoza is very hard to defend; my idea of the kitchen stove is not an idea of the effects of the kitchen stove on my body-actual. But suppose the mind corresponds to the body-cosmic; it is quite defensible to say that perception is the proprioception of the body-cosmic. The clarity of that perception is certainly bound up with the degree and kind of causal interaction between the elements of the body-cosmic (and not just between the body-actual and other parts of the body-cosmic, but also between different 'external' parts of the body-cosmic, e.g. television and aerial, thermometer and atmosphere, etc.).

Insofar as we interact causally with all of nature, but to different degrees, the body-cosmic has no clear boundaries – it has the form of a cross, not a circle; but it can be said to be extended to the degree that direct and indirect causal interaction between the body-actual and its world is increased – not just *any* interaction, however, but that which serves to maintain the equilibrium of the system. The more we are sensitive to the world around us, and the more we control it, the more it is part of us. Now let us consider the implications of this for Spinoza's derivation of morality from the drive for self-advantage, the *conatus*. (3) When we hear self-advantage praised, and assessed only insofar as it is rational or irrational, we are apt to think in terms of that most irrational of human vices, 'economic rationality'. We think 'self-advantage' means increasing one's bank balance, and that it is done rationally if it is done with the minimum productive labour. But of course for Spinoza rationality is not the means to self-advantage, rationality is the definition of self-advantage. Thus at *Ethics* IV, p. 26:

> What we strive for from reason is nothing but understanding; nor does the Mind, insofar as it uses reason, judge anything useful to itself except what leads to understanding.

> (Curley, p. 559)

Under the attribute of extension, this is matched by p. 38:

> Whatever so disposes the human Body that it can be affected in a great
> many ways, or renders it capable of affecting external Bodies in a
> great many ways, is useful to man; the more it renders the Body capable
> of being affected in a great many ways, or of affecting other bodies,
> the more useful it is; on the other hand, what renders the Body less
> capable of these things is harmful.
>
> (Curley, p. 568)

Since this increase in understanding, equivalent to the extending of the body-
cosmic, is aided not hindered by the same development in others, rational self-
advantage is for Spinoza inherently a co-operative, not a competitive good.

But on the basis of my interpretation of the human body as the body-
cosmic, we can take Spinoza's system even further away from egoism than
he wants to go. For I take it that Spinoza recognises the existence of part-
conatuses (conatuses of parts of the body-actual) which, while they may be
harmful if they override the conatus of the individual as a whole, have legitimate claims to balanced satisfaction within that conatus. But if the conatus
of the individual as a whole is not that of the body-actual but of the body-
cosmic, then conatuses of parts of the body-cosmic, whether or not within
the body-actual, can enter their claims. Not only those of other people
(for other people are included in anyone's body-cosmic), but of animate
and inanimate parts of our civic and natural environment. So that, to the
extent that my active and passive powers are increased, *the world* becomes to
a greater degree *my world* – more of the universe becomes more closely incorporated into my body-cosmic; correspondingly, its claims on me are greater.
The limit of this process – approached from an infinite distance – would
be the identity of the personal conatus with that 'providence' which preserves
the whole universe in its complex interaction (or to translate into Freudian,
of libido with Eros).

As an interpretation of Spinoza, this would be far-fetched, for he is undeniably anthropocentric:

> Apart from men [*homines*] we know no singular thing in nature whose
> Mind we can enjoy, and which we can join to ourselves in friendship, or
> some kind of association. And so, whatever there is in nature apart from
> men, the principle of seeking our own advantage does not demand that
> we preserve it. Instead, it teaches us to preserve or destroy it according
> to its use, or to adapt it to our use in any way whatsoever.
>
> (IV Appendix XXVI, Curley, p. 592)

(So far as his theory of perception is concerned, on the other hand, it cries
out to be interpreted in terms of the body-cosmic – as do the more 'mystical'
parts of his thought, if they are to be given any rational sense.)

Nevertheless, I don't think the idea of a conatus of the body-cosmic is an implausible view of human motivation. Our attitude to death bears witness to that. We fear the dissolution of our world, rather than of our body-actual. We care what happens to its components after our death: 'to part is to die a little'; that is not a metaphor, but a literal truth: to die is to part altogether. On the positive side, not only love but such things as intellectual curiosity and the love of beauty fit better with this hypothesis than with many others. And I don't think there is anything utopian about it. It is not, for instance, a claim that we are 'naturally altruistic', but that the ontology on which the egoism/altruism dichotomy makes sense is a false one.

Freedom in the common world

This conception of our place in the world has several consequences for our thinking about freedom. In the first place, it commits us to an 'in gear' rather than an 'out of gear' conception of freedom: a freedom that pre-supposes that we interact causally with the world, and a freedom which is enhanced as our active and passive powers in that interaction are increased – i.e. our powers on the one hand to affect the world in various ways, and on the other, to be affected by more of the world in more ways. Causal laws, while they constrain what we can do, also enable us to do what we can do; we could not act at all where they did not operate. More or less freedom, then, means more or less effective interaction in one's world – not disengagement from the causal processes operative in the 'outside world', as in Cynic, Stoic and Kantian ethics, and in Cartesian, Kantian and Sartrean metaphysics. Since causal laws are a function of the structures that exist in the world, and there are alternative possible structures in some aspects of the world (e.g. economic structures), more or less freedom may also involve more or less congenial structures. But more freedom never involves escaping causal interaction, freewheeling.

Secondly, the conception of the inorganic body, and hence the non-privacy of the body, undermines the idea that individual rights or freedoms could have some 'natural' basis in an ontological boundary between individuals. There is no such boundary. The world is a common world. Even the body-actual of each is part of the body-cosmic of all, and thus others may in principle have some legitimate claim over it. If there are boundaries within which an individual may do as they please, these are socially demarked boundaries. They may differ in different societies, and, though one way of drawing them may be better or worse than another, none are 'natural' or 'unnatural'.

So, thirdly, all freedom, as freedom to interact with and hence change the world – which is never just 'my' world but everyone's world – all freedom, I say, is to a greater or lesser degree *freedom to transform the common world*. It is important to note that this is *to a greater or lesser degree*. Certainly, I am more causally enmeshed with some parts of the world than with others.

My body-actual has a unique part in determining how close a part of me (i.e. of my body-cosmic) any given entity is. But it does not follow that nothing outside my body-actual can be closer to me than my body-actual. I am far more causally dependent for my existence and essence on some beings outside of my body-actual – including some other people – than I am on some parts of my body-actual. The causal/existential 'closeness' or 'distance' of various things is relevant when we come to decide where to draw the lines between people's freedoms, which powers to prioritise, and so on. Nevertheless, that which we are apportioning in such line-drawing is always power to transform the common world. And so it is always pertinent to ask whether a given exercise of freedom – a given transformation of the common world – is with or without common consent.

Now let us consider a few commonplace examples: the question of 'passive smoking' for instance. The anti-no-smoking lobby typically uses libertarian language, as if, whatever might be said for 'no smoking' it is unambiguously a restraint on freedom, and not an increment of freedom. Another example is that I am free to walk a dog on Southampton Common, but not free to take my child for a picnic there without risk of his being frightened by dogs, or infected with toxocara from dogs' turds. Most people's assumption is that the former freedom is a straightforward freedom, the latter something else. In these cases there is a little more awareness now, in reaction against the 'libertarian' culture of Thatcher's Britain, that the freedoms from smoke and uncontrolled dogs are real cases of freedom. But it is still taken for granted that the onus is on the advocates of these freedoms to prove their case; the smokers' and dog-walkers' freedoms are treated as the obvious ones. The cards are stacked against freedoms to live in a congenial common world, and for freedoms to transform the common world without common consent. And this bias is not just a matter of custom,[7] it is backed up by liberal political philosophy, and the whole ontology of the isolated but mobile individual that underlies it.

Motor traffic is a similar, and more far-reaching, case. Restraints on motorists' freedom are deeply resented, yet nothing transforms our common urban world more (aside from wider planetary effects), and this transformation is the effect of thousands of unconnected decisions, plus the public authorities' adaptation to them. It is not a *common* decision, even in a purely aggregative sense, for each individual's decision to buy a car or use it on a given occasion is made in the absence of the alternative option (a communal transport policy) which could only be made available by a common political decision. Were the same individuals to make a common decision, and hence have the alternative before them, the result might be quite different. My case is not just that there should be no absolute freedom to transform the common world without common consent, but that there should be much more freedom to transform the common world *with* and *by* common consent.

Here I come to the ambiguity of freedom referred to in the title; many political issues concern the area of conflict between two sets of freedoms: in political terms, we may distinguish *market freedom*, which is the power money gives its possessor to transform the common world without common consent (this I call *dispersed* freedom); and *civic freedom*, i.e. the freedom to co-determine with one's fellow-citizens a common project for the common world – whether a project of conservation or of transformation. This I call *gathered* freedom. In calling market freedom dispersed, I mean in the first place that power, though inherently social, is assigned to individuals to use without regard for others affected. But there is more to it than that. Actions the effects of which loom large in the worlds of their agents and small in the common world (decorating one's house, for instance) may well be best dispersed in this sense. But here the claim to take *that particular* power out of the remit of common agreement is dependent upon the closeness to the individual of this bit of their world, its marginality to any other individual. Money-power, however, is dispersed in another sense too. It is unconnected with the particularity of the one who possesses it; it may equally well be power over their own or somebody else's house, their cup of tea or a tea plantation on the other side of the earth, time on TV or time at a private clinic. Finally, it is dispersed in that it escapes even its possessor as the market constrains their decisions and transforms the consequences of those decisions.

Hence it may be said to be dispersed in three dimensions: socially, in that social power is exercised by individual agents in separation; temporally, in that it is power to get what one wants now, but not to plan for a congenial world in which to live out one's days; and spatially, in that it is dislocated from the agents' place in the world. Gathered freedom, by contrast, is gathered socially, in that common decisions are made about the common world; spatially, in that a community exercises its common power over *its* common world, i.e. the world from its perspective, the parts of the world that are existentially/causally closest to it. And temporally in that it is exercised with consideration for the past and future of a community, not only for some instant gain.

Perhaps a simple example will clarify the contrasts between gatheredness and dispersedness in the spatial and temporal dimensions (I assume it is clear enough in the social dimension). Suppose a firm of developers buys a part of a street in order to develop it for different – more profitable, obviously – uses. The other residents object, since the character of their street will be ruined. But since the boundaries of their properties will not be transgressed by the developers, their plea is treated as unreasonable; the space in which they live is treated as dispersed into proprietary plots. As a result of this presupposition that the only freedom worth having is dispersed freedom, it is impossible for anyone settling in a neighbourhood to do so (with any degree of confidence) as part of a project of their life as a whole, since the power to transform or conserve the material character of the neighbourhood is not with them and their neighbours, but at the caprice of the market. So one's freedom to live as one chooses is short term, and in any case not freedom to live in a congenial world one has collaboratively chosen, but freedom to move about an alien world in pursuit of congenial bits.

Having sketched the ambiguity of freedom, I can perhaps make it sharper, and at the same time remove the grounds for some objections. My view that we are all, even in our bodies-actual, parts (to a greater or lesser degree) of the bodies-cosmic of all, might suggest the Sadean slogan 'everyone belongs to everyone else', which of course in the Sadean context means that everyone has the right of use and abuse over the bodies-actual of everyone else. That Sadean Republic is not viable because it squanders its most precious resource: the bodies-actual of its citizens. The freedom in Sade's republic is dispersed freedom, in just the sense that market freedom is, but extended to the world of bodily encounter, sexual and/or violent. The *gathered* exercise of our mutual ownership is something quite different: the sort of mutual care and common responsibility of all for the well-being of the body-actual of each, suggested by St Paul's 'we are members one of another'. This does commit us to what Mill described as a monstrous principle: that which 'ascribes to all mankind a vested interest in each other's moral, intellectual, and even physical perfection'.[8]

Now I would like to conclude by working out more explicitly the difference between gathered and dispersed freedom with reference to the production and use of common resources, 'political economy'. It is well known that one of the contrasts in Marx's work is that between the production of exchange-value and the production of use-value. I think that both Marxists and ecological critics of Marxism have underestimated the radical nature of the difference between the dispersed economic rationality that governs exchange-value production, and the gathered economic rationality that would govern use-value production.

For, if the goal of production is to bring into being things or states of affairs useful to people, then in the first place, not just the 'product' in the narrow sense – that which, in exchange-value production, is to be sold – has to be considered, but also every effect that the production process has – including effects on the workers' health and state of mind, the environment, and so on. Many of these 'products' will have a negative use-value. For exchange-value production, whatever is inessential to the realisation of exchange-value is left out of account, but in use-value terms, there could be no rational justification for such tunnel vision. Secondly, use-values have no common quantitative measure. *Calculation* could therefore have no place in deciding between different production projects. The community would have to decide what to produce and how without any quantifiable grounds for the decision. This does not of course mean that their decision would be arbitrary. They would have to ask themselves the question: what sort of world do we want to live in as a result of our productive activities?

The desires and self-understanding and information of the community concerned will determine the answer. That is far from arbitrary. But no sort of quantitative 'cost-benefit analysis', even if spiked with a few imponderables and restyled 'comprehensive weighing', can help.

It is curious that the apparent 'objectivity' of exchange-value calculation – which is nothing but the structurally rooted denial of the people's power to choose their conditions of life – has attracted some who believe themselves to be democrats. For instance:

> With no objective criterion by which to judge the merit of competing economic alternatives, the determinant necessarily becomes the subjective preference of those who hold power.
>
> (Nigel Swain, 'Hungary's Socialist Project in Crisis', *New Left Review* 176, 1989)

But that is not, as he suggests, undemocratic. It is one necessary condition of economic democracy. The other is that 'those who hold power' should be answerable to the people. If the people prefer to bow before an 'objective' measure, that is simply abdicating their power and responsibility – like tossing a coin. For what is measured by the objective measure is something quite other than the people's well-being. In a bureaucratic command economy at least *someone* is deciding; to make that decision process democratic is one thing; to abdicate it in favour of market forces and the sort of calculability that only makes sense under conditions of the alienation of human powers into market forces, is something different.[9]

Use-value planning then is an exercise in gathered freedom in the threefold sense (social, environmental, temporal) – a community deciding the future of its material environment. Insofar as each person is asking themselves, not 'what can I get?', but 'what sort of world do I want to live in?' and hence 'how shall we care for our inorganic body?', our self-understanding as beneficiaries of the productive process is not as *consumers*, but as *dwellers in the world as transformed by our labour.*

This in turn has consequences for the controversy about 'growth'. Marxist theory has a concept of technical progress, e.g. the shortening of necessary labour time; more specifically, in its analysis of capitalism, it has the concept of the increasing organic composition of capital; but 'growth' in the usual, consumer-oriented sense has no equivalent in Marxist science. In exchange-value terms, there can of course be no overall growth, since exchange-values express fractions of the total social labour, so that the total exchange-value produced, by definition = 1. In use-value terms, one could speak of growth unambiguously only if more of some kinds of use-value were produced without any reduction in other kinds, or any increase in negative use-values. But in practice, there is always gain and loss, and no commensurability between them. However, one specific combination of use-values may be more congenial for the people who live with them than another. The nearest we

can get to a synonym for 'growth' in a socialist economy would be something like 'making the world a more congenial home for people'[10].

Am I jettisoning exact ideas in favour of vague ones? In some cases, yes;
exact but false for vague but true ones. The concept of a *consumer*, for instance,
may be exact enough in its place: we consume bread and cheese and tea and
beer. But it is simply inapplicable to such 'products' as education, health
care and the environment. Whatever could be the product and whoever could
be the consumer of schooling, for example? There is no answer which is
not both misleading and offensive. Yet this language is in increasingly
common use, obscuring such facts as that schooling takes up a large part
of people's lives, that it can be inherently rewarding or frustrating, that it
starts when we are relatively dependent and finishes when we are relatively
independent.

This paper has been guided by the belief that differences about values are
at bottom differences about ontology – not as a technical philosophical discipline, but as the ontology implicit in everyone's 'commonsense'. That the
free market seems acceptable to so many people today indicates that freedom
is spontaneously identified with dispersed freedoms, and the lost possibilities of gathered freedom are not taken into account. That this is so indicates
the prevalence of a number of atomisms (social, temporal, spatial: the
atomisms that make dispersedness in these dimensions appear the norm)
in 'commonsense' ontology. I am proposing the foregrounding of the
notion of the inorganic body, the body-cosmic, as the alternative to those
atomisms.

Notes

1 In German: 'Sie entfremdet dem Menschen seinem eignen Leib, wie die Natur ausser
   ihm, wie sein geistiges Wesen, sein *menschliches* Wesen.' Marx and Engels, *Werke,
   Erganzungsband, Schriften bis 1844, Erster Teil*, p. 517.
2 I adopt this phrase from Mesmer Partridge's narrative in Michael Westlake's novel
   The Utopian. It refers to the body as that enclosed by one's skin. I contrast it with
   the 'body-cosmic', as I prefer to call the inorganic body, since it is not entirely
   inorganic. I hope it goes without saying that 'cosmic' is simply a way of forming an
   adjective from 'world', and has no occult meaning.
       On the 'objective/subjective' issue, I take it that the parts of a person's body-
   cosmic exist objectively and have mutual causal relations, for the most part
   independently of that person's existence; they are parts of his or her body-cosmic to
   the extent that their causal interaction with each other and his or her body-actual
   is constitutive of his or her being.
3 This is the term that Brentano adopted from Aquinas to denote the relation of the
   mind's objects to the mind. When as a student I attended Hidé Ishiguro's lectures
   on this topic, she warned us against thinking that 'inexistence' was a negative
   concept, like 'non-existence'. At the time, we all thought the warning unnecessary
   to native English speakers, but I rather think that a recent semantic shift has made
   it necessary.
4 *The Voice of Experience*, p. 28.

5 Douglas Odegard, 'The Body Identical with the Human Mind: A Problem in Spinoza's Philosophy', in Mandelbaum and Freeman (eds), *Spinoza: Essays in Interpretation*.

6 Cf. Heidegger's notion of our spatiality as 'making the farness vanish – that is, making the remoteness of something disappear, bringing it close.' *Being and Time*, p. 139. When we see something distant, by virtue of our seeing it we make our own being partly constituted by it: it becomes part of us, not by anything we do to it – it remains unchanged – but by becoming part of the world that the perceiver is.

7 The feeling that a customary freedom is more sacrosanct than a new freedom is one which should be respected. But this distinction is not the same as the one I am making. The 'obvious' (dispersed) freedoms are not always the customary ones. The motorist's freedom, for example, violates countless customary freedoms.

8 See 'On Liberty', in *Utilitarianism*, p. 222.

9 I am not making any 'existentialist' point against the objectivity of grounds for choice. We may have – and may reason about – objective grounds for choosing one 'possible world' rather than another. The point is that there will be a number of competing alternatives, each with their objective grounds, and no mathematical aids to the choice between them.

10 Pre-capitalist societies have both an immensely slower rate of technical progress, and much less tendency to insist on 'maximum efficiency' in the use of labour than capitalist ones. It is not obvious that these are disadvantages, whatever other disadvantages such societies had relative to capitalism. The obsolescence of still-working equipment, whether in production or 'consumer durables', is one form of waste attendant upon too-fast progress; redundancy of human skills is another. It might well be rational for a socialist community to take it easy where innovation is concerned. Likewise, 'overstaffing' in e.g. a hospital may make for a much higher level of friendliness and good humour and willingness to do favours, and hence of healing care, than time-and-motion-studied efficiency. One should always be suspicious of talk about 'disguised unemployment', whether this refers to the leisure of the Athenian citizen to attend the theatre and the assembly, or that of the modern worker to chat at work. Such talk pre-supposes an idea of efficiency that makes no sense unless one assumes that work is nothing but an unwanted means to an external end, and has no effects other than the production of that end.

References

Curley, Edwin (trans. and ed.), *The Collected Works of Spinoza*, vol. 1, Princeton University Press, Princeton, 1985.

Heidegger, Martin, *Being and Time*, trans J. Macquarrie and E. Robinson, Blackwell, Oxford, 1967.

Laing, R.D., *The Voice of Experience*, Penguin, Harmondsworth, 1983.

Macmurray, John, *Interpreting the Universe*, Faber & Faber, London, 1936.

Mandelbaum, M. and Freeman, E. (eds), *Spinoza: Essays in Interpretation*, Open Court, La Salle, Illinois, 1975.

Marx, K., *Early Writings*, Penguin, Harmondsworth, 1975.

Marx, K. and Engels, F., *Werke: Erganzungsband: Schriften bis 1844, Erster Teil*, Dietz Verlag, Berlin, 1968.

Mill, J.S., *Utilitarianism*, Fontana, London, 1962.

Westlake, Michael, *The Utopian*, Carcarnet, Manchester, 1989.

2   Value, rationality and the environment*

Today most people on the Left are aware that ecological damage, and the threat of ecological disaster, are among the foremost contradictions of capitalism, second only to the impoverishment of the Third World. In addition to ecology in the strict sense, the damage done to the material environment of our everyday lives proceeds, subjecting us, I believe, to an all but irresistible debasement of our personal, aesthetic and political attitudes (of which more below). For myself, I have been made acutely aware of this damage since moving to Southampton: the claustrophobia (for a non-motorist) of a city cut off on its landward side by a motorway; the new urban motorway, cutting a swathe through Swaythling and decapitating St Denys;[1] the destruction of any unity in the City Centre by hard-to-cross roads, car parks, and self-enclosed shopping malls; the University's plan (now dropped) to destroy the local haunts of wildlife at Lord's Wood by siting a second campus there; and the local press regularly bringing news of fresh instances of planning blunders, planning oversights, and 'constructive co-operation between public authorities and private enterprise'.

It is commonly thought that there are few resources in the classics of what I still insist on calling 'scientific socialism', for explaining and remedying these harms. Some socialists, like many non-socialist Greens, have adopted instead a hostility to science, to reason, and to the dominion of humankind over nature. In this paper, I want to suggest that one of Marx's central distinctions – between use-value and exchange-value – can provide the basis of the theory we need. However, I do not limit myself to the use of these terms in Marxist political economy. To the production of use-value and of exchange-value, there correspond two kinds of practical rationality, which have their effects in morality, aesthetics, politics and science, as well as economics.

The production of use-value and of exchange-value

Marx's *Capital* opens with a distinction between use-value and exchange-value. Every commodity is a use-value, i.e. 'a thing which through its

* 'Value, Rationality and the Environment', in *Radical Philosophy*, no. 66, 1994, pp. 3–9.

qualities satisfies human needs of whatever kind' (p. 125). Use-values are 'the material content of wealth, whatever its social form may be' (ibid.). But not every use-value is a commodity, since not all have exchange-value:

> This is the case whenever its utility to man is not mediated through labour. Air, virgin soil, natural meadows, unplanted forests, etc. fall into this category. A thing can be useful, and a product of human labour, without being a commodity. He who satisfies his own need with the product of his own labour admittedly creates use-values, but not commodities.
>
> (p. 131)

Marx notes that:

> In English writers of the seventeenth century we still often find the word 'worth' used for use-value and 'value' for exchange-value. This is quite in accordance with the spirit of a language that likes to use a Teutonic word for the actual thing, and a Romance word for its reflection.
>
> (p. 126n)

I am tempted to adopt this terminology, but resist on the grounds that one can talk about concrete objects as 'use-values', but hardly as 'worths'. And Marx himself uses 'use-values' to refer to the things themselves, rather than the values they possess by virtue of their relations. They are use-values by virtue of their objective properties, though the discovery of these properties is 'the work of history' (p. 125).[2]

Use-value, Marx tells us, is the qualitative aspect of value. This does not of course mean that use-values cannot be counted or measured. But no quantity of one use-value can be equated with a quantity of another. The question 'how many bottles of beer are worth the same as one Bible?' is senseless in use-value terms: the uses are different, hence their worth incommensurable. Yet in the market they will be exchangeable in a definite ratio, mediated by money. In this connection, Marx quotes Aristotle more than once: to the effect that different goods are naturally incommensurable, and made artificially commensurable by money (*Capital*, p. 151; *Ethics*, pp. 120–21); that 'twofold is the use of every object. . . . The one is peculiar to the object as such, the other is not, as a sandal which may be worn and is also exchangeable' (quoted *Capital*, p. 179n); and he refers to the two distinct arts generated, for Aristotle, by this use-value/exchange-value distinction: economics, the art of procuring use-values for the household or the state; and chrematistics, the art of money-making (*Capital*, pp. 253–54). It would be in the interests of accuracy if the economics departments in most universities were re-styled 'Departments of Chrematistics'.

On one matter, however, Marx criticises Aristotle: for Aristotle, the commensurability necessary for exchange is made possible simply by the artificial device, money. For Marx, this is only surface appearance. At bottom, exchange-value expresses 'value', the quantity of labour-time embodied in the product. There are contexts in which I would want to defend Marx's theory of value but, for the purposes of this paper, I don't need to. Just as Marx often gives examples in which a price expressed in money stands in for labour-based value in the point the example illustrates, so we can bracket off the price/value distinction for the present purpose, and hence avoid having to take sides in the controversies between neo-Marxist and paleo-Marxist economics.

Granted this, I may describe my project as distinguishing the type of rationality inherent in economics from that inherent in chrematistics, and in each case generalising the type beyond this particular use; and suggesting that it is the chrematistic type of rationality which is the principal enemy of the environment. But of course the two types of rationality do not hang in a historical vacuum. In both pre-capitalist and socialist societies as defined by Marx, the motive of production is the procurement of use-values. In capitalism it is the augmentation of capital, which for each individual capital means maximising monetary returns and minimising monetary costs. There are two aspects to Marx's case against capitalism: that it is exploitative, and that it is irrational *in terms of use-value rationality*. The environmental destructiveness of modern capitalism is an instance of this irrationality in use-value terms – an irrationality inherent in what is usually called 'economic rationality' (i.e. chrematistic rationality).

Chrematistic rationality

In the passage on chrematistics, Aristotle mentions that, while use-value production has a limit (enough bread to feed the city is enough bread to feed the city), 'riches, such as chrematistics strives for, are unlimited' (*Politics*, quoted *Capital*, p. 253n). It is surely no accident that the conception of happiness upheld by Aristotle is a conception of something which has certain attainable (with good fortune) necessary conditions, which conjointly are sufficient conditions – and if happy, what else can we need? By contrast, an influential group of moral theories indigenous to capitalist societies regards human desires as infinite. A finite being with infinite desires looks like an evolutionary mistake. Why is such a conception so widespread?

The structure of the reasoning is the same in (for example) utilitarian ethics and in chrematistics. Its features are (1) mathematical calculability, which in both cases requires qualitatively different goods to he translated into commensurable quantities; in order to achieve this, (2) a value external to the object valued is postulated; a value which is of the same kind in the case of all valued objects, and which confers their value on them. In the case of chrematistics, money; in the case of utilitarianism, pleasure-and-the-avoidance-of-pain (the hyphens are necessary, otherwise it becomes obvious that two qualitatively different values are already involved). This externality, by at once atomising and homogenising all goods, both licenses quantifiability and abolishes limits. It also imposes a sort of tunnel vision on the practitioners of this kind of practical reasoning. This is obvious in the case of chrematistics. Only those effects of the production process which are saleable are the product; only what costs or brings in money goes into the calculation. Hence environmental effects, among other things, are invisible.

What of utilitarianism? Let us first consider its symbiosis with chrematistics in modern times. Jevons' *The Theory of Political Economy* makes use of utilitarianism in a way which looks like collapsing the two into a single system, while making ultimately untenable distinctions between the two. He includes pleasure and pain among the fundamental concepts of his science, and appeals to the authority of Bentham for treating a 'moral science' (i.e. a social science) mathematically. Yet in one way he is on firmer ground than Bentham – or would be if he recognised the limits circumscribing his own discipline. For he recognises that pleasure and pain cannot in themselves be measured; but 'their effects' can – i.e. quantitative transactions in a money economy. And indeed these can be measured. But Jevons shows no inkling of the values lost to view by this approach and not because of any pretence to value-neutrality. Jevonian chrematistics is both frankly prescriptive and pretty close to claiming a priori necessity:

> Although . . . the beneficent results of Free Trade are great and unquestionable, they could hardly be proved to exist a posteriori; they are to be believed because deductive reasoning from premises of almost certain truth leads us confidently to expect such results, and there is nothing in experience which in the least conflicts with our expectations.
>
> (p. 88)

One and a half million Irish people's lives sacrificed on the altar of Free Trade through the export of grain during the potato famine might have been thought a posteriori evidence enough against it, but a dogma claiming to be 'almost as self-evident as are the elements of Euclid' (p. 90) can hardly lay itself open to such refutation.

Jevons feels the need to point out the relation of economics to ethics (pp. 91–93), and adopts the following position: he accepts the modification of utilitarian ethics in terms of 'higher' pleasures which ought to take precedence over lower ones, and in its name rejects Paley's dictum 'pleasures differ in nothing but in continuance and intensity' (p. 92). How then can his purely quantitative discipline operate with pleasure and pain, rather than simply with money values? His answer is:

> It is the lowest rank of feelings which we here treat. The calculus of utility aims at supplying the ordinary wants of man at the least cost of labour. Each labourer, in the absence of other motives, is supposed to

devote his energy to the accumulation of wealth. A higher calculus of moral right and wrong would indeed be needed to show how he may best employ that wealth for the good of others as well as himself.

(p. 93)

Now if pleasures and pains are measured by their effects on the market, and higher pleasures *actually do* override lower ones in some cases, then the economist cannot abstract from them in this way. What the passage quoted suggests is that Jevons believes that 'higher' considerations may come into play in deciding what to do with one's money once acquired, while economic (i.e. chrematistic) rationality reigns untroubled by such considerations in the matter of acquiring the money. But in truth, by the time the economic process is over and the moral one begins, the damage has been done. For the manner in which certain values are prevented from having economic effects is not that intimated in the last quote. It is rather that all effects of the production process that are extrinsic to the goal of augmenting capital are systematically excluded from consideration, however intensely pleasurable or painful they may be. Almost by definition, environmental values fall into this class.

In fact Jevons quickly forgets the limit he has placed on economics, and reverts to treating it as equivalent to the utilitarian moral calculus. Thus on p. 101: 'Pleasure and pain are undoubtedly the ultimate objects of the calculus of economics'; 'By a *commodity* we shall understand any object, substance, action or service, which can afford pleasure or ward off pain' such as birdsong, prayer, or scratching an itchy spot, no doubt – but when have these had measurable economic effects?

So far I have been looking at equivocations about the scope of economics: in one breath it claims the whole of practical reason for its kingdom, in the next it exiles higher values to the kingdom of ethics, which it has just annexed.

The next question is whether utilitarian ethics, despite its structural identity to this kind of economic reasoning, can restore the exiled values and so offset the tunnel vision of production for exchange. I take it that the attempt to do so is precisely what is called 'cost benefit analysis'.

As an undergraduate, I attended a lecture on cost benefit analysis by a professor of economics. When costing an urban motorway, he told us, purely economic calculation would ignore the deaths it would cause. Cost benefit analysis rectifies this. But to do so it must solve the difficult problem of pricing the heads of the victims. The first suggestion is to measure the pain of death by its hypothetical economic effect: we ask how much money the victims would have given for the privilege of staying alive. Since the answer would be *all they've got*, millionaires and paupers figure quite differently in such calculations, and the siting of the end of urban motorways downtown is strongly indicated. An alternative would be to ask about the value to the economy as a whole of the deceased, calculating this as: how much more would this person have contributed to the economy than taken out of it, had they lived an average lifespan? This, we were told, had the consequence that the average woman over 25 had a price on her head – her death would count as a benefit, not a cost. These proposals were presented, of course, with some irony. But the implication was: nevertheless, if we are not satisfied with the monetary goals of pure economics, we must travel this road. Lives must be priced. And the truth is that there is no way of doing so that is not either offensive or arbitrary.

Of course, a decision must be taken one way or the other in such cases. And it is always possible to dress up one's decision as an assigning of numerical values. To say 'the value of lives is one thousand pounds each' is simply to say 'we won't let road accidents put us off unless the purely economic considerations are fairly evenly balanced'; to value them at ten million each is to say 'stuff your motorway'. Just as, if after a night's revelling a fellow reveller greets you with 'where on a scale of one to ten is your headache this morning?', and you answer 'eight', you are not reporting a reading taken from an inner algometer, just saying, 'lousy, though I've had worse'.

This is all leading to the point that, while utilitarian ethics may pick up some values that chrematistics ignores, it is still afflicted with tunnel vision. It picks up some non-money values, but only insofar as they can be forced into the same straitjacket as money values: mathematical calculability and the externality of value to object. This disqualifies utilitarianism from giving an adequate account of environmental ethics, since:

1   Where some value is in its inherent nature *not* amenable to mathematical calculations, the attempt to mathematise it will almost always devalue it relative to those values that can be quantified by some agreed procedure.
2   By treating values as external to the objects valued, the manner in which environmental goods are valued is falsified and trivialised.

Let us take the example of Southampton University's plans for a second campus in Lord's Wood. The case against is best expressed as: Southampton is a better place to live with one University campus and one large wooded area inhabited by badgers, deer etc., than it would be with two campuses and no such area.[3] That, I think, would gain fairly wide assent. But once the economic advantages of university expansion are pitted against the pleasure of walkers, the balance will look different. This is partly because professional calculators will always wave their hands at the vagueness of the latter; partly because, when the value of Lord's Wood is reduced to experiences in the heads of walkers, it is trivialised. When people enjoy Lord's Wood they are not enjoying experiences in their heads, they are enjoying Lord's Wood.

Aristotle's point about limited and unlimited aims is also apposite here. Universities and woodlands are both use-values, but universities are also economic agencies, and as such may have unlimited ambitions. Woodlands close to a city inevitably fall under the covetous eyes of powerful economic agencies, and have little power of resistance. Chrematistic rationality has powerful agents as its bearers – use-value rationality not so. Those powerful agents may acquire indefinitely large returns for their use of these woodlands; but a walk in the woods is just a walk in the woods. Bad rationality drives out good.

So far I have been considering chrematistic rationality as (a) a feature of the economic structure of capitalism – the *necessary* form of rationality for agents within that structure; (b) the reflection of this in economic theory, which identifies chrematistic rationality with practical rationality as such; (c) the generalisation of this view in utilitarian ethics. Two other features of chrematistic rationality are relevant to environmental ethics.

In the first place, it is embodied in the material environment which capitalism has built for us, and so comes to structure our lives willy nilly. It becomes the 'objective spirit' of our age, and so to a degree constrains our moral as well as our economic practices. Our urban habitat is moulded by an obsession with economical use of time and space to produce an end product: a convenient interior to an individual housing unit. The end-benefit is isolated from its environment and history: to enjoy it, one has to forget its context in time and space. Behind double-locked doors, there is peace, clean electricity and high speed gas; venture outside and a judge just might regard you as an accomplice of your attacker. Thus modern housing areas invert the metaphor of the whited sepulchre; inside, clean and neat and perhaps even comfortable; outside – ugliness, dirt, decay. Bourgeois housing developments express the same ethos in their privileged way: the ugly convenience of a house built round its garage, and the false rurality of developments that make the real countryside recede further and further. Transport policy expresses and enforces the same values. The self-fulfilling assumption is that travel is necessarily unpleasant, a mere interval, to be kept as short as possible, between being behind one set of locked doors and another.[4] The public sphere is drained of value; it becomes the sphere of unpleasant means to ends outside itself, just like wage-labour. Its violence is then re-enacted for pleasure, with the obsessiveness of a recurring nightmare, in the safety of the private sphere. (Almost any other historical society, I think, would have been shocked speechless by the proportion of their time that the average modern spends watching images of slaughter, or reading accounts of slaughter, for pleasure.)

Finally, there is the effect of chrematistic rationality on science. Its homology with certain theories in the natural sciences has often been noted, but this does not impress me. The natural sciences are too well tested to be impugned by such considerations, and their results are morally and politically neutral. At most it may be that areas of reality which do not have the form of quantifiability and externality of relations have been under-theorised. But the way in which the sciences are applied is a different matter. That they are often applied in environmentally reckless ways is well known. I am among those who hold this to be the fault, not of science, but of its commercial or military use. But one feature of that use is interesting also from the point of view of the philosophy of science. The results of sciences are taken up and used *in an abstract state*. Instead of the sequence 'abstract science → concrete science (i.e. scientific knowledge applied to a concrete reality) → practically applied science', we get the abridged sequence 'abstract science → practically applied science'. Thus the knowledge that, say, irradiation inhibits certain processes of decay in organic matter gets lifted straight out of midstream science and applied commercially in food storage, in disregard to the way this mechanism interacts with others in the process of providing food for people. This is so taken for granted that it is not noticed what is happening: the product of science is being put to use before science has finished its work on it. Since this unfinished product has a market value, its inherently unfinished state is missed. Before a product of science can be a (positive) *use-value*, on the other hand, it must be the concrete knowledge *of* some concrete use-value.[5]

Use-value rationality

The inadequacies of chrematistic rationality will already have suggested by contrast the nature of use-value rationality. Different use-values must be recognised as qualitatively different and hence not interchangeable in any fixed proportion. Calculation disappears from moral reasoning, and is put in its place – unable to deliver a final decision – in economic reasoning. There is no way to measure the harm of deceiving someone against the harm of hurting them (when these are alternatives), the good of forgiving wrongs against the good of punishing them, the preservation of cultural values against the equalisation of wealth, the need of a city for water against the need of a village not to be evacuated to make way for a reservoir. We can and must make these choices, of course, and the act of doing so may be thought to assign an ordinal number to alternatives, but not a cardinal number.

In evaluating a plan for a motorway, one would take into account not only costs saved, but lives lost, and such imponderables as the feeling of being boxed in by motorways surrounding one's town. The uselessness of cost benefit analysis for such a decision has recently been acknowledged with the invention of 'comprehensive weighing'. Now the sort of reasoning involved in use-value production *could* be called comprehensive weighing. However, what has in fact appropriated that title looks to me more like cost benefit analysis with a few unassimilated qualitative blobs in it. It is still conceived as something one could be *trained* in, rather as cost benefit analysts are trained. But that sort of training is just what makes people *bad* at qualitative decision making. Inevitably, they will look on the qualitative blobs as intractable problems, obstacles to a 'rational' solution. If they start taking the blobs seriously, all the quantitative work done on the rest of the values is wasted.

Secondly, while things may be desired as a *means* to realising their exchange-value, the use-value of anything is (in one sense) a real quality of it, intrinsic to it. But of course only those properties make something a use-value which make it useful to people. An onion is a use-value because it can be eaten, a landscape because it can be seen. One can sum up these two aspects of use-values by saying that they are inherent in our world. Not in *us*, as are the utilitarian values of pleasure and pain. We enjoy a meal, not a series of sensations in our taste buds; we love beauty, not the eye of the beholder; we relieve suffering, not the pity of the reliever; we seek knowledge, not the having of that knowledge by any individual. Or at least, the state of mind that values itself rather than its object, though it may occur, is rare and derivative, not to say corrupt and self-defeating. And goods or harms may occur without any consciousness of them; a person is harmed if they are deceived, even if no *further* harm ensues, and they never become aware of the deception.

Use-values are inherent in *our* world. By saying this I bracket off – though I do not necessarily deny – possible goods that are independent of the existence of people. It is we who value use-values, but that does not mean that we value them for some end external to them. Just as an individual's desires may not be self-referential (e.g. one may desire certain things to occur after one's death), so we may value things which will produce no further benefit to any human, other than that the valued things exist. Consider here the question of our treatment of animals. Kant thought we should not be cruel to animals because such cruelty corrupts its agents. But if cruelty corrupts, that can only be because it is taking pleasure in something evil. And that is evil, not because it corrupts us, which would be circular, but because it hurts the animal. Conversely the only good desired in an act of kindness to an animal may be the animal's well-being.

These examples of use-value rationality have so far been mainly 'moral' rather than 'economic', even though use-value rationality, like chrematistic rationality, gets its name from its economic infrastructure. But the division between the moral and the economic, whose blurring I criticised in the chrematistic case, really is a fuzzy and relative one in the case of use-value rationality, because of its deliverance from tunnel vision. To this I now turn.

In reasoning about which use-values to produce, it is not only *saleable* effects of the production-process that meet the eye. Indeed the distinction between the product of a labour-process and its side-effects drops out as soon as we consider that process in use-value terms: To evaluate a labour-process for its productivity of use-value is to evaluate it in all its concreteness and for all its effects. Effects of the process on the worker and the environment, effects of the goods turned out on the well-being and life-style of the community, and so on. The cost of every car produced includes its contribution to the boredom of the machinists, the slicing up of the countryside, the garagisation of cities, the pollution of the air, the likelihood of squirrels getting run over and cyclists getting broken arms, and so on.

Economic choice is no longer between commodities, but between worlds. No kind of mathematical calculation can be of any assistance here. We have to ask: given the material resources that are to hand, what sort of world can we make that will be found good by the people of this civilisation?[6] What does the good life for us require by way of houses, streets, parks, shops, workplaces, urban space, rural landscapes, public buildings, ways of getting from one place to another, food, drink, household utensils, clothes, rivers, seas, air, plants, animals, sounds, smells?

I deliberately include in this list some things which might now be thought of as objects of consumption, some not. This kind of question cannot be asked so long as we think of our relation to the product as *consumption*. We consume, literally, food and drink. Metaphorically, we may be said to consume fuel, paper, etc. We do *not* consume transport, health care, education, forests, music, the spirit of place. Our relation to each of these things is quite different. If we want to sum them up, and arrive at a generalised notion of ourselves that may take the place in a socialist economy that 'the consumer' does under capitalism, the concept would have to be something like 'dweller in the world as transformed by our work'.

Of course, as in any kind of practical reasoning, various values, positive and negative, are brought to mind and a decision made with regard to them. But instead of assigning them arbitrary numerical values and doing sums, possible combinations of the values are considered as complex modifications of the world. Each value contributes to the whole, not as an addition to or subtraction from a sum, but as a qualitatively distinct aspect of a concrete whole. The decision before us is then which of these possible wholes to bring about.

Of course much (though not all) work will still be undertaken to meet needs for consumable material objects. These will be one set of values, to be reckoned alongside the cost in terms of concrete work required (and not *abstract labour*, see *Capital*, pp. 131ff.), the resources thereby depleted, and any environmental effects. Certain kinds of environmental effect will enter the reasoning in a fairly obvious way; I mean the *big* environmental issues on which the future of our planet depends. But many subtler environmental issues are brought into play by the notion that we are choosing not which commodities to produce, but what world. We have to start asking ourselves questions like: does walking along that road, or travelling in that bus, make us feel peaceful or anxious and aggressive; how would the situation of our town be changed by the building (or demolition) of a box of motorways round it; what relations of houses to streets make for good neighbourliness; what sounds do we want to hear during our everyday activities – and many more, even subtler questions. This is not as easy as doing sums, and we shall inevitably fall far short of success in it. But having seen the successes of modern capitalism in these matters, who's worried about failure?

Finally, we come to the question how science is to be applied in accordance with use-value rationality. Abstraction is necessary in science if testing, measurement and exactness are to be possible; but the aim of science is not to explain what goes on in the laboratory, where these abstractions are realised. It is to explain what goes on in the concrete conjunctures of the world, and 'the concrete is concrete because it is the union of many determinations' (Marx). To this end, the various abstract strands have to be plaited together again – not indeed in one vast system of nature,[7] but in many little systems. To apply science at all, it must be applied in open systems, and this means systems in which many processes, known through many sciences, work together. To apply science *with adequate knowledge of that to which it is applied*, one must apply concrete conjunctural science, the union of many abstractions. In demanding full-circle science, not the wresting of abstract midstream results, use-value rationality may well take up some romantic or holistic themes, without becoming anti-science or in any way interfering with the sciences' freedom of inquiry. It simply requires science to finish its job, just as we would not let a builder leave slates loose and live wires exposed, or a chef serve us half-cooked chicken. The proposal is moderate enough in conception, but revolutionary in application, given the present organisation and use of the sciences. It means that new knowledge of the laws of nature will not by itself give rise to new technologies. All-round knowledge of a concrete domain of nature is first required. Of course, our knowledge will always be finite, so damaging applications will always be possible; but many would be avoided.

Postscript

Virtually any socialist argument will be countered by reference to the recent history of the Soviet Union and Eastern Europe. On the issue in hand, I think some pre-emptive response is needed.[8] For use-value production means planned production as opposed to the market, and those economies that were planned have now opted for the market.

First let me say that, while I rejoice in the achievement of democratic liberties by those countries, I see nothing to rejoice about in their new economic order or situation. But I grant that the failures of their economies under planning were real enough too. Here I am going to stick my neck out and say that the chief failing was the opposite of what it is often said to be. It was not their failure to catch up with the west. Given where they started from, their record in this respect, until the 1980s, was much better than it could have been under other economic systems. But partly because they were so geared to this aim, and partly because of the over-centralisation which was itself largely a consequence of this aim, their record in human terms was not so good, and in ecological terms was disastrous.

In explaining this bad record, the foremost cause was that they were (and are) nation-states. As such they compete on the world market as producers and also compete militarily as powers. This subjects them to the same compulsion to accumulate that capitalist firms experience. If we want a scientific term for these economies, variously called 'existing socialism', 'state socialism' and 'state capitalism', it would be *national socialism*, had not that phrase already been taken by an altogether more sinister movement.

In relation to global ecological problems – acid rain, deforestation, greenhouse effect, etc. – such competing agencies, be they corporations or states, will always be more or less subject to tunnel vision. Only for global agencies does this supreme use-value without exchange-value – the habitability of the planet Earth – come into view as an over-riding concern. At the same time, centralised planning in nation-states is too remote from the knowledge by acquaintance of local problems by local communities, to be sensitive to the use-values at stake in such planning. Nation-states, east or west, are in some ways too large, in some ways too small, to plan use-value production effectively. Having made this two-edged criticism, I am perhaps obliged to make specific suggestions, even at the risk of appearing utopian (a fault which I regard as very grave – but here my sketch is only meant to indicate the general direction of desirable change).

Most positive planning needs to he done by small, democratic command economies (which does not preclude market relations at the corner shop and jobbing builder level). How small? Well, a city can hardly be divided into several separate economies, and some cities comprise some millions of people. But ideally, a state of one million people is too large. On the other hand some planning needs to be legislated and policed on a worldwide scale, including much negative planning (e.g. prohibiting atmospheric pollution or the destruction of rain forests), and inter-state trade and investment needs to he controlled in the interests of global equalisation and the prevention of market-compelled productivity-drives. For in use-value terms the drive for unlimited growth would appear not as a sign of a healthy economy, but as a cancer on the body politic.

Notes

1   Districts of Southampton on the west bank at the River Itchen.
2   The concept of use-value is almost exactly equivalent to that of the ready-to-hand (*zuhanden*) in Heidegger's *Being and Time*.
3   For simplicity of example, I am leaving out other aspects of this real issue. It is my opinion that taking them all into account would on balance strengthen the case against a second campus on Lord's Wood. (Since writing this particular plan has been shelved.)
4   On this attitude to space, let me quote C.S. Lewis, writing on the advantages of growing up in a no-car family:

> The truest and most horrible claim for modern transport is that it 'annihilates space'. It does. It annihilates one of the most glorious gifts we have been given. It is a vile inflation which lowers the value of distance, so that a modern boy travels a hundred miles with less sense of liberation and pilgrimage and adventure than his grandfather got from travelling ten. Of course if a man hates space

and wants it to be annihilated, that is another matter. Why not creep into his coffin at once? There is little enough space there.

(*Surprised by Joy*, p. 127)

5 The special role of general practitioners in medicine also illustrates the need for concreteness in applied science.

6 These questions need the qualifications 'for the people of this civilisation', 'for us', and so on, so as to avoid turning into utopian questions about the best society absolutely. The somewhat holistic way of asking questions, which use-value rationality cannot shirk, puts it at risk of a kind of utopianism, exemplified frighteningly by Trotsky's remarks on future environmental planning:

> The imperceptible, ant-like piling up of quarters and streets, brick by brick, from generation to generation, will give way to titanic constructions of city-villages, with map and compass in hand.
>
> (*Literature and Revolution*, p. 249)

This loathsome vision (and I speak as an admirer of Trotsky on many matters) exemplifies the metaphysical attitude behind utopianism: the desire for an environment which, instead of incarnating our regional histories, in each case unique, springs fully formed from the mind of a calculator – expressing an unhistorical conception of humankind as a mass of worldless individuals. Trotsky assures us that 'Most likely, thickets and forests and grouse and tigers will remain, but only where man commands them to remain' (p. 252). But if people were infected by this titanic vision, we can be sure that they would have no time for merely 'natural' tigers, and would prefer to decorate the world with geometric shapes, 'compass in hand'. I would hope that this rootless notion of originality, being no more than an aesthetic effect of chrematistic rationality, would disappear from a use-value-rational world, to be replaced by a preference for the almost imperceptible transformation of deeply assimilated traditions. If so, the danger inherent in 'holistic' planning would be avoided. It would be holistic not in the sense that totally new wholes would be planned, but that it would be contrived that the integration of the newly produced elements into the pre-existing whole should form a preferable whole.

7 Cf. Engels' remarks in the Old Preface to *Anti-Dühring* about the dialectical nature of Greek thought, the necessity for science to pass through an undialectical phase in modern times, and the consequent need for dialectic to restore its concreteness:

> Among the Greeks – just because they were not yet advanced enough to dissect, analyse nature – nature is still viewed as a whole, in general. The universal connection of natural phenomena is not proved in regard to particulars; to the Greeks it is the result of direct contemplation. Herein lies the inadequacy of Greek philosophy, an account of which it had to yield later to other modes of outlook on the world. But herein also lies its superiority over all its subsequent metaphysical opponents.
>
> (*Dialectics of Nature*, pp. 45–46)

Engels is fully aware of the practical necessity of such scientific attention to the interconnectedness of natural laws in concrete particulars:

> Let us not, however, flatter ourselves overmuch on account of our human victories over nature. For each such victory nature takes its revenge on us. . . .

> The people who, in Mesopotamia, Greece, Asia Minor and elsewhere, destroyed the forests to obtain cultivable land, never dreamed that by removing along with the forests the collecting centres and reservoirs of moisture they were laying the basis for the present forlorn state of those countries. . . . Thus at every step we are reminded that we by no means rule over nature like a conqueror over a foreign people, like someone standing outside nature – but that we, with flesh, blood and brain, belong to nature, and exist in its midst, and that all our mastery of it consists in the fact that we have the advantage over all other creatures of being able to learn its laws and apply them correctly.
>
> (ibid., p. 180)

8   Though it is my opinion that recent events in Eastern Europe, while they have altered the polemical situation, do not in themselves require us to make any revisions in socialist thinking. The events there in Stalin's time *did* necessitate rethinking; but to suddenly embark on such rethinking now smacks of time-serving. To give a historical analogy: it is as if someone became disillusioned with the ideals of 1789, not because of the Jacobin terror or the corruption of the *Directoire* or the aggressions of the Empire, but because Napoleon lost the battle of Waterloo.

Of course, other developments may require socialists to rethink, and some do – notably ecological ones.

References

Aristotle, *The Nicomachean Ethics of Aristotle*, ed. and trans. Sir David Ross, Oxford University Press, London, 1954.

Engels, F., *Dialectics of Nature*, Progress Publishers, Moscow, 1934.

Heidegger, M., *Being and Time*, trans J. Macquarrie and E. Robinson, Blackwell, Oxford, 1967.

Jevons, W.S., *The Theory of Political Economy*, Penguin, Harmondsworth, 1970.

Lewis, C.S., *Surprised by Joy*, Fount Paperbacks, 1977.

Marx, K., *Capital*, vol. 1, Penguin, Harmondsworth, 1976.

Trotsky, L.D., *Literature and Revolution*, University of Michigan Press, Ann Arbor, 1960.

3   Unhewn demonstrations*

Compell the Reasoner to Demonstrate with unhewn
   Demonstrations.
Let the Indefinite be explored, and let every Man be Judged
By his own Works. Let all Indefinites be thrown into
   Demonstrations,
To be pounded to dust & melted in the Furnaces of Affliction.
He who would do good to another must do it in Minute
   Particulars:
General Good is the plea of the scoundrel, hypocrite & flatterer.
For Art & Science cannot exist but in minutely organized
   Particulars
And not in generalizing Demonstrations of the Rational Power.
                              William Blake, 'Jerusalem'[1]

This article is intended as a contribution to critical realist philosophy, not
a criticism of it, but my starting point is a paradox about the critical realist
corpus, and my conclusion a rather surprising practical consequence of it.
Indeed the conclusion involves incorporating into a scientific realist position
some views which are normally associated with romantic or Green critiques
of science, though there is nothing essentially antiscientific about them.[2]

The motivation of critical realist work has mainly been the rectification
of method in the human sciences. Roy Bhaskar in particular is explicit about
his desire that critical realism shall do this underlabouring not only for the
work of science but for the work of human emancipation. This could hardly
be claimed if critical realism limited itself to theorizing the natural sciences,
and indeed it has been in the human sciences that critical realism has had
most impact. Yet the central and most fundamental argument of critical
realism has been an argument from the possibility and necessity of experiment in science – and there are no experiments in the human sciences.

The central argument to which I refer goes as follows. In experiments, we
make nature do what it would otherwise not have done. We do so in order

* 'Unhewn Demonstrations', in *Radical Philosophy*, no. 81, 1997, pp. 22–26.

to find out how nature produces the effects that it does spontaneously, when we are not making experiments. How can such experiments yield such knowledge, rather than just the knowledge of what happens in the experiments themselves? And why is it necessary to force nature in this way, rather than just observe what nature would do without our interference?

Bhaskar's answer, which forms the basis of critical realism, is that an experiment isolates one mechanism of nature from the others. Under normal (non-experimental) conditions, the course of events is co-determined by a number of mechanisms working together. By preventing some of these mechanisms from working, or keeping their operation constant, or measuring and discounting their operation, an experiment isolates *one* mechanism, and shows what it is. We may assume that when no experiment is going on, the same mechanism works, but in conjunction with others.

An experiment, in other words, abstracts from certain mechanisms to identify others. It does not just do so in thought, but makes the abstraction real. It gives rise therefore to abstract laws – laws which would predict how something behaves *other things being equal*, but do not predict how anything will behave in the real world where other things never are equal. Other things are only equal when we artificially make them equal – and that is just what an experiment is. Experiments give rise to what may be called the abstract sciences, since they are each about one set of laws which we have discovered by abstraction. They are not about particular entities of one sort or another. Physics is not specially about the physical world; chemistry is equally about the physical world. Chemistry is not about 'chemicals' in the sense that the chemical industry produces chemicals. It is about the chemical aspect of the whole physical world, including living organisms, for instance.

Bhaskar's argument confirms and explains the importance of experiments for the abstract sciences, but it also shows that the laws defining those sciences are not actualized; nothing is more fundamental to the physical sciences than the law of inertia, which states that bodies tend to remain at rest or in uniform motion in a given direction. But nothing in the universe has ever remained at rest or in uniform motion in a given direction. This is no skin off the physicists' noses though, for although a cricket ball does not exemplify inertia, we need the law of inertia alongside the law of gravity and the laws governing air resistance in order to explain its flight.

Now some natural sciences – for instance geography, meteorology, medicine – are about particular entities. They may be called the concrete sciences. When making the distinction between abstract and concrete sciences, Husserl says that abstract sciences 'are *nomological* in so far as their unifying principle, as well as their essential aim of research, is a law', whereas in concrete sciences 'one connects all the truths whose content relates to one and the same object, or to one and the same empirical genus'. He tells us that 'the abstract or nomological sciences are the genuine, basic sciences, from whose theoretical stock the concrete sciences must derive all that theoretical element by which they are made sciences'.[3]

It is only by getting the relation between the abstract and the concrete sciences right that we will be able to understand the position of the human sciences. The abstract sciences – for example, physics and chemistry – are self-standing in the sense that they can justify themselves experimentally, and so don't need to rely on the concrete sciences in which they are applied in order to vindicate their claims. But there are no such self-standing abstract sciences in the human world. Instead, there are abstract parts of sciences whose whole connection with reality is at the concrete level.

Husserl's reference to the 'genuine' sciences as abstract reflects (surprisingly for him) what might be called common sense in a positivistic culture; but another apparently contradictory idea goes along with this as part of positivistic common sense: that only the concrete is real. It is quite widely taken for granted that only the abstract sciences are real sciences, but that only the concrete world really exists. We are then at a loss to explain how the abstract sciences map onto the concrete world. Critical realism denies both poles of this contradiction. The mechanisms corresponding to the laws of the abstract sciences are also real, hence:

	Domain of real	*Domain of actual*	*Domain of empirical*
Mechanisms	/		
Events	/	/	
Experiences	/	/	/

Note that this diagram[4] is *not* saying that mechanisms are somehow more real than events or experiences, as is sometimes alleged, but just that they are also real.

But the concrete sciences are real sciences too, or at any rate they are an essential part of the body of knowledge outside of which the abstract sciences would make no sense. For while the concrete sciences can certainly draw on the knowledge yielded by the abstract sciences, they can also do quite a few things that the abstract sciences can't, and without which things being done all science would lose its point.

In the first place, they have in their practical dealings with their objects a source of knowledge independent of the abstract sciences. Second, they can carry out a depth analysis of concrete beings, which abstract sciences cannot. And third, they can draw practical conclusions from their knowledge. I shall return to these points with reference to the human sciences.

Let me illustrate this with reference to a practical discipline, which, while it would not normally be described as a science, can be more or less scientifically done, and which brings out many of the strengths and weaknesses of the concrete sciences. I refer to the teaching of singing, particularly operatic singing.[5]

I have said that concrete sciences have two sources of knowledge: what they borrow from the abstract sciences and what they pick up from practical experience. They also have two tasks which abstract sciences cannot undertake, namely depth analysis and practical conclusions. They are tied to the practice in which they are applied in a way that the abstract sciences are not, since the latter have their own internal practice in experiment. I have elsewhere called practical concrete sciences 'epistemoids'. Some are quite science-like in their rigour and explanatory power; others, like the one chosen here, are much more problematic. But this is a matter of degree, not of kind.

First of all, a singing teacher is or has been a singer herself. She knows what it feels like. Here is some knowledge 'in a practical state', as Althusser would say, which however she must put into words if she is to teach it. I am not denying that some non-verbal communication may take place (for instance, feeling each other's bodies to see what happens when some specific vocal or respiratory instruction is carried out), but the teaching would not get far without the medium of language. But 'putting it into words' is a genuine problem in communicating practical knowledge of this sort. It is often done by asking the pupil to imagine him- or herself doing something that he or she could not literally do. For instance: 'pretend your voice is coming out of the back of your head'; 'sing from the top of your head and make the sound come down your nose'; or 'draw the sound in'. Taken literally, of course, these instructions would be nonsense. But they succeed in telling the singer how to make it feel, and hence what to do.

However, some instructions sound plausible enough to be quite easily taken as literally true, as descriptions of what can take place in the singer's body, though a physiologist could show that they are not. For instance: 'use your sinuses' (i.e. make your sinuses contribute to the sound by their vibrations). Now apparently the vibration of the sinuses cannot appreciably contribute to the sound. However, if the singer sings in such a way that she can feel her sinuses vibrating, she will be singing in the right way. Sometimes the description of how it feels is the opposite of what is physiologically the case. Thus a singer may be advised to 'make more space' when singing high notes. But the action which feels like making more space actually makes less space in the singer's throat. This does not vitiate the instruction as a direction in teaching, since it is understood and the required effect produced. Nevertheless the physiologist should not be entirely ignored by the singing teacher. His or her findings do make certain judgements possible about good and bad practice, since it can be discovered physiologically that certain singing techniques do harm to the vocal cords, and so on. Sometimes such information could have been discovered or guessed at by a good singing teacher on the basis of experience, but not necessarily. Physiology can correct singing practices in ways that phenomenology can't – yet it would be absurd to think that it could replace the phenomenological knowledge that the singing teacher has. One could never become a singer or a singing teacher by studying the physiology of the vocal organs.

Similar considerations apply in psychoanalysis, whose raw data are entirely phenomenological, but some of whose abstract parts sound like speculations about neurology and sexology. Those biological sciences do not vitiate the practice of psychoanalysis when they appear to conflict with it, yet it would be obscurantist for psychoanalysis to ignore their findings. Freud's meta-psychology has a status much like the metaphorical physiology used by singing teachers. At certain points – for instance, the concept of instinct or drive which Freud explicitly says is a border-concept between the biological and the psychological sciences – a tie up with physiology is useful and helps to confirm or refute the metapsychological theory. At others it would be inappropriate to take the psychoanalytical idea physiologically and look for confirmation or refutation from physiology, since the concept may be justi-fied phenomenologicaly, by its clarification of the patient's self-experience. For instance, Freud's distinctions between clitoral and vaginal orgasms are neither contradicted by claims that all female orgasms are clitorally trig-gered, nor confirmed by claims about the G-spot. They are based on the self-experience of some women whom Freud analysed, and make no physio-logical claims.

These points may I think be generalized to the concrete sciences: their concepts are arrived at partly by retroduction from practical experience – 'how can we explain the way things seem in practice' – and partly borrowed from the abstract sciences. By these two methods, the concrete sciences build up a stock of abstract concepts of their own. But here we may note a difference between concrete natural sciences like meteorology and concrete human sciences like psychoanalysis. The borrowings are in both cases from natural sciences since only in these are there experiments. This means that the human sciences can learn far less by borrowing than can the natural concrete sciences. This is what justifies my claim that the human sciences relate to their objects only through their concrete parts, even though there is some input from experimental sciences into human sciences and disciplines (e.g. from physiology into psychoanalysis or singing teaching). That input is alien in a way that the input from physics to meteorology is not.

Now let us look at what one of the only three people with a credible claim to have founded a human science says about the relation of abstract-ness to concreteness. I refer to Marx (the other two are Freud and Chomsky). Marx sometimes stresses the importance of abstraction in science, while at other times he seems to be quite rude about it. Most of his followers follow either one or the other of these examples, but it may be that the two can be reconciled. First, it should be mentioned that for Marx as for Kant, the term 'abstraction' often refers to a process rather than a result:

abstracting from something, bracketing it off. Now to one rude remark about abstraction:

> First of all, an abstraction is made from a fact; then it is declared that the fact is based on the abstraction. That is how to proceed if you want to appear German, profound and speculative.
>
> For example: Fact: The cat eats the mouse.
>
> Reflection: Cat = nature, Mouse = nature;
>
> consumption of mouse by cat = self-consumption of nature.
>
> Philosophical presentation of the fact: the devouring of the mouse by the cat is based upon the self-consumption of nature.[6]

Here the point about abstraction is that it gives you poorer, less specific information than more concrete language. Wherever abstraction means no more than leaving something out in order to arrive at a more general and less specific description, Marx is rude about it.

But in the section on the method of political economy in the 1857 introduction, he says that to start with 'the real and concrete', e.g. the population, commits the same error, since 'The population is an abstraction if I leave out, for example, the classes of which it is composed'.[7] We should therefore start by moving analytically towards 'ever thinner abstractions', and then put them together again in their due order to arrive at 'the population again, but this time not as the chaotic conception of a whole, but as a rich totality of many determinations and relations'.[8] We arrive at this full conception of a concrete entity by showing the relations between its features which taken separately would be abstractions, but of which the real concrete entity is composed: 'The concrete is concrete because it is the union of many determinations, hence unity of the diverse.'[9]

Good abstraction consists in specifying the many interrelated aspects of something, and this is how a concrete science should proceed; bad abstraction consists in ignoring the specificity of something, to subsume it under some more general concept. Thus a social scientist who wanted to provide knowledge of Britain in the 1990s should analyse out the many aspects of that society and show how they are related; and not abstract from many of its specific features in order to place it in a statistical population of somewhat similar societies, and produce statistical data about them. If social science were an experimental science, it would be possible to actualize these abstractions and test them separately – for example, to test what the effect of exposure of British capital to Continental competition would be in the absence of trade unions. But it is not. Hence 'in the analysis of economic forms neither microscopes nor chemical reagents are of assistance. The power of abstraction must replace both.'[10] We make abstraction in thought – 'experiments in thought' – and cannot do more than this. But we stay with the concrete reality which we are analysing and try to tease out as many details as we can, rather than ignoring details in order to subsume it under generalizations. The abstract parts of good social science are speculative explanations of concrete particulars, which are tested only by their capacity to explain those concrete particulars. To take them out of their use in such explanation and use them to compare different concrete particulars in the attempt to arrive at 'statistical causality' is always a mistake, since the other determinants of events and differences are being ignored without their having been rendered ineffective as in a real experiment. Statistics has an important place among the descriptive preliminaries of social science; information about the simultaneous increase in unemployment and crime may be the starting point of a fruitful social-scientific analysis. But the analysis itself must focus on concrete particulars, and retroduce explanations from them. It cannot read off the explanations from the statistical correlations. But if statistics has no explanatory role in social science, neither has any other form of mathematics, since we cannot measure abstract forces without actualizing them as is done in an experiment.

To return, then, to the original paradox: the analysis of experiment has not been useless for the human sciences, since it shows something very general about the real world, namely that it is structured and stratified, that the concrete really is a union of many determinations, and hence that abstraction and analysis are appropriate methods of developing knowledge of concrete beings. But it also shows that where experiment is not possible, this analysis and abstraction is not measurable, and is testable only by its capacity to explain the minute particulars of concrete entities. It shows, in short, the ontological similarity of natural and human sciences – they are both analysing concrete structured wholes and explaining them in terms of the abstractions arrived at – and also the methodological dissimilarity of natural and human sciences: the latter cannot use mathematics and should look rather to paradigms like Freud's analysis of the Rat Man (or any full psychoanalytic case-history), or Trotsky's *History of the Russian Revolution*. In short, social science can exist only 'as minutely organized particulars, and not in generalizing demonstrations of the rational power'.

Now to the question of practical applications. Many of the concrete sciences are inseparably tied to a practice (for example, medicine to healing, psychoanalysis to therapy, Marxian theory to working-class politics), but whether this is so or not, all sciences, abstract or concrete, deliver their discoveries into a world of ongoing practices which they often transform in some way. I want to argue in conclusion that as a matter of scientific ethics and good public policy, abstract sciences ought never to be allowed to influence practice directly, but only through the assistance they give to concrete sciences. This applies not only to natural sciences, where it has important ecological implications, but also with respect to the abstract and concrete parts of human sciences.

Abstract sciences can yield practical advice of a sort; for instance, 'here is a way w to make product x with half the labour that it took before'. This may justify the conclusion: 'other things being equal, we should make x by process *w*.' But other things are not equal and in this sort of case that is crucial. Process *w* may also deplete a scarce resource or cause pollution or produce sickness in the workers. To establish whether this is so, we need a concrete study of the process in context – environmental, human, economic and so on. *That* study *may* yield real practical advice, without the 'other things being equal' clause. However, it is a feature of our economic system that the 'other things being equal' clauses of the practical advice of abstract sciences are not taken seriously – the advice is carried out as if it were conclusive, which only the advice of a concrete scientific study can even approximate to being. This is a feature of modern economic life because if the 'other things' do not relate to profitability, they are equal to the commercial appliers of science – all equally indifferent. But it is important to notice that *all* advice from abstract science is subject to an other-things-being-equal clause, just because it is abstract, having abstracted from some of the other things that affect the outcome. An economic system that systematically applies science in an abstract state is a systematically irresponsible system.

There is a tradition of hostile criticism of science which makes very similar points to those that I have been making. Blake in some moods is part of that tradition. Today it often comes from those within the Green movement who blame science rather than its commercial use. There is also a tendency within 'postmodernism' to counterpose the practical concrete knowledge of (for instance) shepherds to the pretensions of the Ministry of Agriculture experts, trained in abstract science. In so far as these tendencies have directed attention to the necessity of concrete knowledge and its sole right to guide practice, they are absolutely right. Yet the fault lies not with abstract science but with the tendency of its commercial and military users to apply science in its abstract state, rather than treating abstract sciences as contributory disciplines whose results must flow together into the sea of concrete science before they are in a fit state to be applied practically.

Since I am claiming that the rationality of the practical application of science depends on following the full sequence *abstract sciences – concrete science – practice* rather than the abridged sequence *abstract science – practice*, I should perhaps say something about what sort of discipline counts as a concrete science, as distinct from an abstract science on the one hand and a practice on the other. I have given examples of concrete sciences such as meteorology and medicine, but it is not always easy to identify them. Whereas abstract sciences are individuated (as physics, chemistry, biology and the like) by the kinds of laws that they discover, and practices are individuated (as agriculture, health care, war and so on) by the aims that they pursue and the means that they use, concrete sciences are individuated by their concrete objects, which may be of greater or lesser scope, so that the concrete science required for a given bit of application of science to practice may not have a ready-made name. To take the instance of pesticides, the abstract science of chemistry is applied in the practice of agriculture. The concrete scientific disciplines which ought to stand between these two would include in their objects the state of the soil, water and air, and various ecosystems dependent on that state. It is a matter of 'practical wisdom' to determine in any given case what the scope of the requisite concrete science should be.

The application of abstract science is irrational and the application of concrete science is rational. But concrete science can never give you what abstract science appears to give: a method of calculating which course of action is rational. For the discovery that *w* is the most economical way of producing *x* can be quantified: it costs half what process *v* had cost. But as soon as a multiplicity of incommensurable reasons for using or not using *w* is delivered by the concrete study of *w*-in-context, we have to make a decision between incommensurable alternatives. Calculation becomes useless. But that is not an objection to basing action on concrete science, for calculation between the actual alternatives was always impossible anyway. It was only because many of the incommensurable values were left out of account or assigned arbitrary commensurable values that the issue looked calculable in the first place. Deciding on the basis of an abstract science just is leaving some things out of account – that is what abstract means. If we have to decide between a motorway and an ancient wood of special scientific interest, there is nothing we can rationally do but sit down and think 'would life be better with a wood and no motorway or with a motorway and no wood?' At which point I can perhaps conclude as I started with a quote from Blake:

> Improvement makes strait roads; but the crooked
> roads without Improvement are the roads of Genius.[11]

Notes

1 William Blake, *Complete Writings*, Oxford University Press, London, 1966, p. 687.
2 An earlier version of this paper was read to the Seminar on Critical Realism organized in the Faculty of Economics and Politics at the University of Cambridge.
3 Edmund Husserl, *Logical Investigations*, vol. 1, Routledge & Kegan Paul, London, 1970, pp 230–31.
4 Roy Bhaskar, *A Realist Theory of Science*, Harvester Wheatsheaf, Hemel Hempstead, 1978, p. 13.
5 I am grateful to Heather Collier for information in this part of the article.
6 Karl Marx and Frederick Engels, *The German Ideology*, ed. R. Pascal, International Publishers, New York, 1969, pp. 114–15.
7 Karl Marx, *Grundrisse*, Penguin, Harmondsworth, 1973, p. 100.
8 Ibid.
9 Ibid., p. 101.
10 Karl Marx, *Capital*, vol. 1, Penguin, Harmondsworth, 1976, p. 90.
11 *Complete Writings*, p. 151.

4 Critical realism and the heritage of the Enlightenment

Roy Bhaskar's article 'Critical Realism, Social Relations and Arguing for Socialism' opens with Kant's famous defining motto of enlightenment *'sapere aude!* Have courage to use your own reason!', and Roy expresses the hope for:

> the dawning of a new enlightenment, a socialist enlightenment which will stand to some future order of things, as the eighteenth-century bourgeois enlightenment stood to the American Declaration of Independence, the French Revolution and the overthrow of colonial slavery for which it helped to prepare the cultural ground.
>
> (*Reclaiming Reality*, p. 1)

This favourable assessment of the Enlightenment is deeply unfashionable, and even recent radical defences of the Enlightenment heritage, such as Alison Assiter's *Enlightened Women*, give the impression of fighting with one's back to the wall. In particular, the commitments to reason, universalism and progress are regarded as untenable. I want to defend these legacies of the Enlightenment and disentangle them from mistakes that often historically went with them, although they need not do so. One comment first to forestall a reaction which almost everything that I write seems to provoke: when I am stimulated to write polemically against a prevalent idea, it is almost always live discussions in seminars or conferences or pubs or political meetings that are the stimulus. I am arguing against positions that I have heard put forward, often by people that I didn't know and have never met again. For this reason my polemics are scant in attributions or textual references. Nevertheless, I think the positions criticised are at any rate close to positions typical of much postmodernist literature, as well as of much contemporary intellectual conversation.

First it may be useful to situate historically the Enlightenment in the 'long' sense – the trajectory of thought which started with Bacon in England and Descartes in mainland Europe, included the self-consciously enlightened movements in Northern Europe and France in the eighteenth century, and culminated in Kant and Godwin. In order to understand how its commitment to reason led in fact – as it need not have done in logic – to foundationalist errors, we need to look at the scholastic philosophy against which it defined itself. That philosophy tended to divide knowledge into two zones, one based on reason and one on authority, to be accepted on trust. Thus Aquinas thought that the existence of God could be proved by pure reason, whereas the Trinity had to be accepted on the authority of revelation transmitted by the Church. Late medieval philosophy took more and more things out of the zone of reason, partly on the grounds of justifiable scepticism about the a priori arguments involved, but with the effect of accepting more and more uncriticisable dogmas. It was necessary to unfetter reason – to insist that every idea passed on by some authority should be open for criticism at the bar of reason. But it was not necessary to reject authority as a source of knowledge. Today even more than in the Middle Ages most of our knowledge is owed to authority – lay people's knowledge of the discoveries of science, knowledge of what goes on in other places, and so on. This is all in order so long as these authorities do not put themselves above rational criticism. What was necessary to unfetter reason was to break down the division of knowledge into a rational zone and an authoritative zone, and recognise that all knowledge presupposes the deliverances of authorities, but that all authorities are subject to rational criticism. Instead, the Enlightenment philosophers tended to accept the division into zones but reject the authoritative zone altogether as dogma and superstition; in doing so they rejected one error of medieval (particularly late medieval) thought – its placing some knowledge outside the scope of rational criticism – but perpetuated the other: the idea that some knowledge could be derived from *nothing but* reason. This is the source of the foundationalism of most Enlightenment thinkers.

Another way of putting it is this: the Enlighteners overestimated what reason can do; but they did not *overvalue* reason. For though reason is not the foundation of knowledge, it is its growing point, and the sole corrective of received opinion. I am using 'reason' in the wide sense, to include not only logic but empirical testing and indeed the testing of authorities on the basis of grounded suspicion. Here Freud is exemplary as both a follower and a corrector of the Enlightenment: reason, or the ego, is a relatively weak contender in human affairs; yet if we want mental health and personal liberation we must rely on and extend its power. Thus, on the one hand, he writes to Jung about Adler:

> I would never have expected a psychoanalyst to be so taken in by the ego. In reality the ego is like the clown in the circus, who is always putting in his oar to make the audience think that whatever happens is his doing.
>
> (*The Freud/Jung Letters*, p. 219)

Yet, on the other hand, he proclaims the emancipatory task of psychoanalysis:

Its intention is, indeed, to strengthen the ego, to make it more independent of the super-ego, to widen its field of perception and enlarge its organization, so that it can appropriate fresh portions of the id. Where id was, there ego shall be. It is a work of culture – not unlike the draining of the Zuider Zee.

(*Complete Introductory Lectures on Psychoanalysis*, p. 544)

Now I shall look in turn at each of the three contentious issues of reason, universalism and progress.

Reason

It is not my aim here to define reason or its place in human life. Elsewhere I have defended Macmurray's notion of reason as the capacity to act in the light of the nature of things independent of us, and hence as the non-anthropocentric principle in humankind; I have also tried to show that the oppositions reason/authority and reason/emotion are misplaced: the opposition is rather between rational and irrational authorities, and between rational and irrational emotions. But here I only want to defend the Enlightenment's high regard for reason, and that regard is centred on three values: intellectual freedom, logical argument and science. Intellectual freedom was a genuinely new value at the time of the Enlightenment. It had to be fought for against the old authoritarianism of the inquisition and the new one exemplified by Hobbes' philosophy. For Kant it is *the* Enlightenment value, and he stakes everything on it politically. Those who reject the Enlightenment today do not as a rule reject this value; indeed, they even reject the Enlightenment in its name, since reason is seen as 'just another authority', telling us what to believe. But we have to ask what it is that is so good about intellectual freedom. One thing is that it is one instance of personal liberty generally. But of course this is not threatened by reason, since reason is not coercion. The Enlighteners, though, thought that something else was good about intellectual freedom – namely, that it enabled people to have open minds, that is, to listen to reasons for revising their opinions. To *reasons* for revising their opinions, not to demands that they do so to keep up with intellectual fashion or some politically or economically powerful but rationally unjustified authority. If intellectual freedom does not mean that, it can just as well be an excuse for complacency about a closed mind. Such an intellectual freedom cut off from commitment to reason has only a small place in the list of personal civil liberties, somewhere lower on the scale of priorities, I would suggest, than freedom to ramble in the countryside.

This brings us to the issue of logical argument. I have heard it argued: logic declares certain arguments to be invalid; that is a way of excluding or suppressing them; so the question to ask about the logician is: why do they want to exclude those arguments? But the nature of an argument is to show that there are good reasons for believing the conclusion. An invalid argument fails to do that; the criterion of success or failure is implicit in the nature of argument. One might just as well ask why a batsman in cricket wants to prevent the ball from hitting the stumps; that is part of what it is to be a batsman in cricket. Of course, a particular batsman may have taken a bribe to lose the game, but being bowled out is a cricketing failure even if it is a commercial success. A bad argument may persuade the voters to vote for you or the customers to buy your product; it is just for this reason that it is so important to be able to point out a bad argument.

In the context of the Enlightenment, the issue is this: you want to refute an accepted dogma; to do so, you must either show it to involve a contradiction or produce some well-founded information which contradicts it. Either way, you must understand that a self-contradictory view cannot be true or that two contradictory propositions cannot both be true. Without this assumption from which all logic follows, it is not possible to criticise any view, and you might as well accept whatever dogma brings you most power or money or self-esteem. So far from logic being another dogma that stifles criticism, it is a condition of the possibility of any criticism of any dogma.

The specific value of science in Enlightenment thinking, apart from as one instance of intellectual endeavour, is as knowledge *applied* for what Bacon called 'the easement of man's estate'. I shall return to this under the heading of progress, but here I shall just comment on the slogan 'knowledge is power', once an optimistic slogan inscribed on trade union banners in the spirit of the Enlightenment. Today, this slogan is almost always used to the detriment of knowledge; as in much classical liberal thinking, power has come to be identified with domination and so seen as something bad. Yet the power that comes with knowledge is not domination, but *pouvoir*, being-able. Power in this sense is more or less a synonym of freedom and not a contrasting term as in liberalism. Domination, on the contrary, requires a lack of knowledge; certainly ignorance or illusion on the part of the dominated, but also I think shallow knowledge on the part of the dominators – an instrumentalist rather than a realist conception of society and human nature, for example.

Universalism

Those who defend the Enlightenment heritage almost always value its universalism and those who attack it condemn it for the same universalism. And certainly the two philosophers whom I mentioned as the culmination of the Enlightenment considered as a historical movement, Kant and Godwin, both made universalism central to their ethics. Yet the relation of the Enlightenment to universalism is less straightforward than its relation to the unfettering of reason. The high value placed on reason ought to lead to universalism, and in the long run, tendentially, it did; nevertheless it is true both (a) that universalism did not originate with the Enlightenment, as the unfettering of reason did – it is implicit and sometimes explicit in the Hellenistic philosophies of late antiquity and in international religions such as Buddhism, Christianity and Islam; and (b) that the great Enlighteners were not always consistent in their universalism. In particular the issue has recently been raised about the racism of some Enlightenment thinkers. And it is certain that racism and indeed the concept of a plurality races, like belief in witches, is a modern not an ancient or medieval phenomenon. When St Anselm (1033–1109), who invented the idea that the death of Jesus was a substitute punishment for the sins of humankind, said that he could not atone for the sins of devils but only those of his own race, he could take it for granted that his readers would understand the human race, not the Jewish race. But modernity is not synonymous with the Enlightenment. There are other specifically modern movements of thought as well – irrationalism, for instance. Racism is much more characteristic of this movement.

However, there have recently been two kinds of attempt to link the Enlightenment with racism; on the one hand there have been attempts to show that if Enlightenment tendencies such as rationalism or empiricism are combined with certain other premises, they can lead to racist conclusions. This is pretty useless. Any philosophical opinion can be combined with some other opinion to generate any moral or political conclusion whatever. The second kind of attempt is worth more serious attention; the digging up of undeniably racist passages in texts by Enlightenment authors. A valuable source of such information is the reader *Race and the Enlightenment* edited by Emmanuel Chukwudi Eze. However, it seems to me that what the offending passages prove is that the racism of some Enlightenment figures was alien to the central concerns of their thought. To take only two examples from Hume and Kant. First, in Hume's essay 'Of the Populousness of Ancient Nations', there is a footnote expressing the opinion that black people are inferior to whites. But what is curious is the relation of this footnote to the main text to which it is attached. For in the main text Hume is arguing that all differences between nations are cultural rather than physical in their causes. The footnote then does not illustrate or support the main argument, but rather contradicts it. Knowing what we do of Hume, it seems reasonable to assume that what he is doing here is admitting to holding an opinion (his racism) which is directly contradictory to the results of his reasoning. The contradiction, like so many in Hume, is left unresolved.

Second, Kant, apart from speculative physical anthropology and various observations on national characteristics, shows racism by his apparently approving reference to Hume's footnote, and by one coarse racist remark which is so incongruous that one wonders if it is an attempt at irony that misfires.[1] But what is in no way compromised by Kant's racism is his idea of human beings as rational beings, an all-or-nothing concept, admitting of no degrees. Kant may have thought – as Hume certainly, if inconsistently, did – that there were different degrees of intelligence between the races, but certainly not degrees of rational nature, on which alone his moral philosophy is based. And this genuine universalism bears political fruit in Kant's uncompromising rejection of imperialism; he says that:

> the *inhospitable* conduct of the civilised states of our continent, especially the commercial states, the injustice which they display in *visiting* foreign countries and peoples (which in their case is the same as *conquering* them) seems appallingly great. America, the negro countries, the Spice Islands, the Cape, etc. were looked upon at the time of their discovery as owner-less territories; for the native inhabitants were counted as nothing.
>
> ('Perpetual Peace', in *Political Writings*, p. 106)

He goes on to praise China and Japan for keeping Western traders out.

It is when we contrast Enlightenment thought with anti-Enlightenment tendencies in modernity that we see the extent to which its universalism is tendentially emancipatory. The Enlightenment-influenced French revolutionaries were the first in modern times to abolish slavery; the anti-Enlightenment romantic Carlyle wanted it brought back; the Kantian T.H. Green got women admitted to Oxford; the anti-Enlightenment romantic G.K. Chesterton tried to stop them getting the vote. The countries where Enlightenment philosophy prevailed and pervaded the culture – the UK, France, the USSR – fought against Nazism; the anti-Enlightenment countries fought for it. When postmodernists ask (as they sometimes do) why European universities are dominated by belief in reason, the answer is that, in so far as this is true (which perhaps it no longer is), it is because the Allies defeated the Fascist powers in 1945.

If it can be granted then that, at least relative to other modern philosophies, the Enlightenment heritage is universalistic, we still have to defend that universalism against its critics. I think that two distinct kinds of criticism of universalism have been made. I take the weaker one first, although it is characteristically more recent. This is the view that supposed universalism is always just one particularism imperialistically claiming universality. Such a phenomenon does really occur, of course. The ideology of imperialism in the literal sense usually includes equivocation between the particular power of the ruling nation and its claims to represent some universal ideal: humanity as Romanity, Moscow as the Third Rome or the Third International, Britain as the policeman of the world, America as the lone superpower and so on. But to unmask these particularisms is to condemn them precisely for being, after all, only particularisms: that the 'mother of parliaments' was not 'the parliament of man, the federation of the world' (in Tennyson's phrase) but the parliament of one European offshore island, that the Third International was not a genuine international like the First and Second, but an instrument of Soviet foreign policy, and so on. If we cannot contrast these shamefaced particularisms with genuine universalism, it is not clear how their unmasking criticises them. But the anti-universalist case rests on *all* universalism being *necessarily* shamefaced particularism. If so, what are we to replace it with? Upfront particularism? But unless there is some universal order into which the various particularisms fit, there is nothing against one particularism dominating another. The false universalism of all civilised empires is at least 'the homage that vice pays to virtue', as hypocrisy has been defined. The Vikings and Huns needed no such mask; they rejoiced in their conquests because they were *their* conquests. And modern particularism is no different. Mussolini's logic was good when he derived from his relativism the right of any party to impose its will on the others if it could.

Critics of universalism as imperialism usually have one group of imperialisms in mind – namely, European imperialism. The Enlightenment is seen as the regional ideology of Europe, being imposed on non-European cultures to which it is alien. Any plausibility that this has is based on focusing on a narrow (mainly nineteenth-century) time span. For the Enlightenment had to make its way in Europe too through struggle against the old European ideologies – against feudalism and ecclesiastical power, against fundamentalism and the early modern craze for witch-hunting – just as in China it had to make its way against Confucianism or in India against the caste system and communalist intolerance. Doubtless there was a time when Enlightenment ideas were already relatively strong in Europe and still weak elsewhere, but there was also a time when they were unknown anywhere, and today they are thoroughly international. A secular politician in India who opposes communalist intolerance is no more a mock European than an English coffee drinker is a mock Ethiopian (since coffee originated in Ethiopia).

All this is not to say that all pre-Enlightenment ideas (whether in Europe or Asia or wherever) are wrong, nor is it to deny intercontinental influences before the Enlightenment. Indeed, medieval European philosophy was in many ways less continentally isolated than modern; after all, its main problem was to integrate the ideas of the Arabic philosophers Ibn Rushd and Ibn Sina with those of the African philosophers Plotinus and Augustine. Nevertheless, it is galling to hear the ideas of the Enlightenment dubbed ethnocentrically European when they have had so many heroic defenders in Asia and Africa, and given that within living memory they were nearly wiped out in Europe.

I have already touched on the second line of criticism of Enlightenment universalism: that diversity is inherently good and universalism destroys it. The postmodernist philosophers' opposition to Enlightenment universalism then appears as parallel to the postmodernist architects' altogether welcome opposition to the international style.

However, universalism and uniformity are not the same thing. I fully accept that diversity is good and uniformity bad. But diversity between philosophies or cultures is only good on condition that they communicate with and to some extent understand one another. If rational life exists on some galaxy millions of light years from here, it will in all probability be very different from ours, but that difference is of no account either to us or to them. If two cultures do meet but totally lack mutual understanding, the case is even worse. There was nothing valuable about the diversity of Saracen and Crusader as they hacked each other to bits. But the encounter of philosophies from those two cultures in thirteenth-century scholastic philosophy was valuable. So, at another level, was the encounter of the English with the Asian tea plant. And today British analytical philosophy has benefited from its recent assimilation of continental philosophy, and will no doubt benefit again from the increasing encounter with Indian and Chinese philosophy which is bound to come. Diversity-in-communication is valuable; diversity in isolation is just fragmented uniformities.

But this high valuation of communication and understanding between cultures is precisely part of universalism. Contemporary anti-universalism tends to deny the possibility of such understanding by its notion of incommensurability. And if cultures cannot understand each other, then any individual is trapped in a single culture and the diversity might as well not exist.

Progress

The Enlightenment idea of progress has three main aspects: (1) the idea that science will lead to the 'easement of man's estate' (Bacon); (2) the idea that freedom of thought will lead to the erosion of cruel and irrational institutions. This finds its classic expression in Kant's political writings; and (3) the idea that humankind is moving towards greater unity, and a more universalistic ethic. This last is actually more characteristic of the dialectical thought that was arguably one of the nineteenth-century inheritors of Enlightenment values – of Hegel, Marx and T.H. Green – than of seventeenth- and eighteenth-century Enlightenment thought. Indeed, the connection between the three aspects of progress only becomes clear with Marx and Engels' materialist conception of history, and in the process certain epicycles are introduced into the account of progress, which remove its appearance of steady linear progression. The following is a brief reconstruction of this account.

Technology – science applied in work – does indeed ease the human estate, primarily by reducing the labour time necessary to produce the means of life. As humankind progresses technologically, this makes more and more total leisure available to society. And leisure in the sense of release from the necessity to spend all one's energy producing the means of subsistence is the necessary condition of participation in arts and sciences and the management of society. As the total leisure available to society increases, it becomes possible for more and more people to participate in these activities. Beyond a certain point of technological advance, probably reached in Europe and North America in the nineteenth century, it becomes possible for all to do so. Hence the possibility of universalism and democracy is inherent in advanced technology – the possibility, not the actuality. Society may decide to give all its available leisure to a barbaric squirearchy who spend it persecuting beautiful animals. It usually does decide, under capitalism, to use all the potential leisure time producing new forms of consumption which deplete the Earth's resources and destroy the pleasures of nature and company which are every person's heritage to make way for expensive artificial pleasures. Society may even decide, as the lunatics who were misgoverning us from 1979 to 1997 did (and their legacy is far from dead), to make the majority of people over fifty and millions under it redundant, while working all the others into early graves. But even though progress only makes universal leisure and thus democracy possible, not necessary, in the long term this possibility tends to some extent to pass into actuality. More people participate in art and science and government today than in the Middle Ages. *Tendentially* history does progress, as Hegel says, from ancient monarchies in which only one is free, through the ancient republics (and one might add, modern liberal democracies) in which some are free, to a possible time when all will be free.

However, for the materialist conception of history, this progress is not a simple linear development. Societies are of different kinds, organised in different modes of production. Each constitutes progress over its predecessor, but within each, progress only occurs until that mode of production has outlived its usefulness. After that, technological progress still occurs, but this 'progress' is in some respects damaging to humankind. Since the bourgeoisie reached the end of its career as a progressive class early in the twentieth century, it has been a century in which many things have become worse, while others have continued to get better. The ecological crisis and the genocidal character of war and tyranny in the century instantiate the former; the advances made by democracy, decolonisation and the emancipation of women instantiate the latter. It can also be argued that the historical bankruptcy of the bourgeois class is the deepest source of the anti-Enlightenment culture that has developed throughout the century. Given these points, there can be a case for a relatively short-term luddism and cultural conservatism, within a long-term commitment to progress through reason, science and universalism.[2]

It has been my main concern to defend aspects of the Enlightenment which I think are valuable and under threat, and which critical realism has inherited. But there are also two ideas associated with most thinkers of the Enlightenment period and many of their successors which I hold to be deeply mistaken. I shall only state and briefly situate these ideas; I have argued against them elsewhere.[3] Oddly, though, these ideas are not rejected by most contemporary anti-enlightenment thinkers who can therefore be said to throw out the baby but retain the bathwater. I refer to anthropocentricity and a group of ideas which, for brevity, I shall denote by the name of one of them, atomism (others include a mechanistic account of causation, an externalist account of relations and physiological reductionism). Both these ideas had advocates among the Greeks, but they acquired a new lease of life and came to prevail for the first time in Enlightenment thought.

It may seem paradoxical to see anthropocentricity as an innovation of the Enlightenment, since this movement of thought starts with the rejection of geocentric cosmologies. But geocentricity is not anthropocentricity. It is not because of its hosting of humankind that the Earth is seen as the centre of the universe by the medievals. Indeed, 'centre' for them does not have the evaluative force that it does for many moderns. The Earth was thought to be in the middle of the universe, as the University of Warwick is in the middle of England. But the most important part of the universe was not the middle, where we supposedly lived, but the top, where angels supposedly lived. And values were not seen as dependent on us, but as inhering in all beings; 'being and good are convertibles' argued Aquinas, meaning that these two terms had different meanings, but applied to the same things. From Descartes on, being is seen as anthropocentric because it is epistemocentric. Modern anthropocentrism is a consequence of the epistemic fallacy.[4] The only philosophers of the seventeenth and eighteenth centuries to avoid this epistemocentrism were the reductive materialists and Spinoza. Spinoza also avoided atomism, but the materialists fell for atomism in a big way. The only non-atomistic tendencies in post-Enlightenment thought are the organic idealists such as Hegel; but these are deeply anthropocentric. The only modern philosophies (as opposed to modern continuations of older philosophies such as Thomism) that avoid both these errors are Spinoza, the dialectical materialists and critical realism. Postmodernism, on the other hand, can be described as atomism and anthropocentricity pushed to their furthest extremes.

Notes

1   The context is an account of how men of different cultures treat women. Kant tells us that:

> Father Labat reports that a Negro carpenter, whom he reproached for haughty treatment of his wives, answered: 'You whites are indeed fools, for first you make great concessions to your wives, and afterward you complain when they drive you mad.' And it might be that there were something in this which perhaps deserved to be considered; but in short, this fellow was quite black from head to foot, a clear proof that what he said was stupid.
>
> (*Race and the Enlightenment: A Reader*)

2   See my *Socialist Reasoning*, Chapter 4, for a fuller account of these issues.
3   For instance, in my book *Scientific Realism and Socialist Thought*.
4   See Roy Bhaskar's book *A Realist Theory of Science*, pp. 36–38, for a definition of the epistemic fallacy.

References

Assiter, Alison, *Enlightened Women*, Routledge, London, 1996.

Bhaskar, Roy, *Reclaiming Reality*, Verso, London, 1989.

Bhaskar, Roy, *A Realist Theory of Science*, Verso, London, 1997.

Collier, Andrew, *Scientific Realism and Socialist Thought*, Harvester, Hemel Hempstead, 1989.

Collier, Andrew, *Socialist Reasoning*, Pluto, London, 1990.

Freud, S., *Complete Introductory Lectures on Psychoanalysis*, Allen and Unwin, London, 1971.

Freud, S. and Jung, C.G., *The Freud/Jung Letters*, ed. W. McGuire, Pan, London, 1979.

Kant, I., *Political Writings*, ed. H. Reiss, Cambridge University Press, Cambridge, 1970.

Kant, I., *Race and the Enlightenment: A Reader*, ed. E.C. Eze, Blackwell, Oxford, 1997.

5   On slave rebellions in morals

Nietzsche's thesis of the slave rebellion in morals is well known. In a nutshell, it is that the dominant strain in European morality is of the type character- istic of slave classes rather than of master classes; that this morality is one of 'sour grapes' – that is, whereas the masters value things which make life good and treat their lack as bad, the slaves treat all that is characteristic of the masters – that is, all the good things of life, power, pleasure, culture, strength, beauty – as evil, and consequently regard themselves as good for lacking those things; further, that the slaves, lacking scope for the exercise of their will to power in the outside world, turn it against themselves, just as some animals in the cat family will pluck themselves if they cannot get whole small animals to pluck and eat. And finally, that as all moralities tend to generate metaphysical systems, the slave morality generates a dualist one, splitting the body and soul into separate entities and postulating another world, more real and better than this one, in which the soul is at home as the body is in this world.

Sometimes Nietzsche seems to be saying that the slave rebellion in morals was a historical event, in which case he identifies it with Judaeo-Christian traditions:

> Christianity, growing from Jewish roots and comprehensible only as a product of this soil, represents a *reaction* against that morality of breed- ing, of race, of privilege – it is the *anti-Aryan* religion *par excellence*: Christianity the revaluation of all Aryan values, the victory of Chandala values, the evangel preached to the poor and lowly, the collective rebellion of everything downtrodden, wretched, ill-constituted, under- privileged against the 'race' – undying Chandala revenge as the *religion of love*.
>
> (*Twilight of the Idols*, p. 58)[1]

This can be called the diachronic reading of the slave rebellion in morals: it is presented as something that happened in a particular time and place, in the ancient Mediterranean world, in the historical religions of Judaism and Christianity.

But Nietzsche also believes that slave morality is alive today in other forms, not only in the religious forms of modern (i.e. Victorian) Christianity and Judaism, but also in the political left, liberalism, democracy, socialism, feminism and anarchism. Some philosophers have interpreted the 'slave rebellion in morals' thesis as the synchronic theory that oppressed classes tend to generate slave moralities, which sometimes (for instance, in modern Europe) come to predominate over master moralities. Some, for instance Scheler,[2] have endorsed Nietzsche's critique of the left as slave morality, while exonerating Christianity from this charge. On the other hand, the German Marxist Karl Kautsky has written in terms reminiscent of Nietzsche's, if less rancorous, about early and medieval Christianity, while disavowing such slave rebellion on behalf of modern socialist movements.

My position in this paper is as follows: I accept that oppressed classes tend to produce slave moralities as described by Nietzsche, although this is not without countervailing tendencies. I also agree that slave moralities are unhealthy. But I think that Nietzsche's history and sociology of ideas is inaccurate. In the first part of the rest of this paper I will criticise his diachronic account of the slave rebellion in morals in the form of the Judaeo-Christian traditions. In the second part, I will look at the synchronic slave rebellion in morals in relation to the political left in nineteenth-century Europe and since. If my contentions are well founded, they will go some way towards vindicating both Judaeo-Christian traditions and the left.

Athens and Jerusalem

I think it is undoubtedly true that, on the one hand, ancient Greek and Roman cultures were cultures of the master class, while on the other Judaeo-Christian culture was a culture of the oppressed. Although Athens at its heyday was a democracy, it was a democracy that excluded slaves, women and metics, and even so the most enduring intellectual legacies of Athens, with the exception of Socrates (whom anyway we know only as co-opted by the aristocrat Plato), represent not the democratic classes but the slaveholding aristocracy. Only the Cynics with their ethic of inner freedom speak with a voice from non-aristocratic classes, and they are marginal to the history of ancient ethics. Jewish culture in its most sublime form, the pre-exilic prophets, is trenchantly on the side of the oppressed.[3] As liberation theologians have noted, kings are not praised for being impartial between rich and poor, but for being on the side of the poor. Whatever the reality of the Jewish monarchy was, its ideal was certainly that the king was a protector of the weak and poor, and a rod of iron to the oppressors.

As for Christianity, at the outset of the Gospel Mary praises God because:

> the arrogant of heart and mind he has put to rout,
> he has torn imperial powers from their thrones,
> but the humble have been lifted high.

The hungry he has satisfied with good things,
the rich sent empty away.

(Luke 1: 52–53)

The past tense should not deceive us, as it has deceived some, into thinking this is meant in some spiritual sense. Hebrew tenses are different: the tense for completed action, which of humans is used for the past, is used for future acts of God since they are seen as already decided. Mary is predicting the inversion of class fortunes as a result of the work of her son.

Jesus himself proclaims the blessedness of the poor and woe to the rich (Luke 6: 20 and 24), and his brother James continues the work with 'a word to you who have great possessions':

weep and wail over the miserable fate descending on you. . . . The wages you never paid to the men who mowed your fields are loud against you, and the outcry of the reapers has reached the ears of the Lord of Hosts.

(James 5: 1–4)

Here we have the class soil for a slave rebellion in morals, but not yet that rebellion itself, for there is no asceticism or inversion of values here. Whether these things ensue is a complex issue to which I will return, but first let us turn to a simpler issue: which of these two cultures – the master culture of classical antiquity or the Judaeo-Christian culture of the oppressed – gives us dualist metaphysics, which Nietzsche supposes to be the consequence of slave morality. Judaism certainly does not. It neither divides the soul into rational and irrational parts, nor holds the soul to be separable from the body, nor impugns the reality of the world perceived by the senses, nor postulates a spiritual world separate from this one. Plato does all of these things. This is the opposite of what Nietzsche would lead you to expect,[4] but it is quite intelligible in class terms: the scholars of Judaea are craftsmen in daily contact with the reality of nature; Plato is from the slave-owning aristocracy, with its contempt for manual labour as slavish and its consequent denigration of the body. Dualism is always the ideology of an oppressing class, which admires itself in the 'mental work' for which it has the leisure and proclaims the autonomy of such work from the 'slavish' body. Granted that Aristotle is less dualist than Plato, even he is more so than Jewish culture. The nearest thing to a philosophical text in the Jewish scriptures – the Book of Ecclesiastes – is so non-dualist that it is tempting, if anachronistic, to call it materialist. It is certainly mortalist.[5] The pre-exilic prophets and Deutero-Isaiah are almost secularist in their hostility to the temple cult and their insistence that true worship of God consists in the practice of social justice.[6]

Christianity is admittedly a more complex case. In common with lower-class Judaism of the first century it looks forward to a Reign of God on Earth in which the dead will be raised, but it does not postulate a separable or naturally immortal soul, nor does it speculate at any length about the details of an afterlife, seeing it instead in terms of a heavenly banquet. It uses language (in Paul's epistles) which could be read as a dualistic anthropology, but the best scholars tell us that it should not be: the flesh is simply the human and the spirit is the divine.

In summary: there is a spectrum of opinions about dualism from the non-dualism of classical Judaism to the dualism of Plato, but the Judaeo-Christian traditions generally are less dualistic than the pagan. This continues into the Latin world: consider St Augustine's polemic against the Stoic hostility to the emotions.[7]

What, then, of the inversion of values and ascetic renunciation of natural goods which are the central features of slave morality? It is uncontentious that these cannot be found in classical Judaism. Christianity again is a more complex case. On the face of it, it seems to invert prescriptions but not to invert values. It urges you to return good for evil (as does Socrates, of course) and to be ready for martyrdom, to give your goods to the poor and to take no thought for the morrow; yet it does not denigrate earthly goods such as health, long life and the enjoyment of festivities. Jesus, unlike John the Baptist, can be plausibly described by his enemies as a glutton and drunkard and keeper of bad company. The miracles stories are all such as to make sense only in a life-affirming culture. The explanation of this unusual combination must be at least partly that the ethic of the New Testament is an *interimsethik*, an ethic for a time of emergency. This is clearly the case of Paul's counsel of celibacy: the point is not to avoid sexual intercourse, but to avoid entanglements with the world at a dangerous and transitional time.

There are, however, two things in New Testament ethics which look like a Nietzschean inversion of values: the assessments of power and of wealth:

> in the world, kings lord it over their subjects; and those in authority are called their country's 'Benefactors'. Not so with you: on the contrary, the highest among you must bear himself like the youngest, the chief of you like a servant.
>
> (Luke 22: 25–26)

> How hard it is for the wealthy to enter the kingdom of God! It is easier for a camel to go through the eye of a needle than for a rich man to enter the kingdom of God.
>
> (Luke 18: 24–25)

This, however, would only indicate an inversion of values if wealth and power were being denounced in absolute rather than relative terms; if, that is, it was being said that poverty and powerlessness were good, rather than that the wealth and power of the wealthy and powerful is at the expense of the poverty and powerlessness of others, and that it is this poverty and powerlessness that is bad. The quotes from Mary and James above tend to show that it is not that good things are being denounced as bad, but that good things are being claimed for those who lack them at the expense of those who monopolise them. In short, the kingdom of God has more in common with a slave rebellion than with a slave rebellion in morals.

I conclude that the New Testament morality is not slave morality; neither is that of classical antiquity, of Socrates, Plato and Aristotle. But that of the Hellenistic period into which Christianity flowed as soon as it went beyond the Palestinian milieu was much closer to slave morality, and subapostolic Christianity was affected by this too. In second- and third-century Christianity, the immortality of the soul and the denigration of the body are endemic. This goes for neo-Platonism and Stoicism and many pagan religious cults as well. It was the spirit of the times. The usual explanation is the powerlessness of ordinary citizens (whether economically oppressed or not) in the Roman Empire, compared with the active role that free citizens could play in the Greek democracies and, to an extent, in the Roman Republic. Christianity also underwent a similar disappointment in the non-happening of the expected return of Christ.

Could it be, then, that though Nietzsche is wrong about biblical religion, he is right that the form in which the slave morality triumphed in Europe was a Christianity which had been transformed into a slave morality? There is some truth in this. But reservations need to be made. If we look at Christian thought in the centuries immediately after the establishment of the Christian religion, we find, on the one hand, Augustine with his doctrine that being as being is good and all evil is the privation of being – the very opposite of slave morality according to Nietzsche. And, on the other hand, we find that, had legislation in the 'Christian Empire' been handed over to the doctors of the Greek Church, particularly St John Chrysostom, it would have constituted a slave rebellion not in morals, but in economics, and we should soon be celebrating the sixteenth centenary of communist civilisation.

Nevertheless, at the popular level many must have found in Christianity a means of reconciling themselves to their oppressed lot, in the hope of an inversion of fortunes in the hereafter. This is the clue to the success of the slave rebellion in morals among the master classes of Europe: in a slave rebellion in morals the slave class had found a substitute for a slave rebellion in reality. So long as slave morality prevailed, the masters could sleep securely in their beds because the slaves had forsworn emancipation as sour grapes. Slave morality was so useful to the masters that they were unable not to come to believe in it. This takes us to my second theme, the relation of slave morality to the modern left.

Slave politics and proletarian politics

If you are a member of an oppressed group, you can do one of two things about it: you can have a slave rebellion or you can have a slave rebellion in morals. If you regard the good things that the masters have as genuine goods and want to redistribute them, you will do the former. The motivation for the latter is different: to retain one's self-esteem as a member of one's oppressed group; this self-esteem becomes bound up with being part of that oppressed group: one is proud of having a manual worker's aversion to high culture and being unlike those 'arty-farty' intellectuals; one is proud of one's feminine aversion to objective research and one claims that objectivity is just male subjectivity. In normal times, these slavish attitudes are enough to keep oppressed groups relatively contented and incapacitated for effective revolt. Revolutionary consciousness and the possibility of emancipation are dependent on the oppressed freeing themselves from slave morality. But it sometimes happens that an oppressed group becomes militant without so freeing itself. When this happens it becomes political, but it is the politics of identity not the politics of emancipation. The aim is to destroy rather than redistribute the benefits of the master class, so that everyone can have the identity of the slave class. This form of politics has historically come very naturally to every non-proletarian oppressed group on all those rare occasions when such groups have been political at all. The hostility to 'superfluities' in Quakerism and Rousseau are cases in point. But if Marx is to be believed, there is a version of communism too which conforms to this model:

> the domination of *material* property bulks so large that it threatens to destroy *everything* which is not capable of being possessed by everyone as private property; it wants to abstract from talent, etc., by *force*. . . . the category of *worker* is not abolished but extended to all men. . . . The crude communist is merely the culmination of this envy and desire to level down on the basis of a *preconceived* minimum. . . . How little this abolition of private property is a true appropriation is shown by the abstract negation of the entire world of culture and civilisation, and the return to the *unnatural* simplicity of the *poor*, unrefined man who has no needs and who has not even reached the stage of private property, let alone gone beyond it.
>
> (*Early Writings*, p. 346)

Kautsky, writing about the heretical communists of the Reformation period, comments that:

> Production was not yet sufficiently developed to provide means for a refined enjoyment of life by the masses of the people. He, therefore, who desired equality among mankind, could see evils not only in luxury, but also in art and science, which, as a matter of fact, were often enough the handmaids of luxury. Communists, as a rule, went further than this. In the face of the vast amount of misery in the world, it seemed to them that not only were arrogance and frivolity sins, but that even the most harmless pleasures were sins also.
>
> (*Communism in Central Europe at the Time of the Reformation*, p. 21)

However much we modern communists may be tempted to romanticise the rustic communist movements of medieval and early modern times, it is likely that, had they succeeded, they would have resembled that one modern triumph of the identity politics of the oppressed, Pol Pot's Cambodia.

By contrast, it is uniquely characteristic of proletarian movements that they have aimed to redistribute wealth and generalise culture, rather than abolishing them. The Russian Revolution, for example, was marked by a respect, almost a deference, for art and science and a serious attempt to make them available to the whole people. This is in striking contrast to the pre-Marxist revolutionaries in Russia who were nihilists about art and science. It is noteworthy that even modern non-proletarian movements of the oppressed have a tendency to revert to slave rebellions in morals as opposed to slave rebellions. This is true of peasant movements, but it is also true of feminism in so far as it has become alienated from the working-class movement. Socialist feminism typically aims at the equal empowerment of women, but much recent feminism simply idealises the real or imagined qualities that women have as a result of their oppression; this is identity politics, or slave rebellion in morals, or putting flowers on one's chains – the three phrases are synonymous.

The synchronic 'slave rebellion in morals' thesis, then, can be accepted by the left in so far as 'left' means relating to working-class politics; slave rebellion in morals is one tendency among the oppressed, offset by another tendency, proletarian class consciousness. The class-conscious worker will share Nietzsche's aversion to slave rebellions in morals because it is a mechanism by which the oppressed are kept oppressed and because it makes them value their chains.

Furthermore, Marx provides answers to two questions that Nietzsche provokes but does not try to answer: why does the slave morality prevail among master classes and how can slave morality be avoided in the future? The master classes adopt slave morality because it is in their interest that slave morality be widely adhered to; and there will be no more tendency to slave rebellions in morals when there are no more oppressed classes.

I conclude that while Nietzsche has identified a genuine mechanism that is operative in the history of ideology, he is wrong in his claim that it is present in Judaism and early Christianity and in modern socialism. He is unable to see this because of his own socio-political commitments: much of what he values depends on the existence of the oppression that generates the slave rebellion in morals and that both the Judaeo-Christian scriptures and modern socialism protest against.

Notes

1   This passage may seem more 'Nazi' than it is, since Nietzsche is in part trying to embarrass 'Christian' anti-Semites by drawing attention to the Semitic roots of Christianity, rather than setting up his own anti-Christian anti-Semitism. Nevertheless, this

chapter of *Twilight of the Idols* ('The "Improvers" of Mankind') contains some atrocious passages, including the claim that breeding a better humankind by cruel methods, including genital mutilation of women, is preferable to the Judaeo-Christian attempt to improve humankind by preaching love and justice.

2   See his nasty, snobbish little essay 'Ressentiment', in Solomon (ed.), *Nietzsche.*

3   For example, Isaiah 10: 1–2:

> Woe to the legislators of infamous laws,
> to those who issue tyrannical decrees,
> who refuse justice to the unfortunate
> and cheat the poor among my people of their rights,
> who make widows their prey
> and rob the orphan.

Also, Jeremiah 22: 15–16:

> Are you more of a king
> for outrivalling others with cedar?
> Your father ate and drank, like you
> but he practised honesty and integrity,
> so all went well for him.
> He used to examine to cases of poor and needy,
> then all went well.
> Is not that what it means to know me? – it is Yahweh who speaks.

There are similar passages in Amos and Micah.

4   Oddly enough, Nietzsche himself praises the pre-exilic prophets – specifically Isaiah – despite their frequent threats of divine retribution against the master class. But he sees the exile as a refutation of their faith in God: 'The old God *could* no longer do what he formerly could. One should have let him go' (*Antichrist*, Ch. 25). Yet the pre-exilic prophets without exception had prophesied that God would bring enemies to punish them for their oppressions. The exile was a fulfilment, not a refutation, of their threats.

5   For example:

> The living know at least that they will die, the dead know nothing; no more reward for them, their memory has passed out of mind. Their loves, their hates, their jealousies, these all have perished, nor will they ever again take part in whatever is done under the sun. Go, eat your bread with joy and drink your wine with a glad heart; for what you do God has approved beforehand. Wear white all the time, do not stint your head of oil. Spend your life with the woman you love, through all the fleeting days of the life that God has given you under the sun; for this is the lot assigned to you in life and in the efforts you exert under the sun. Whatever work you propose to do, do it while you can, for there is neither achievement, nor planning, nor knowledge, nor wisdom in Sheol [the grave] where you are going.
>
> (Ecclesiastes 9: 5–10)

6   For instance, Isaiah 1: 11–17.

7   See *City of God*, Book XIV, Chapter 9.

References

Augustine, Aurelius, *City of God*, Penguin, Harmondsworth, 1972.

Kautsky, K., *Communism in Central Europe in the Time of the Reformation*, Augustus M. Kelley, New York, 1966.

Marx, Karl, *Early Writings*, Penguin, Harmondsworth, 1975.

Nietzsche, Friedrich, *Twilight of the Idols and Antichrist*, Penguin, Harmondsworth, 1968.

Solomon, R. (ed.), *Nietzsche*, Doubleday Anchor, Garden City, New York, 1973.

6 The right rebellion in the wrong cause

Heidegger, technology and the market

As is well known, Heidegger's *Being and Time* focuses on the kind of sight and knowledge involved in work, rather than that involved in passive looking, and tries thereby to escape the errors of the last three hundred years of Cartesian philosophy. It is on this achievement that his reputation rests. But it often happens that a philosopher earns his reputation by one work but exercises influence by quite different ones. Many who have not read *Principia Mathematica* are induced by its authority to take Russell's advice about marriage and morals seriously. Heidegger's influence today lies mainly in his critique of the technological world view and his grand narrative of the history of ideas. At the risk of greatly oversimplifying what Heidegger has to say about these issues, I intend to summarise Heidegger's views as four hypotheses, three of which I will defend. I will argue that these hypotheses cannot be explained as Heidegger does, but require a Marxian account of ideology to make sense of them. The four hypotheses are:

1 That the essence of the technological world view is to regard the whole of reality – natural, human or cultural – as a 'standing reserve', a stockpile of materials for production; see 'The Question Concerning Technology', *Basic Writings* (hereafter *BW*), pp. 298–301; (since 'standing reserve' sounds unnatural in English, I shall usually use the term 'stockpile').
2 That the essence of modern science is the mathematicisation of nature (*BW*, pp. 302–4).
3 That (1) explains (2) (*BW*, pp. 302–3).
4 That the roots of this technologism are in a 'productivist metaphysics' inherited from the Greeks ('Letter on Humanism', *BW*, p. 220).

Let us look at these in turn.

(1) Already in 1844, Marx was writing 'the dealer in minerals sees only the commercial value, not the beauty and peculiar nature of the minerals; he lacks a mineralogical sense' (*Early Writings*, p. 353). One and a half centuries on, we call our ability to teach and write 'marketable skills', and talk about

the 'throughput' of students in the university. Perhaps two recent facts can illustrate the increasing dominance of this world view – one of them a trivial annoyance, the other a monstrous atrocity. The first is the fact that, when you get the speaking clock on the telephone, you are given the 'time sponsored by Accurist' – time itself has become a marketable product. The second is the fact that, in many South American cities (outside Cuba), 'street children' are murdered to put their organs on the transplant market. Despite the immeasurable moral disparity of these two facts, they equally illustrate the standing reserve mentality. This may throw light on a remark of Heidegger's for which he has been fiercely condemned:

> Agriculture today is a motorized food industry, in essence the same as the manufacture of corpses in gas chambers and extermination camps, the same as the blockade and starvation of countries, the same as the manufacture of atomic bombs.
>
> (Quoted in Wolin, *The Heidegger Controversy*, pp. 290–91)

I see no reason to call this 'a gruesome equation of incomparables', as Wolin does. Heidegger is not saying that all these evils are equivalent, any more than I am saying that about the speaking clock and child murder; he is saying that they all express the same attitude, reducing everything to parts of a stockpile. I may add that in several ways Wolin himself shows moral insensitivity in the passage where he criticises this remark of Heidegger's. For aside from the question of factory farming, Heidegger has mentioned real atrocities against civilians – starvation and nuclear bombing – which Wolin makes light of by contrast with the 'specifically German responsibility' for death camps. This sort of Kraut-bashing serves merely to ease the conscience of Anglophone liberals who, after all, have at various times been responsible for starving one and a half million Irish civilians to death under Lord Russell's Liberal government and wiping out whole cities and subjecting future generations to the horrific effects of radiation under Truman's presidency. These crimes are surely comparable to the Holocaust. Factory farming, of course, is not, but it is still a wrong. To gloss it as 'the production of higher yield crops', as Wolin does, is a cop-out. In passing, it should be said that the often-repeated slander that Heidegger has never condemned the Holocaust, even in retrospect, is refuted by this passage. These points are meant to support Heidegger's diagnosis of the ontological outlook of the present age; the aetiology is more questionable, as we shall see.

(2) Galileo is supposed to have said: 'if it is quantifiable, quantify it; if it is not quantifiable, still quantify it'. This approach has been very fruitful in the natural sciences and Heidegger does not deny that, within their limits, they disclose being. What may have been lost for knowledge through this approach is another matter. But in the human sciences, I think it is demonstrable that quantification has no explanatory role (I have argued this

elsewhere). In so far as they do use quantification, this is always a sign that crucial qualitative distinctions are being ignored. And the practice of modern politics applies the theory of quantified social science. For instance, as a result of 'reforms' imposed by international financial institutions, the Ghanaian economy has increased the amount of money it acquires to pay these same bankers with. That is a hard quantitative fact, which hides the soft qualitative fact that this is done by producing timber instead of food, which causes local people to starve, forest peoples to be evicted from their homes and rainforest to be cut down with disastrous effects on the environment. It is because the forest and its peoples are seen as a stockpile, a means of producing monetary and therefore quantifiable revenue for these bankers, that the calculations that show this inhuman outcome to be 'economically rational' can be made: 'does not man himself belong even more originally than nature within the standing-reserve? The current talk about human resources, about the supply of patients for a clinic, gives evidence of this' (*BW*, p. 299). For the sort of non-economic rationality which would take into account the claims of forest dwellers to live in their homes and of all of us to have air to breathe, mathematical calculation would be useless. Every building housing an economic policy-making institution ought to have inscribed over its entrance Blake's motto 'Bring out number, weight & measure in a year of dearth' ('The Marriage of Heaven and Hell', in *Complete Writings*, p. 151).

Mathematicisation is possible only if qualitative distinctions are ignored, and that happens because all entities are measured by the same yardstick – the single, external quality of their potential use for profit-making. As the seventeenth-century economist Nicholas Barbon puts it:

> One sort of wares are [*sic*] as good as another, if the value be equal. There is no difference or distinction in things of equal value. . . . One hundred pounds worth of lead or iron, is of as great a value as one hundred pounds worth of silver or gold.
>
> (Quoted in Marx, *Capital*, pp. 127–28)

At the time this was a revolutionary idea; Barbon's background was indeed a revolutionary one – bourgeois revolution, of course. He was the son of Praise-God Barebone, after whom Cromwell's nominated parliament was named.

In passing, it is worth mentioning that Macmurray has a very similar account to Heidegger's of the basis of the use of mathematics in science, in a utilitarian attitude to 'stuff' – see his book *Interpreting the Universe*.

It will be clear from my examples that I think that Heidegger is on the right lines about the stockpile attitude, the a priori application (often misapplication) of mathematics in modern science and the basis of the latter in the former. His fourth point, though, seems to be almost the exact opposite of the truth: so far from the Greeks inaugurating a productivist metaphysics, they failed mainly in underrating the place of production in epistemology and metaphysics. There are also *ad hominem* reasons why it is an odd view for Heidegger to hold. In the first place, if the ancient Greeks had made production the model for everything, it would have been craft production, not industrial technology. Yet Heidegger himself is insistent that craft production does not express the stockpile attitude as industrial technology does. Modern technology 'puts to nature the unreasonable demand that it supply energy which can be extracted and stored as such. But does this not hold true for the old windmill as well? No' (*BW*, p. 296). On the following page he goes on to contrast the wooden bridge built across the River Rhine by craft technology with the damming of the Rhine for hydroelectric power by industrial technology. To give any plausibility to the hypothesis of a productivist metaphysics stemming from the Greeks and issuing in the stock-pile attitude, one would have to obliterate that distinction. Heidegger is, of course, acutely aware of the differences between Greek and modern technology and naturally prefers the Greeks, yet in the end he treats the continuity as more important than the break. 'For technology does not go back to the *techne* of the Greeks in name only but derives historically and essentially from *techne* as a mode of *aletheuein*, a mode, that is, of rendering things manifest' (*BW*, p. 220).

Furthermore, as I said at the outset, Heidegger's own masterpiece *Being and Time* takes work – mainly productive work – as the paradigm of our relation with the world. It treats as the great error of modern philosophy, from Descartes on, its tendency to take 'just looking' as the paradigm case of sight and knowledge, rather than the 'looking around' (*umsicht*) of practical life and the worker's knowledge of his or her materials. One might say that Heidegger's starting point is 'I use a hammer to mend a shutter, therefore I am', and he consequently concludes that what I am is Being-in-the-world rather than a thinking thing.

It is arguable that Descartes' mistake here is inherited from the Greeks, although he gets more enmired in it than they did, for the Greeks too prioritised purely contemplative knowledge over that inherent in practice. Compare the views of John Macmurray, the closest UK philosopher to Heidegger, but one who, unlike Heidegger, had benefited from deep study of Marx. According to Macmurray, the error of the Greeks was that, because their society was a slave one which devalued handwork as slavish and over-valued 'pure' contemplative knowledge as aristocratic, they based their epistemology on the latter and hence arrived at a dualist metaphysics. Macmurray contrasts this unfavourably with the ancient Hebrews whose society was the least class divided of civilised societies in antiquity. Their scholars were also handworkers. They did not, in fact, develop an explicit epistemology and metaphysics, but implicit in their culture is a work-based epistemology and a non-dualist metaphysics which, according to Macmurray, it should be our task to develop. It shows in the absence from Hebrew thought of any conception of a soul that could exist separately from the body, so that when the idea of an afterlife enters their religion, it can only take the form of belief in resurrection. It shows in the fact that even knowledge of God is conceived by them not as theory but as inherent in practice. As Jeremiah tells the king:

> Did not your father eat and drink, and do judgement
> and justice, and then it was well with him?
> He judged the cause of the poor and needy;
> Then it was well with him:
> Was this not to know me? Saith the Lord
> (Jeremiah 22: 15–16)

Along with this goes a denial of the distinction between sacred and secular, and the aim of a fully classless society, both explicit in prophets like Amos and Isaiah. In Plato, by contrast, we have an aristocrat's contempt for hand-work and the knowledge inherent in it, and not only a dualism of body and soul, but a three-way splitting of the soul to match the three classes in his ideal society. This is recognised by Zimmerman:

> Max Scheler has argued, for example, that the Greek institution of slavery was what enabled philosophers such as Aristotle to view the natural world in terms of teleological forms rather than merely as an instrument for human ends. Hence the hierarchical social structure made it possible for Plato and Aristotle to shift from the pragmatic, ready-to-hand orientation of the lower classes to the theoretical, present-at-hand orientation of the elites.
>
> (*Heidegger's Confrontation with Modernity*, p. 158)

– even though he does not pick up on the use-value/exchange-value or production-for-use/production-for-money way of distinguishing Greek metaphysics from modern, of which more later.

The tradition leading from Plato to Descartes is precisely the tradition that marginalises production from epistemology and metaphysics; the explicit working out of the idea that knowledge is itself a form of production we owe to the modern Jewish philosophers Spinoza and Marx. In short, the view that Greek philosophy set us on the road of productivist metaphysics is not only untrue, it is the direct opposite of the truth, like so many of the shibboleths of postmodern thinking. (Derrida's idea that Western thought prioritises speech over writing is another such falsism.) As for the view (see *BW*, pp. 158ff.) that Aristotle's hylomorphism – the idea that all things are formed matter – is productivist, this is surely wrong. It was almost certainly suggested to him by his studies of animal organisms. It is also interesting that this hylomorphism survived as the dominant doctrine about the way things are until commerce came to dominate Europe and hylomorphism was abandoned as an obstacle to the ideologies of commerce – that is, precisely to the stockpile attitude. Descartes' idea that it is legitimate to exploit animals unrestrictedly, for instance, depends on seeing them as machines rather than organisms (hylomorphs). One might even characterise the sort of technology that Heidegger objects to as the sort that does not regard the form of the entities with which it deals, but treats them as if they were formless matter.

However, the commonplace of Marxist discussions of the Greeks – that they neglected production as a theme for thought because they thought productive labour was fit only for slaves – is not the whole story of the relation between society and philosophy in ancient Greece as understood by Marxists. But before we return to this issue, there is a problem to be cleared up about the third point in Heidegger's account of the origins of the technological outlook.

As Heidegger himself points out, there is a paradox in that the mathematicisation of nature by science is supposed to result from the technological conception of reality as a stockpile; yet mathematical physics emerges in the sixteenth and seventeenth centuries, while technology in the industrial sense has to wait until the eighteenth and nineteenth centuries:

> But after all, mathematical science arose almost two centuries before technology. How, then, could it have already been set upon by modern technology and placed in its service? The facts testify to the contrary. Surely technology got under way only when it could be supported by exact physical science. Reckoned chronologically, this is correct. Thought historically, it does not hit upon the truth.
>
> (*BW*, p. 303)

> modern technology, which for chronological reckoning is the later, is, from the point of view of the essence holding sway within it, historically earlier.
>
> (*BW*, p. 304)

Heidegger lets this paradox stand unresolved. The Marxist solution is that both the stockpile concept and mathematicisation flow not from particular techniques used in the production process, but from the fact that production has come to be for the market rather than for use. It is the spirit of commerce, not of technology, that treats nature and humankind as raw materials and believes all distinctions quantifiable because they are all obliterated by that eminently quantifiable universal medium, money. Although the Industrial Revolution first started in England in the mid-eighteenth century, Tudor England was already a capitalist country, not a feudal one. The labour shortage following the Black Death had transformed the serfs into wage-labourers; many of the feudal aristocrats whose ancestors had come over from Normandy with William the Bastard had killed each other in the Wars of the Roses, saving the people the trouble; self-sufficient food-producing villages were being destroyed to produce wool for the export market; the commercially successful landowners were being ennobled, creating a new aristocracy, bourgeois to the marrow of its bones; the high geographical mobility that is characteristic of modern English life dates from this time, not from the Industrial Revolution. The feudal tie between peasant and land had gone and both were now part of the stockpile. It is against this background and the contemporary emergence of capitalist relations of production in the Low Countries and northern Italy that both the stockpile attitude and modern science emerge as components of the 'modern world outlook'.

The solution of Heidegger's paradox shows what is the truth underlying his critique of modernity: that modernity, as capitalism, is dominated by exchange-value-driven production, not use-value-driven production. I have written at some length about this Marxist distinction elsewhere, so here let me just summarise it:

1 The difference of use-value between two commodities – which is what makes them different commodities – is qualitative, not quantitative. For instance, the difference in use-value between a cheese sandwich and a pocket calculator is not that one is more or less anything than the other, but that you cannot eat a pocket calculator or add up with a cheese sandwich. The difference in exchange-value is purely quantitative: one costs more or less than the other. If you want either of them only to sell, you can easily decide which you would rather have by arithmetic; if you want them to use, you decide non-calculatively, by deciding what you want to do – eat or do a sum.

2 Exchange-value production leaves out of account whatever does not effect profit; it is therefore systematically indifferent to the environment, workers' welfare, and so on.

3 The pursuit of use-values is inherently limited, that of exchange-values inherently unlimited; the feudal lord will rob his serfs to support his gluttony, but his stomach can only hold so much; the capitalist's bank account has no such limitations.

4 Exchange-values are extrinsic to the valued object, use-values intrinsic. The use-value of an object is internally related to the work of its production as a specific kind of work – that is, baking produces bread, carpentry produces wooden goods, and so on. The exchange-value is an external end: work gets money.

Marx, who was always ready to acknowledge his intellectual debts, refers to Aristotle as the originator of the use-value/exchange-value distinction. Aristotle is also the teacher of all those moderns who rebel against the dominant exchange-value metaphysics. This suggests that it is worth taking another look at the relation between philosophy and society in ancient Greece.

First of all, the idea of some Marxist scholars (for instance, George Thomson in *The First Philosophers*) that the classical philosophers and in particular Plato are straightforwardly ideologists of the slave-owning class needs qualifying. Certainly Plato came from that class; I have suggested that his contemplative view of knowledge and his dualist metaphysics reflect this, as more obviously does his attack on democracy. But Plato was also the disciple of Socrates. And whatever the views of the historical Socrates about democracy, he was from the craftworker class and his whole style is uniquely formed by Athenian democracy. It reflects a society where ordinary peasants and craftworkers could spend time in the theatre and the public assembly; the dialogue form, taken over and immortalised by Plato, has its origin in the cut and thrust of street-corner debate, which is perhaps even today more characteristic of the Greeks than of any other European people. Ellen Wood, a Marxist scholar who disagrees with Thomson about the extent of slavery in ancient Athens, claiming that it was a peasant and craftworker democracy to which slavery was peripheral, also claims that Plato's thought, though the classical statement of the anti-democratic position, takes a form which is made possible only by Athenian democracy (see her book *Peasant-Citizen and Slave*). That form – dialectic in its old sense – defines all that is best in Western philosophy ever since.

The second complication is more directly pertinent to the matter in hand. Aside from the contrast between the ideologies of the slave-owning aristocracy and of the craftworkers of Athens, there is another ideological division running through the greatest period of Greek philosophy – that marked by Aristotle's contrast (in *Politics*, Books 1 and 2) between the art of household management, 'economics', which aims at producing use-values, and that of wealth-getting, 'chrematistics', which aims at producing exchange-values and brings in its wake the disreputable consequences that we have seen. This reflects the fact that Athens was on the cusp of the transition between a craft economy producing and exchanging use-values, and an economy in which the market, while not all-pervasive as in capitalism, had a much more influential role. Money and exchange existed in the older economy too, but in Marxist terms, their function was in the transaction C–M–C (commodity–money–commodity), not M–C–M (money–commodity–money) (see *Capital*, pp. 247ff.). That is, sandalmakers sold a commodity (sandals) for money and used the money to buy another commodity (say, bread), while bakers sold bread and bought sandals. This was motivated by the fact that you cannot eat sandals or wear bread on your feet. In the commercial economy, on the other hand, exchange is governed by the transaction M–C–M: you start with money, buy a commodity, and sell it for money – *more* money, of course, being the motivation. Although there is exchange in both economies (and of course use-values are produced in both economies, otherwise people could not live), C–M–C economies are use-value-driven and M–C–M economies are exchange-value-driven. In C–M–C transactions the motive is qualitative (a different commodity), in M–C–M transactions it is quantitative (more money). C–M–C exchange is limited – when you have the commodity you want, you enjoy it. M–C–M exchange is unlimited –

when you have more money, you lay it out to get more still. Neither form of exchange held exclusive dominance in the economy of Athens, and this is reflected ideologically in the Platonic dialogues, in the conflict between Socrates who represents the use-value-producing craft view, and the sophists who represent the exchange-value-producing commercial view. Take Plato's *Republic.* While there is no doubt that much of the Socrates of that dialogue is really Plato (for example, the theory of forms, the three-class state, the noble lie, the eugenic gang-bangs), I suspect that the conflict over the nature of work is a genuine Socratic/sophistic disagreement. For Socrates, a shepherd is someone who looks after sheep, a doctor is someone who heals the sick, a sandalmaker is someone who makes sandals and a baker is someone who makes bread. A *good* shepherd, doctor, sandalmaker or baker is one who does that thing well. For the sophists there is one goal of all these crafts: money. A good anything is a profit-making anything. Parodying Bentham: profit being equal, push-pin is as good as poetry. This, of course, affects Socrates' and the sophists' respective views of philosophy: for Socrates it aims to discover truth, for the sophists to develop transferable skills.

The real ancestors of the stockpile attitude are neither the craftworker Socrates nor the aristocrat Plato, but the sophists. It is a commercialist metaphysics not a productivist one. One consequence is that Heidegger's *Being and Time* does not fall under the axe of his own critique of the modern world outlook. Taking work rather than gawping as our fundamental way of relating to the world does not commit us to a stockpile attitude. For the model of *Dasein*'s Being-in-the-world in *Being and Time* is indeed work, but work as concrete not abstract labour, the labour that produces use-values, not exchange-values (see Marx's *Capital* for this distinction). This point is, I think, missed by those (for example, Zimmerman) who defend *Being and Time* from the charge of productivism on the grounds of its craft (pre-industrial) description of work; it is not the level of technology that is essential, but its goals.

But what, then, of Heidegger's distinction between craft and technological production? It does seem intuitively plausible that there is a real difference of attitude to nature expressed in the damming of the River Rhine for hydroelectric power and, for instance, the use of a river to drive a water mill. The stockpile attitude seems present in the one and not in the other. Yet water mills, while characteristic of the feudal mode of production, did operate for some hundreds of years in market economies; and hydroelectric power stations, while first built in capitalist societies, could exist in a use-value-driven communist society. Can the intuitive distinction be mapped on to the use-value/exchange-value distinction? To spell out the intuitive distinction: a water mill uses the force of the river, but leaves the river much as it was; the dam transforms the river into something else. The damming of the Rhine thus involves a loss that is not involved in the water mill. But that loss does not show up in exchange-value-based calculations. It is an ironic fact that the overuse of hydroelectric power in the Soviet Union, which was the cause of some of the environmental disasters that haunt that part of the world today, was the result of a method of economic calculation that took only exchange-value into account – that is, which used the kind of criteria endogenous to capitalism. A use-value-driven system of planning might still lead to the building of hydroelectric power stations. But the decision process would take into account the intrinsic value of the river system, setting it against the incommensurable value of increased electricity generation and deciding between them not on the basis of any countable units of value, but of an opinion about whether the world (or that part of it) would be a better place to live in with the untransformed river and less electricity, or with the transformed river and more electricity. Only those who lived in that part of the world would be in a position to make such a decision. It could not be made on the basis of written information. This example will serve to differentiate two notions of the sort of knowledge that planning and management generally should require: storable abstract information by which alternatives can be assigned numerical values which will give rise to a calculable optimum choice; or concrete personal experience by which incommensurable alternatives can be assessed for their contribution to a whole lifeworld. If it is worthwhile using a Marxist theory of history to rescue Heidegger from himself, this is partly because any kind of socialist planning that is to be better than a state-run imitation of planning within a capitalist corporation will depend on an existentialist style of management replacing the utilitarian one which is increasingly pervasive.

The term 'the right rebellion in the wrong cause' has been applied to the Jacobite rebellion of 1745. Scotland, particularly the Highlands, was being oppressed and devastated by the English Whig oligarchy and its Scottish quislings. A rebellion was well in order. But the cause for which the Scots rebelled was to reverse what has been called the one clear benefit that Scotland ever received from English rule: the ousting of the House of Stuart. Likewise, Heidegger's rebellion against the stockpile attitude is fully justified and perhaps the most needed rebellion in the world today. But the source of this attitude is not science or technology, it is commercialism.[1] I say 'commercialism' rather than 'capitalism' for two reasons. First, capitalism has two defining characteristics: it is a market economy and it is a society divided into propertied and propertyless classes. I am opposed to both, but it is only the former that I am concerned with here. I do also hold that 'market socialism' – that is, the rectification only of the latter feature – would generate most of the same evils as capitalism – environmental disaster, unemployment, Third World poverty and the arms race, for instance. Second, the ideology of capitalist society has not historically been a seamless web. One component in it has always been commercialism, with its metaphysical corollaries of atomism, reduction of quality to quantity, of organism to mechanism and of internal relations to external relations, and its ethical corollary of belief that various sorts of maximising behaviour can be rational.

But generally there have been other components too in the ideology of capitalist societies: religious or humanistic limits on what can be bought and sold, for example; or belief in the intrinsic worth of certain activities with internal goals, such as art, science and scholarship. Commercialism today has become totalitarian commercialism, the dogma that commercial values are the only values, and the domination of every area of life by commerce. This all-pervasive ideology is the principal enemy of every decent person.

In the light of the idea that what Heidegger was really up against was commercialism, I would now like to take another brief look at his critique of inauthentic existence in *Being and Time*. When Heidegger asks the 'question of the "who" of Dasein' – that is, of humankind – he is asking in what the constancy of the self consists (p. 152). Later, he will discuss the authentic self-constancy of resoluteness (pp. 369–70). But in 'everyday Being-one's-Self' this is conspicuous by its absence. Our everyday self-constancy is provided by others (p. 166), but in a particular way. After the section describing our essential sociality, our 'Being-with' (s. 26), he characterises our everyday relations as 'distantiality', although the German word *Abständigkeit* (which shares a root with *Selbständigkeit*, self-constancy) suggests the colloquial English expression 'standoffishness'. Examples given are the cases in which 'one's own Dasein has lagged behind the Others and wants to catch up in relationship to them' or 'one's Dasein already has some priority over them and sets out to keep them suppressed' (pp. 163–64) – cases of keeping up with the Joneses, one might say. Standoffishness, then, is a relation in which one's inequality with others is an issue. Yet this inequality is not that of a personal relationship (for example, master and slave), and likewise precludes equal personal relationships (friend and friend). Nor is it any qualitative difference, as expressed in a person's originality; that sort of inequality gets levelled down (p. 165) into an averageness where all are the same. This is precisely both the kind of inequality and the kind of equality that are characteristic of market relations between people.

Under the sway of this standoffishness, an alienation of human powers takes place, which Heidegger sums up in his famous phrase *'das Man'* – 'the "they"':

> Dasein's everyday possibilities of Being are for the Others to dispose of as they please. These Others, moreover, are not *definite* Others. . . . The 'who' is not this one, not that one, not oneself [*man selbst*], not some people [*einige*], and not the sum of them all. The 'who' is the neuter, *the 'they'* [*das Man*].
>
> (p. 164)

The rule of *das Man* is also characterised by both the sort of freedom and the sort of unfreedom that pertain to market economies: standoffishness is such that we stand in subjection to others (p. 164). Not to any particular other, however: personal dependency is precluded; so is dependency on the collective, since *das Man* is not the sum of people (p. 164). *Das Man* has coercive power without its being personal power or the power of any kind of agency; just such is the power of the market. 'In Dasein's everydayness the agency through which most things come about is one of which we must say that "it was no one"' (p. 165).

The later description of idle talk and curiosity (ss. 35 and 36) also looks like a description of the market in news and information and sightseeing, as opposed to the knowledge and sight which are rooted in exercising skills and dwelling in a place: information as exchangeable merchandise rather than as experience in a craft and familiarity with a neighbourhood. The polemic against inauthenticity is a polemic against the spirit of commerce penetrating our ways of relating and talking.

I have focused on inauthenticity as manifested in relations between people, but it could also be argued that the part of Heidegger's description of inauthenticity that concerns our relation to things rather than people is a description of means/end inversion – an absorption in things rather than in one's potentiality for being, just as the market pushes saleable 'things' to the fore, presents them as the essence of our being and represses the awareness of any other potentiality for being (compare my essay on authenticity in my book *Being and Worth*).

Now Heidegger makes it quite clear that authenticity does not mean egoism or isolation, nor the snobbish separateness of a superman, nor the priggish separateness of a Pharisee.[2] It is a modification of everyday Being-in-the-world and Being-with-Others. Yet there has been a persistent tendency to read it as somehow an anti-democratic ideal. This is because of the tendency to identify democracy with that most undemocratic of all institutions, the market. The most undemocratic institution, that is, for in the market the outcome is arrived at from human actions, yet arrived at without anybody choosing it, often contrary to every desire that was expressed in the actions whose resultant the state of the market is. In short, it exhibits counter-finality. By contrast, even an undemocratic authority – a hereditary monarch, for example – makes decisions that can be criticised and opposed by others who in consequence have some possible input into the outcome. A market is uniquely impervious to human preferences, even though they are its input. Furthermore, the market, while the most inegalitarian of all economic mechanisms in its effects on wealth distribution, has its own sort of egalitarianism in that it suppresses differences of quality and treats all effective demand as equal. The plea for authenticity is a plea for the sort of freedom, equality and self-constancy that the market destroys, and against the sort of freedom, equality and self-constancy that the market promotes. That is the right rebellion.

Notes

1 This right rebellion for the wrong cause goes some way towards explaining Heidegger's wrong rebellion for a wrong cause – namely, his support of the Nazis in the mid-1930s. It should also be said that no one in 1933 knew which promises Hitler was going to keep and which he would break. Heidegger, like many Germans, clearly thought that he would keep his 'workerist' and 'green' promises and break his anti-Semitic ones. Of course, it was the other way round. But there was more excuse for a German philosopher voting Nazi in 1933 than for an English philosopher voting Tory in the 1990s, after eighteen years of unrelieved evil.

2 For instance, on snobbery and priggishness as the manifestation of *das Man*:

> we shrink back from the 'great mass' as *they* shrink back; we find shocking what *they* find shocking.
>
> (*BT*, p. 164)

On the absence of isolation from among the salutary effects of anxiety:

> Anxiety individualizes Dasein and thus discloses '*solus ipse*'. But this existential 'solipsism' is so far from the displacement of putting an isolated subject-Thing into the innocuous emptiness of a worldless occurring, that in an extreme sense what it does is precisely to bring Dasein face to face with its world as world, and thus to bring it face to face with itself as Being-in-the-world.
>
> (*BT*, p. 233)

On the sociality of authenticity:

> Dasein is authentically itself only to the extent that, as concernful Being-alongside and solicitous Being-with, it projects itself upon its ownmost potentiality-for-Being rather than upon the possibility of the they-self.
>
> (*BT*, p. 308)

> Resoluteness, as *authentic Being-one's-Self*, does not detach Dasein from its world, nor does it isolate it so that it becomes a free-floating 'I'. And how should it, when resoluteness as authentic disclosedness, is *authentically* nothing else than *Being-in-the-world*? Resoluteness brings the Self right into its current concernful Being-alongside what is ready-to-hand, and pushes it into solicitous Being-with-Others.
>
> (*BT*, p. 344)

References

Aristotle, *Politics*, in *The Basic Works of Aristotle*, ed. R. McKeon, Random House, New York, 1941.

Blake, William, *Complete Writings*, Oxford University Press, London, 1966.

Collier, Andrew, *Being and Worth*, Routledge, London, 1999.

Heidegger, Martin, *Being and Time*, trans J. Macquarrie and E. Robinson, Blackwell, Oxford, 1967.

—— , *Basic Writings*, Routledge, London, 1978.

Macmurray, John, *Interpreting the Universe*, Faber & Faber, London, 1933.

Marx, Karl, *Early Writings*, Penguin, Harmondsworth, 1975.

—— , *Capital*, vol. 1, Penguin, Harmondsworth, 1976.

Plato, *Republic*, Penguin, Harmondsworth, 1955.

Thomson, George, *The First Philosophers*, Lawrence & Wishart, London, 1972.

Wolin, Richard (ed.), *The Heidegger Controversy*, MIT Press, Cambridge, Mass. and London, 1993.

Wood, Ellen, *Peasant-Citizen and Slave*, Verso, London, 1989.

Zimmerman, Michael, *Heidegger's Confrontation with Modernity*, Indiana University Press, Bloomington and Indianapolis, 1990.

7 Sartre: intimations of authenticity

Elsewhere (in the supplement to my *Being and Worth*) I have discussed Heidegger's conception of authentic existence and argued that authenticity is a virtue and not a self-regarding virtue. In Sartre's case, it is not so easy. Authenticity is a fundamental concept and perhaps the projected ethical goal of *Being and Nothingness*, but while Sartre describes its opposite – bad faith – in some detail and with great plausibility, he says little about authenticity. Yet, despite his good measure of agreement with Heidegger, Sartre's authenticity cannot quite be Heidegger's authenticity, since the opposite – bad faith – is not quite the same as Heidegger's 'inauthentic existence'. They have something in common: in both cases there is the idea of *ponziopilatismo*, disavowing one's actions. But in Sartre's bad faith the cognitive aspects are much more up front than in Heidegger's inauthenticity. Bad faith is self-deception. The motive for avoiding bad faith is therefore clearer than the motive for avoiding inauthenticity: you cannot maintain a choice of bad faith with full awareness of what you are doing, any more than you can say 'it is true, but I don't believe it'.

Sartre's examples are usually of someone disavowing their freedom in some way: the girl on her first date who neither responds to nor rejects her companion's gesture of taking her hand, but leaves it there like a thing; the waiter who, not content with waitering, puts on an act of being (nothing but) a waiter; the doctor who reveals his bad faith in the first two words of his speech: 'we doctors . . .'. We all recognise these means whereby we deny the freedom of choices that we nonetheless consciously make.

The possibility of avoiding this bad faith, and the mystery of Sartre's inability to discuss it, are raised by Sartre's footnote to his main discussion of bad faith:

> If it is indifferent whether one is in good or in bad faith, because bad faith reapprehends good faith and slides to the very origin of the project of good faith, that does not mean that we can not radically escape bad faith. But this supposes a self-recovery of being which was previously corrupted. This self-recovery we shall call authenticity, the description of which has no place here.
>
> (*Being and Nothingness*, p. 70, note 9)

Can we discern, from Sartre's account of bad faith to which he restricts himself here, what authenticity would be like? The easiest part of this is to refute the idea that Sartre has made bad faith inescapable, despite this protestation. Take his example of the man who, despite the fact that all his sexual relations have been with other men, will not call himself a homosexual (*Being and Nothingness* (hereafter *BN*), pp. 63–65). In so far as he says 'I am not a homosexual' he is in bad faith, denying his own past actions. But his friend who wants him to 'come out' is actually urging another form of bad faith upon him – that of identifying himself with his facticity (in this case, past actions) at the expense of his possibility (the open future in which he may freely choose whether he acts as he has in the past or not). The question is then levelled at Sartre: 'if the man says he is a homosexual he is in bad faith, and if he says he is not a homosexual he is in bad faith, so what is he to say?'. However, this question Sartre can answer. It all turns on Sartre's definition of a for-itself (a human agent, a person) as a being who is what he or she is not and is not what he or she is. This is not, of course, a denial of the law of contradiction, but means: in so far as I am anything – my race, sex, social position, physical stature, past – that is my facticity. But what is essential about me as a person is that I am not just my facticity but my capacity to transcend my facticity towards my possibilities. I am not my facticity as an inkwell is an inkwell, for an inkwell has no possibilities. But neither am I my possibilities as an inkwell is an inkwell, for I am them in the mode of having to be them – that is, they are to be realised by my actions, they are not yet real. If the homosexual who comes out means to say 'I am a homosexual as an inkwell is an inkwell – that is, that is my essence and it determines my possibilities' – then he is in bad faith; and if by saying that he is not a homosexual he means to say that he is not a homosexual as an inkwell is not a paper-knife, i.e. it could be true that he is a homosexual but it is false, then he is in bad faith. But if he says 'my past acts have been homosexual but my future is open and what I do is up to me', then he is not in bad faith. To express it linguistically, the bad faith lies in the noun form; if the avowal of homosexuality took a verbal form – 'I sleep with other men' – there would be no bad faith. But, of course, the essence of the point is not about language but about attitudes. The attitude of avowing one's facticity but not identifying oneself with it, defining oneself by one's possibilities but not taking the will for the deed, is a perfectly possible attitude and is not in bad faith.

The fact that Sartre has called one kind of bad faith 'good faith' (the homosexual coming out) has confused some people. Such good faith indeed he sees as another form of bad faith. But this does not mean that there is no alternative to bad faith, as we have seen, and in the above quote Sartre introduces the notion of authenticity to give it a name without calling it 'good faith'.

So far so good. But there is a real paradox in Sartre's intimations of authenticity. The first form of this paradox arises when we compare Sartre's account of the value-properties of objects in *The Transcendence of the Ego* (hereafter *TE*) with that in *BN*. In *TE* he tells us:

> I pity Peter, and I go to his assistance. For my consciousness only one thing exists at that moment: Peter-having-to-be-helped. This quality of 'having-to-be-helped' lies in Peter. It acts on me like a force. Aristotle said it: the desirable is that which moves the desiring. At this level, the desire is given to consciousness as centrifugal (it transcends itself . . .) and as impersonal (there is no *me*: I am in the presence of Peter's suffering just as I am in the presence of the color of this inkstand; there is an objective world of things and of actions, done or to be done, and the actions come to adhere as qualities to the things which call for them).
>
> (*TE*, p. 56)

Here Sartre is arguing against the 'self-love' moral psychology which postulates some self-referential motive behind the pitying of Peter. To-be-helpedness is a property of Peter, not something projected by the helper as a means to some end of his or her own (peace of mind, a sense of their own virtue, or whatever). But in *BN*, value appears as something projected by us and the attitude that treats values as adhering to objects appears as 'the spirit of seriousness', which Sartre regards as inauthentic, as a form of bad faith:

> But the principal result of existential psychoanalysis must be to make us repudiate the *spirit of seriousness*. The spirit of seriousness has two characteristics: it considers values as transcendent givens independent of human subjectivity, and it transfers the quality of 'desirable' from the ontological structure of things to their simple material constitution. For the spirit of seriousness, for example, *bread* is desirable because it is necessary to live (a value written in an intelligible heaven) and because bread *is* nourishing.
>
> (*BN*, p. 626)

It is certainly paradoxical to hold both that value is located in the object rather than the subject, and that it is dependent on the subject rather than on the nature of the object, but I don't think it is actually contradictory. He explains his position as follows:

> [value] can be revealed only to an active freedom which makes it exist as value by the sole fact of recognizing it as such. It follows that my freedom is the unique foundation of values and that *nothing*, absolutely nothing, justifies me in adopting this or that particular value, this or that particular scale of values. As a being by whom values exist, I am unjustifiable.
>
> (*BN*, p. 38)

Yet he can still go on to say:

> Ordinarily, however, my attitude with respect to values is eminently
> reassuring. In fact I am engaged in a world of values. The anguished
> apperception of values as sustained in being by my freedom is a secondary
> and mediated phenomenon. The immediate is the world with its
> urgency; and in this world where I engage myself, my acts cause values
> to spring up like partridges.
>
> > (*BN*, p. 38)

The metaphor of partridges is very suggestive: as one steps into the field,
the startled partridges spring up. One caused this by stepping into the field.
But one did not expect or intend to startle the partridges. Likewise, one's
choices cause values to be, but these values are not consciously projected or
decided upon. But reflectively, we discern with appropriate existential
anguish that we put them there. Here the metaphor breaks down; the
partridges had to be in the field in order to be startled, but values for Sartre
would not be there but for our choices.

But the paradox comes close to a contradiction when we bring in the question of authenticity. In *TE* Sartre had been treating the unreflective life of
non-self-referential values as the authentic life; it is reflection that poisons
desire according to this text (*TE*, p. 59: 'it is not my fault if my reflective
life poisons "by its very essence" my spontaneous life. Before being "poisoned"
my desires were pure').

This is not the traditional contrast between selfishness and altruism, for
that takes place on the reflective level. If unselfishness means 'self-denial',
pursued for its own sake or for some ulterior motive such as a good conscience
or a reward in heaven, it is as much poisoned as any other self-referential
desire. The point is rather that, for Sartre in *TE*, consciousness is pure, empty
directedness towards the object, so everything that moves one belongs to the
object, not the subject. That is the point of the reference to Aristotle.
Consciousness itself is empty of any motivating force: it is desire by virtue
of being consciousness of the desirable. It is bad faith (although Sartre does
not yet use that term) to attribute contents, states, qualities, etc. – any sort
of inner realities – to oneself, although reflective consciousness quite naturally
(if not quite inevitably) does it:

> Doubts, remorse, the so-called 'mental crises of consciousness' [*conscience*]
> etc. – in short, all the contents of intimate diaries – become sheer *perform-*
> *ance*. And perhaps we could derive here some sound precepts of moral
> discretion.
>
> > (*TE*, p. 94)

The ego as the possessor of states and qualities is fictional:

> Everything happens, therefore, as if consciousness constituted the ego as
> a false representation of itself, as if consciousness hypnotized itself before
> this ego which it has constituted, absorbing itself in the ego as if to
> make the ego its guardian and its law.
>
> (*TE*, p. 101)

This is Sartre's first description of bad faith, and he goes on to describe the
alternative, a type of reflection that is not hypnotised in this way:

> But it can happen that consciousness suddenly produces itself on the
> pure reflective level. Perhaps not without the ego, yet as escaping from
> the ego on all sides, as dominating the ego and maintaining the ego
> outside the consciousness by a continued creation.
>
> (*TE*, p. 101)

But if the ego is recognised as fictive, the motivating forces fictively ascribed
to it must be recognised as in the objects of consciousness. Some sort of
realism of values is required at the 'pure reflective' as at the unreflective level.
But in *BN* he seems to be saying that the unreflective attitude is inauthentic
and only reflection brings about a passage to authenticity which involves
recognising oneself as the source of one's values (see *BN*, p. 39). Perhaps
Sartre has changed his mind between writing *TE* and *BN*, but the paradox
continues, I think, into *BN* itself. As a preliminary, a few brief words are
required about Sartre's account of desire as a lack.

In the section 'The For-Itself and the Being of Value', the lack involved
in any human desire is analysed into three elements. If we see a crescent
moon, we may say that the darkened area of the moon is lacking. This is
because we transcend the crescent moon towards the full moon, 'the lacked'.
In human desire, there is always the existent (the desirer) corresponding to
the crescent, the lacking (the object desired) corresponding to the darkened
area of the moon, and the lacked (the totality composed of the existent and
the no-longer-lacking) corresponding to the full moon. Thus:

> In order to constitute it as hunger or thirst, an external transcendence
> surpassing it toward the totality 'satisfied hunger' would be necessary,
> just as the crescent moon is surpassed toward the full moon.
>
> (*BN*, p. 87)

So that:

> Everything which is lacking is lacking to . . . for . . .
>
> (*BN*, p. 88)

If I am hungry, a meal is lacking *to* me (the existent), *for* satisfied hunger (the lacked).

But it is not as straightforward as this. We might think that the totality satisfied-hunger is an attainable goal, but the lacked is said to be something that haunts all desires as their norm, but cannot be realised:

> Thus this perpetually absent being which haunts the for-itself is itself fixed in the in-itself. It is the impossible synthesis of the for-itself and the in-itself; it would be its own foundation not as nothingness but as being and would preserve within it the necessary translucency of consciousness along with the coincidence with itself of being-in-itself. It would preserve in it that turning back upon the self which conditions every necessity and every foundation. But this return to the self would be without distance; it would not be presence to itself, but identity with itself. In short, this being would be exactly the *self* which we have shown can exist only as a perpetually evanescent relation, but it would be this self as substantial being. Thus human reality arises as such in the presence of its own totality or self as a lack of that totality. And this totality can not be given by nature, since it combines in itself the incompatible characteristics of the in-itself and the for-itself.
>
> (*BN*, p. 90)

The 'in-itself-for-itself' is Sartre's most technical expression for the godlike self-coincidence that haunts us as the ideal end of every desire. The French is '*en-soi-pour-soi*', which suggests that the ordering of terms should be inverted in English as 'for-itself-in-itself'. It refers to that which (impossibly) has the character of the for-self – it desires, feels, intends – but has it in the way that in-itselfs have their properties. Sartre holds that this sort of totality is known to the European philosophical tradition as 'God'; a being who combines the freedom of the for-itself with the lacklessness and unchangeability of the in-itself. While it is true that classical philosophy has conceived of God as both free and unchangeable, this has usually gone with regarding God as outside of time, which, provided it is a coherent notion, does seem to take away the supposed contradiction. Also, God's freedom has sometimes been conceived, not as Sartrean natureless freedom, but as meaning that he acts entirely from his own nature. However, if God's freedom is conceived along the lines that Sartre conceives human freedom, only infinite – in other words, if it means that God can at any time choose to do anything – then it really is incompatible with changelessness and having an eternal nature or essence. And this is how Sartre conceives of the notion of God: as a being combining the incompatible predicates of Sartrean freedom and essentiality, and therefore as an impossible being. Hence Sartre is, of course, an atheist, but, more to the point, one who believes that human beings all want to be this impossible being, God – that is, the for-itself-in-itself. Hence our fate is to be 'an unhappy consciousness with no possibility of surpassing its unhappy state' (*BN*, p. 90).

But since this unrealisable desire is not one desire alongside others, but something that haunts all our particular desires, it would be better to say, not that we desire to be God absolutely, but that, with respect to any desire x, we want to be the god of x. Sartre gives the example of suffering:

> This norm or totality of the affective self is directly present as a lack *suffered* in the very heart of suffering. One suffers and one suffers from not suffering enough. The suffering of which we speak is never exactly that which we feel. What we call 'noble' or 'good' or 'true' suffering and what moves us is the suffering which we read on the faces of others, better yet in portraits, in the face of a statue, in a tragic mask.
>
> (*BN*, p. 91)

First-person suffering always confronts us with the choice of living it this or that way, so that the actual experience of suffering is always partly of something chosen, while we would like the suffering to be altogether an unchosen given:

> The suffering which I experience . . . is never adequate suffering, due to the fact that it nihilates itself as in itself by the very act by which it founds itself. It escapes as suffering towards the consciousness of suffering. I can never be *surprised* by it, for it *is* only to the exact degree that I experience it. Its translucency removes from it all depth. I cannot observe it as I observe the suffering of the statue, since I make my own suffering and since I know it. If I must suffer, I should prefer that my suffering would seize me and flow over me like a storm, but instead I must raise it into existence in my free spontaneity.
>
> (*BN*, p. 92)

One would like to be, in other words, the god of suffering.

Now let us return to the concrete examples of the threefold analysis of lack. I am thirsty; a pint of beer is lacking to me. What is the lacked? Not, it seems, the simple totality made up of me and a pint of beer which I am drinking. What is lacked is my being Bacchus, my being The Beer Drinker, as in a statue. Why? Because what thirst achieves when it is satisfied is its own cessation; but unreflective desire never aims at its own cessation:

> Actually it is not exact to say that a Thirst tends towards its own annihilation as thirst; there is no consciousness which aims at its own suppression as such. Yet thirst is a lack, as we pointed out earlier. As such it wishes to be *satisfied*; but this satisfied thirst, which would be realised by synthetic assimilation in an act of coincidence of the For-itself-desire or Thirst with the For-itself-reflection or act of drinking, is

not aimed at the suppression of thirst. Quite the contrary the aim is the thirst passed on to the plenitude of being, the thirst which grasps and incorporates repletion into itself as the Aristotelian form grasps and transforms matter; it becomes eternal thirst.

(*BN*, p. 101)

Sartre may go too far in saying that no consciousness aims at its own suppression. Severe pain surely does. But certainly, if our example is not a man dying of thirst in the desert but a walker on a sunny day looking forward to the next village where there is a pub: if someone offered to magically remove his thirst, he would not accept the offer.

However, is the lacked in thirst really the eternal thirst that Sartre speaks of? One might object that, phenomenologically, what one experiences when one has just had a refreshing drink is something qualitatively different from both thirst and the absence of thirst which might very well be called 'satisfied thirst'. There is a gap between Sartre's correct observation that desires do not typically aim at their own cessation and the claim that we want the godlike state of being desire-in-itself. Nevertheless, that is what he does claim.

Thus Sartre teaches us to regard every desire as having two aims: the appropriation of the concrete object of desire, the lacking, which is attainable (for example, getting my pint); and being the lacked, which is not.

Now what attitude is Sartre recommending, for he is certainly recommending things here, not merely describing. Suppose someone says 'My desires are not haunted by any unrealisable ideal; when I am thirsty, I get a drink, and then I am satisfied'. This is perhaps 'common sense' on this side of the Channel. If, as Nietzsche said, 'Men do not pursue happiness, only Englishmen do', perhaps Sartre might say 'Men do not seek the lacking rather than the lacked, only Englishmen do'. But he would add that such Englishmen are deceiving themselves – that is, they are in bad faith. And he can make a case, if not conclusively for the proposition that we pursue the lacked for-itself-in-itself, at least for the proposition that we do not just pursue the lacking. Whatever else it is that we want apart from what is concretely lacking, there is at any rate something. Let us take the example of food, since the diuretic properties of beer make it quite possible to go on drinking for quite a long time without thirst being satisfied – which is perhaps a Sartrean reason why beer drinking is so appealing. Unless one is literally starving, to want a meal is not to want hunger to cease. Before a special meal, one may go without food in order to get up a good hunger. One may well want to prolong the meal and be disappointed that when one has had enough one is no longer hungry. But more than this, a meal is not just about eating. When it is shared, it is about table fellowship. When of a particular national cuisine, it signifies that nationality. Borrowing Barthes' terms, we can say that souvlaki with horiatiki salad signifies Greekness, dum ghosht with basmati rice signifies Indianness, slimy boiled carrots with soggy boiled cabbage and floury boiled potatoes signifies Englishness, and so on. Likewise and more polysemically with drinks: bitter signifies not only Englishness but tradition, folksiness and artisanhood, while lager signifies Europeanness, up-to-dateness and yuppiedom. I have chosen the cases of food and drink as the hardest to present in this way; it is obvious that clothes are chosen not for comfort or to keep off the elements but for what they signify. As Nietzsche remarks, no woman has ever caught a cold if she knew she was well dressed, even if she was hardly dressed at all. And, quite obviously, every sexual desire is rich in polysemic symbolism.

However, although Sartre may be able to show that we do not just desire the lacking, it is not so easy to show that we desire the lacked in Sartre's sense. If I drink beer I want to be in a public place with dark, heavy, natural textured decor and to drink out of a pint glass, not a half-pint one, and so on. One could trace the symbolic connection of all these things with the polysemic desire to drink beer. But one does not need to posit a desire to be Bacchus or, more prosaically, simply to be 'a beer drinker' as opposed to drinking beer. This motivation *may* be present; the character in one of Simone de Beauvoir's novels who hates Pernod but likes drinking Pernod could probably be better described as not wanting to drink Pernod, but wanting to be a Pernod drinker, because of the image of a Pernod drinker in postwar French society, not because all desires aim at the for-itself-in-itself. Anyway, the polysemic desire to drink beer is not analysable into the desire to quench one's thirst on the one hand and the desire to be a beer drinker on the other. In between, there is the desire to enjoy a certain type of atmosphere, to participate in certain traditions, and so on.

Now there is a certain attitude which recognises the polysemic symbolism of human desires, but urges that we kick this habit. Sartre quotes – and describes as unsatisfactory and even shocking – the dictum 'make love to a pretty woman when you want her just as you would drink a glass of cold water when you are thirsty' (*BN*, p. 388). But something similar, though not applied to sex, is a feature – perhaps the least attractive feature – of English puritanism. Clothes need not be brightly coloured to keep the rain off, so everyone wears black or grey; churches need not be beautiful to worship God in, so they produce the ugly decency of the English chapel. This attitude survives in a secular form in Tony Benn's drinking fine sherry out of a cracked teamug and in 1960s architects providing all mod cons in matchbox-shaped tower blocks. But despite the unattractiveness of this puritanism, one can see why someone might adopt it. First, what is symbolised in the symbolic rather than necessary features of the objects that we want is very often some sort of snobbery. Designer clothes are 'cool' because they are expensive; they signify money. Quaker plainness of dress and manners was originally an adherence to the dress and manners of the peasant or artisan class against the signifiers of bourgeoisdom or aristocracy.

Second, the symbolic aspect of objects of desire is exploited by advertising. The huge and successful advertising campaign that made lager the fashionable beer to drink in England had to change the signification of lager from femininity or effeminacy with which it was associated in the 1960s to machismo. But of course the motivation of this multi-million pound campaign was that lager can be produced cheaper and sold dearer than bitter. This situation in which, while the physical qualities of a commodity and hence its capacity to satisfy 'brute needs' remains constant, its symbolic qualities are manipulated by advertisers for the sake of profits, applies in every sphere of modern life. To the extent that people are aware of this, they do not want to be dupes and hence may try to kick the habit of choosing for the sake of the symbolic aspects of their choice.

But third – and most Sartreanly – there seems on Sartre's account to be two reasons why acting for the sake of the lacked rather than the lacking is in bad faith. The first is that the lacked, unlike the lacking, can never be attained. I get my beer but I don't get to be Bacchus. But pursuit of the unrealisable is self-deception and so in bad faith. The second is that if we formulate the difference between wanting the lacking and wanting the lacked as that between wanting to drink beer and wanting to be a beer drinker, we are back with the original concept of bad faith: it is not bad faith to wait at tables in a café, it is bad faith to be a waiter; it is not bad faith to sleep with one's own sex, it is bad faith to be a homosexual – just as, of course, it is not in bad faith to sleep with the opposite sex, but it is in bad faith to be a heterosexual. Sartre's attitude to his own writing illustrates this: as a child, long before he wanted to write, he wanted to be a writer. Later, he came to have some things that he wanted to write, but he was careful to avoid being a writer. Hence his objection to being called '*maître*' by café waiters and General de Gaulle, and his refusal of the Nobel prize for literature. It seems from this that he thought that to be authentic one had to kick the habit of desiring to be a writer or a beer drinker and rest content with writing and drinking beer – which aligns Sartre with the puritan position.

I may say that when I first read *BN* this is how I interpreted Sartre – as exposing the bad faith in the way that we pursued in the first place and for the most part a logically unobtainable goal, so that we might kick this habit and pursue only concrete empirical 'lackings'; one can read the section on concrete relations with others in this way too. But this would be paradoxical, as he goes to great lengths to show us that it is the lacked, not the lacking, that we desire and that it is self-deception (bad faith) to deny this.

In fact, in the ethical section of the conclusion to *BN*, Sartre seems to be saying that, although the desire for the lacked is unfulfillable, authenticity involves recognition that it is this, not the lacking, that we pursue:

> Many men, in fact, know that the goal of their pursuit is being; and to the extent that they possess this knowledge, they refrain from appropriating things for their own sake and try to realize the symbolic appropriation of their being-in-itself. But to the extent that this attempt still shares in the spirit of seriousness and that these men can still believe

that their mission of effecting the existence of the in-itself-for-itself is written in things, they are condemned to despair; for they discover at the same time that all human activities are equivalent (for they all tend to sacrifice man in order that the self-cause may arise) and that all are in principle doomed to failure. Thus it amounts to the same thing whether one gets drunk alone or is a leader of nations. If one of these activities takes precedence over the other, this will not be because of its real goal but because of the degree of consciousness which it possesses of its ideal goal; and in this case it will be the quietism of the solitary drunkard which will take precedence over the vain agitation of the leader of nations.

(*BN*, p. 627)

The drunkard knows that he wants to be drunk as a for-itself-in-itself, drunk as the god of drunkenness; the politician thinks she is acting for the good of the people. The example is appealing because we know that politicians give themselves out to be working for the public good when this is not the case. But would the politician who knew himself or herself to be aiming at being a politician as an inkwell is an inkwell be preferable? I have a feeling that Hitler wanted to be the leader of Germany much more than he wanted to lead Germany. But Abraham Lincoln, I think, wanted to liberate the slaves more than he wanted to be the liberator of the slaves. And by the criterion in *TE* – the non-self-referentiality of desires – that looks more authentic, as well as more politically admirable.

In fact, it is possible to resolve the paradox as it appears in *BN*. The solution is that authenticity consists in being aware both that what we really want is not the lacking but the lacked, and that what we will get is not the lacked but the lacking: I write in order to be a writer knowing that I won't get to be a writer, but I will get to write books; I drink in order to be Bacchus knowing that I won't get to be Bacchus, but I will get drunk. This leads to a certain ironical detachment with respect to all one's desires, which is quite unlike the popular image of authenticity, but I think really is the intimation of authenticity that we get in *BN*. It is curious that an existentialist very different from Sartre presents a similar ethic of holding back from complete absorption in one's actions. I refer to Heidegger's friend, the Protestant theologian Rudolf Bultmann, who never tires of quoting Paul's advice (1 Corinthians 7: 29–31) that those who have wives should be as though they had none, those who rejoice or mourn should be as though they were not rejoicing or mourning, those that buy goods should be as though they did not buy them, and so on. Of course, Paul was writing at a time of persecution and transition, but the constant repetition of this passage as the conclusion of all Bultmann's arguments suggests that his notion of how to live is: whatsoever thy hand findeth to do, do it with half thy heart!

But to return to Sartre, this reflective attribution of an underlying self-referential desire – the desire to be the lacked – is quite incompatible with the account which I have taken as an intimation of authenticity in *TE* (although Sartre does not use the word in this context). In *TE*, self-referential reflection poisons desire. In a sense, Sartre has come round in *BN* to a view resembling the self-love moralists whom he criticised in *TE*, except that in place of ordinary self-interest he has put the desire to be the lacked, the for-itself-in-itself, a god. Admittedly, he gives a non-self-referential twist to this in places, as in the last quote, where he says 'their pursuit is being', or in the famous passage:

> Every human reality is a passion in that it projects losing itself so as to found being and by the same stroke to constitute the In-itself which escapes contingency by being its own foundation, the *Ens causa sui*, which religions call God. Thus the passion of man is the reverse of that of Christ, for man loses himself as man in order that God may be born. But the idea of God is contradictory and we lose ourselves in vain. Man is a useless passion.
>
> (*BN*, p. 615)

However, phrases like 'found being' and 'that God may be born' should not mislead us into thinking that we are dealing with a non-self-referential desire; the aim is that the agent shall appropriate being, shall be a god.

I conclude that the intimations of authenticity in *TE* and those in *BN* cannot be reconciled. Those in *BN* are internally consistent, but not plausible in that, while Sartre shows that we desire something more than the concrete objects of our desires, he does not show that it is to be the for-itself-in-itself; also, in that the sort of ironic make-believe he seems to be advocating as the authentic way to live our desires does not seem to be required by honesty or to be a plausible ideal. There remains the distinction, which I think is a useful and morally relevant one, between wanting to drink, to write or to sleep with people of one or the other sex, and wanting to be a drinker, writer, homosexual or heterosexual. The latter does involve a form of self-referentiality or vanity that is best done without; but in kicking this habit, we do not lose the symbolic dimension of our desires as such.

References

Collier, Andrew, *Being and Worth*, Routledge, London, 1999.
Sartre, Jean-Paul, *The Transcendence of the Ego*, Noonday Press, New York, 1957.
—— , *Being and Nothingness*, Methuen, London, 1957.

8   Sartre's mistaken approach to Marxism

In the postwar years, Sartre moved closer to Marxism politically. I entirely applaud that movement. He also felt it necessary to revise his philosophy to make it a version of Marxism, which issued in his monumental and almost unreadable book *Critique of Dialectical Reason*. This, I think, was a mistake for three reasons: his earlier philosophy (*Being and Nothingness*) was on most points compatible with Marxism as it stood; the issue on which it is not compatible with Marxism escaped Sartre's notice; and the new philosophy of the *Critique* really is incompatible with and inferior to Marxism.

To start, let us get out of the way two crass mistakes, one made by many English-speaking critics of Sartre's Marxism and the other by Sartre himself. The critics often express surprise that Sartre should be attracted to Marxism on the grounds that 'the philosophy of *Being and Nothingness* is individualistic and Marxism is not'. The first thing wrong with this is that 'individualism' does not mean one thing but many, several of which are mutually incompatible. None of the senses in which Sartre's existentialism is individualistic are senses in which Marxism is not. Sartre was never a liberal and neither was any other existentialist, although almost every other political position has been represented by some existentialist. The second thing is that precisely the focus of *Being and Nothingness* on individuals takes it out of the sphere where it could have conflicted with Marxist theory. In so far as *Being and Nothingness* is about individuals and Marx's theories are about societies, they can no more conflict than can Darwin's theory of evolution and Einstein's theory of relativity.

The crass mistake of Sartre's is that he thought that, in order to defend Marxism, he had to show that history was dialectical a priori, rather than simply exemplifying dialectical processes as a matter of empirical fact. But Marxism is most decidedly an a posteriori dialectic.

My next point is that there is no need to depart from the philosophy of *Being and Nothingness* (hereafter *BN*) in order to give an account of class. In that book, class for the most part appears as part of the facticity of the for-itself – that is, as one of the facts about a person that does not stem from their current choice of possibilities. Facticity, Sartre claims, does not determine what possibility one chooses, but it does restrict the range of one's possibilities. Just as a man cannot bear children and a blind person cannot become a film critic, so a proletarian cannot (in France at Sartre's time) become a doctor. This is Sartre's example. The crucial one for Marx is that a proletarian cannot work without selling his or her labour power. This does not by itself make the proletarian choose class-conscious politics, but it does make it possible to do so and, if as is likely, the proletarian projects aims to which their proletarian status is an obstacle, it makes it rational to do so as a means to emancipation from those obstacles. And this is enough at the individual level, if combined with Marx's class analysis of society which is entirely compatible with it, to ground class politics in Marx's sense.

But it is not all that Sartre says about class. In one place Sartre comes closer than at any other to allowing that facticity does feed into our projection of our possibilities, rather as Heidegger sees a link between our thrownness and our projection (fore-throwing). Indeed, Sartre uses the term 'thrownness' here:

> I am not only thrown face to face with the brute existent. I am thrown into a worker's world, a French world, a world of Lorraine or the South, which offers me its meanings without my having done anything to disclose them.
>
> (*BN*, p. 514)

There follows a subtle account of the way we live these worlds, through the example of language. These worlds, as lived, are not encountered as constraints because we are too much inside them: 'for whom do the laws of language exist? . . . they are not for the one who speaks, they are for the one who listens' (p. 517). I recall my French teacher at school telling us how, as a student, he had sat in on a class in English at a French school. The teacher had picked out one boy and asked him (in English) 'What happens to "some" after a negative?' My teacher, as a native English speaker, had been totally puzzled by the question, but the French boy, who had done his homework, answered straight away 'It becomes "any"'.

Now one might say, but doesn't the worker encounter his or her proletarianness as a constraint precisely in the inability to become a doctor? I think we have to distinguish two things here. There is the structural fact that his social position is that of a worker who consequently must sell his labour power, cannot afford to study medicine, and so on. And there is his lived workerishness which is not encountered unless through the other. Thus, in the case of Jewishness, Sartre says:

> Because *I am a Jew* I shall be deprived – in certain societies – of certain possibilities, etc. Yet I am unable *in any way* to feel myself as a Jew or as a minor or as a Pariah. It is at this point that I can react against these interdictions by declaring that race, for example, is purely and simply a

collective fiction, that only individuals exist. Thus here I suddenly encounter the total alienation of my person: I am something which I have not chosen to be.

(*BN*, p. 524)

The point here is not, I think, that one is an assimilated Jew who regards himself or herself as to all intents and purposes a Gentile, but whom the Nazis nevertheless class as a Jew; rather, one may be a thoroughly Jewish sort of person – eating kosher food, speaking Yiddish, and so on, yet doing so without encountering one's Jewishness; just as when running for a bus one does not think 'here am I running for a bus' but 'there is a bus which must be caught', so one thinks not 'here am I eating kosher food' but 'that bagel and lok is to be eaten, that bacon sandwich is to be avoided'. The reflective sense of identity comes when one encounters oneself in the eyes of the other: 'Aryan restaurant, no Jews admitted'. Now this sort of constraint can be encountered by the worker as well as by the member of an oppressed race: 'No overalls in the lounge bar'. However, this is not the main form of constraint encountered by the worker – the main form is the sheer facticity of the worker's structural position: not his or her workerishness, but his or her proletarianness. Take again the example of the worker who is not able to become a doctor: actually, this could be for two sorts of reason. Due to the proletarianness of the worker, he or she cannot raise the funds to study medicine; or, due to the worker's workerishness, they will do badly in interviews with snobbish interviewers.

Alongside class there is something that has recently been dubbed 'classism', although this is really only a pretentious word for snobbishness. The danger here is that class will be reduced to classism. For instance, there is more classism (snobbishness) in the UK than in the US, but the US is at least equally a class-divided society as the UK. Those who use the term 'classism' think of it as an analogy with racism: as essentially a set of bigoted attitudes. But the difference is that, if we take away those attitudes, the constraints of race have gone, but the constraints of class have not. There could be a society without racial oppression that contained black people and Caucasians and Jews, or a non-sexist society in which there were men and women, but not a society without class oppression that contained proletarians and capitalists. Proletarianness is neither a physiological given ontologically anterior to society, as skin colour or Y-chromosomes are, nor a result of encounters with other individuals within society which define one's identity. To abolish class oppression is to abolish class.

This raises a question about Sartre's account of class consciousness, for in one passage he compares class and national consciousness: 'One can "be-in-order-to-be French", "be-in-order-to-be-a-worker"':

the Zionist Jew resolutely assumes himself within his race – that is, assumes concretely once and for all the permanent *alienation* of his being;

in the same way the revolutionary worker by his very revolutionary project assumes a 'being-in-order-to-be-a-worker'.

(*BN*, p. 531)

The idea here seems to be that all of these projects are cases of consciously taking up an identity originally conferred by others – hence the reference to assuming alienation. How the Zionist would respond to this I leave to Zionists to answer. But the class-conscious worker is, in the first place, responding not to the identity conferred in encounter with the snob, but to the position he or she holds in the class structure, as one who has access to the means of labour only by selling their labour power to another. And in the second place the revolutionary proletarian is not at all project-ing 'being-in-order-to-be-a-worker', but 'being-in-order-to-no-longer-be-a-proletarian'. This brings out very clearly the fact that the politics of emancipation and the politics of identity are diametrically opposed.

However, while Sartre's own description of class consciousness may be flawed, his recognition of the sheer facticity of class as a set of limits to an individual's possibilities leaves a place for an account of class structure at the level of social analysis – a level that Sartre does not engage with here, but for that very reason leaves open for a Marxist analysis. In this respect, *Being and Nothingness* is much more compatible with Marxism than the *Critique of Dialectical Reason*, which does engage with the social level and on that level gives an account of groups, but leaves no place for an account of structures. Marxist class analysis is in the first place a theory of structures and only after-wards a theory about groups.

However, there is a concrete account of a kind of class consciousness in *Being and Nothingness* which, while itself quite perceptive, seems to involve a doctrine that really would undermine the Marxist project, although Sartre never seems to recognise this. It is necessary to quote quite a long passage here:

> It is on the day that we can conceive of a different state of affairs that a new light falls on our troubles and our suffering and that we *decide* that these are unbearable. A worker in 1830 is capable of revolting if his salary is lowered, for he easily conceives of a situation in which his wretched standard of living would not be as low as the one which is about to be imposed on him. But he does not represent his sufferings to himself as unbearable; he adapts himself to them not through resigna-tion but because he lacks the education and reflection necessary for him to conceive of a social state in which these sufferings would not exist. Consequently *he does not act*. Masters of Lyon following a riot, the workers at Croix-Rousse do not know what to do with their victory; they return home bewildered, and the regular army has no trouble in overcoming them. Their misfortunes do not appear to them as 'habitual' but rather *natural*; they are, that is all, and they constitute the worker's condition.

They are not detached; they are not seen in the clear light of day, and consequently they are integrated by the worker with his being. He suffers without considering his suffering and without conferring value upon it. To suffer and to *be* are one and the same for him. His suffering is the pure affective tenor of his non-positional consciousness, but he does not *contemplate* it. Therefore this suffering cannot be in itself a *motive* for his acts.

(*BN*, p. 435)

'Motive' here translates '*mobile*'. Readers of the English text of *Being and Nothingness* can easily be confused by Hazel Barnes' inconsistent translation. She always translated *mobile* as 'motive' and *cause* as 'cause', but she sometimes translates *motif* as 'motive' and sometimes as 'cause', although Sartre explicitly distinguishes it from both. The correct translation of *motif* is 'reason', in the sense of the reason for an action. For Sartre, reasons and motives are objective and subjective correlatives in that the reason for the Lyons workers' revolt was that their wages were lowered, and the motive was the consciousness of that fact as a reason for revolting. The fact was only a reason because they had the motive. But if we want to describe the nature of their motive, surely the natural description of it is 'suffering'. It is because they are suffering that the lowering of their wages is a reason for revolt. Sartre is therefore going too far when he says that the worker confers no value on suffering and that suffering cannot be a motive for his acts. The point is rather that, because the workers have an inadequate idea of the causes and hence the possible cure of their suffering, the acts which it motivates are limited and ineffective. But acts it certainly does motivate: the riot that made the workers masters of Lyons. Sartre concludes that no factual state can determine consciousness to apprehend it as a lack. The workers' suffering – which can be spelt out in factual, partly physiological terms as a certain quantity and quality of food, shelter, and so on – cannot by itself determine them to experience the lack of a socialist republic in which they would not be exploited, but it can certainly determine them to experience a lack of adequate wages.

Now it is clear enough from the way that Sartre describes the Lyons workers' revolt that he thinks it would have been better if they had had sufficient knowledge of social constraints and possibilities to project their emancipation. But it is not clear why. For Sartre's denial that there are factual motives or, what is the same thing, his denial that there is such a thing as human nature, seems to indicate a radically 'autoplastic' ethic – an ethic of changing one's desires rather than changing the world. Sartre says, with apparent approval 'Descartes . . . recognized both that the will is infinite and that it is necessary "to try to conquer ourselves rather than fortune"' (*BN*, p. 482). He returns to this in his essay 'Cartesian Freedom', where he paraphrases this idea as 'if I do not have the power to perform such and such an action, I must abstain from desiring to perform it' (*Literary and Philosophical*

Essays, p. 173). Indeed, for Sartre there is actually no question of *trying* to change one's desires, since there are no unfree forces (e.g. passions) in the soul, passions being for Sartre as much free acts as volitions. It would seem to follow that we are infinitely adaptable and consequently invulnerable to harm from outside; we can have no reason to want to change the world. Sartre does not draw these conclusions, but he leaves us no grounds for rejecting them. Marx, since he believes in human nature, does. This may sound strange to many who, perhaps even under the subliminal influence of Sartre, have come to believe that Marx too denied the existence of human nature, but, purely from the standpoint of Marxology, no one can reasonably defend that view since Norman Geras' book *Marx and Human Nature: Refutation of a Legend*. This is the real difference between Marx and the early Sartre that goes unnoticed by Sartre when he comes to revise his thought to accommodate it to Marxism.

References

Geras, Norman, *Marx and Human Nature: Refutation of a Legend*, Verso, London, 1983.
Sartre, Jean-Paul, *Being and Nothingness*, Methuen, London, 1957.
—— , *Literary and Philosophical Essays*, Hutchinson, London, 1955.
—— , *Critique of Dialectical Reason*, New Left Books, London, 1976.

9 Berdyaev's socialism

When Berdyaev was expelled from Russia in 1922, he was no doubt regarded by the Soviet authorities as an enemy of socialism; but when Gorbachev was about to give way to Yeltsin, Soviet academics who a year or two before had been orthodox communists were attacking Berdyaev for 'failing to recognise the truth of capitalism'. Berdyaev's prophecy that the bourgeois spirit could come to Russia via the communists had come true.

This is not just (though no doubt it is also) a matter of successive generations of uncomprehending bureaucrats. Berdyaev's writings about socialism are complex and, to the unwary, ambiguous. In this essay I want to help put the record straight – to a large extent, in Berdyaev's own words. I will argue that Berdyaev was unambiguously a socialist, and try to show how he agreed and disagreed with other socialists. Of course, it is unquestionable that he was a socialist in his student days and he was exiled to the far north of Russia by the Tsarist government for his socialist agitation. The question is whether he was a lifelong socialist, for he certainly became more critical of Marx and of socialist movements in later years. Yet he remained in Russia and taught there after the Revolution until his exile, and in exile always held aloof from counter-revolutionary *emigrés*.

First, a record of his positions for or against (or apparently for or against) Marx, Soviet Russia and socialist proposals.

Marx

Berdyaev's statements about Marx can be divided into the following four points:

1   his general assessment of him;
2   his opinion and interpretation of his economic theory;
3   his opinion and interpretation of his politics; and
4   his opinion and interpretation of his philosophy.

General assessment

Berdyaev's general assessment of Marx was expressed as follows:

> My admiration for men of genius did not cease when I became ideo-
> logically hostile to them: such, for example, was the case with Marx.
>
> (*Dream and Reality* (hereafter *DR*), p. 84)

> I have asked myself more than once what impelled me to become a
> Marxist, albeit an unorthodox, critical and free-thinking one; and why
> I should still have a 'soft spot' for Marxism.
>
> (*DR*, p. 117)

Berdyaev goes on the speak of the superiority, both in social analysis and
cultural standard, of Marxism to earlier Russian socialist movements, and
concludes:

> I remember distinctly the tremendous impression produced on me by
> the sheer genius of Marx when I first read him. I accepted his critique
> of capitalism without reservation. I realized that his insight into purpose-
> ful conflict as a part of the structure of things was pregnant with
> enormous revolutionary possibilities.
>
> (*DR*, p. 118)

From these passages one has the strong impression that, despite later disagreements with Marx, Berdyaev did not just admire his 'genius', but believed
he had made real breakthroughs. Those breakthroughs are primarily in the
area of the critique of the capitalist economy.

Opinion and interpretation of Marx's economic theory

Berdyaev discusses his interpretation of Marx's economic theory in *The Origin
of Russian Communism*:

> The strength of the economic factor in human life is not an invention
> of Marx, and he is not to blame for the fact that it has so great an influ-
> ence on ideology. Marx observed this in the capitalist society of Europe
> which surrounded him. But he reduced it to a theory and gave it a
> universal character.
>
> (*The Origin of Russian Communism* (hereafter *ORC*), p. 97)

> Marx discovers in capitalism a process of dehumanization which makes
> man* dependent upon the products of his own creation. To this is due

---

*   The word 'man' in all Berdyaev quotes means humankind; the Russian word cannot be
read as referring only to the male sex.

Marx's brilliant doctrine about the fetishism of goods. Everything in history and in social life is the product of human activity, human labour, human conflict. But man falls victim to illusory, deceptive consciousness, as an effect of which his own activity and labour presents itself to him as an objective world of things on which he depends.

(*ORC*, p. 98)

Here Berdyaev seems to be entirely endorsing Marx's economic theory; he sees economic determinism as true of capitalism, but, I take it, not true universally, for Berdyaev comments: 'His mistake lay in taking the particular for the general' (*ORC*, p. 97). I think Berdyaev means both that Marx rightly saw the primacy of economics in capitalism but wrongly generalised it to other societies and that he generalised this primacy from a principle of analysis of society (historical materialism) to a universal metaphysical principle (dialectical materialism). Elsewhere, he expresses a similar point as a dilemma:

There remains in [Marx] a rooted duality of thought: Is the turning of man into a function of the economic process a sin and an evil of past capitalist exploitation or is it the ontology of man?

(*ORC*, p. 182)

Put this way, at least, I think we can say that the reading which Berdyaev would approve (the former one) is the correct one. But he reads Marx's theory of fetishism and reification in a very particular way: as objectification taking place in consciousness, rather than as disempowerment taking place in the social structure. I believe that this is a misreading of Marx, for Marx denied that labour was the source of all wealth, saying that nature was equally the source of wealth; and if this is true, monopolisation of resources by the possessing class disempowers labour from without, it is not self-disempowered from within. But Berdyaev's reading of Marx, which he endorses, is that 'man, by his own activity, can always dissipate this phantom world of capitalist economics' (*ORC*, p. 99). Of course, for Marx too it is possible to get rid of the capitalist economy and its laws, but only by a revolution. Seeing through it as appearance is not enough. There *is* a place for such seeing through in Marx's theory. Social relations of power over the labour of others are the 'truth of' money. One does not understand the role of money in society until one understands this. Likewise, one does not understand the production of wealth unless one abstracts from money and sees it in terms of work and goods. Any economist will be the better for seeing through the illusions generated by money and capital. But seeing through these illusions will not make them go away. Berdyaev's formulation suggests that it will. Granted, Berdyaev always recognises that cognitive illusion and its rectification are never merely cognitive. Other things than cognition have to change. But this hardly adds up to the radical break between the cognitive enlightenment that can be had by reading *Capital* and the social liberation that requires the state to be seized and the expropriators expropriated. Berdyaev stresses this reification theory as the 'different side' of Marxism from his determinism and associates it with the young Marx's inheritance from German idealism. It is really only the young Marx that Berdyaev ever praises philosophically, as distinct from with regard to economics. There is another aspect of Berdyaev's idealist reading of Marx:

> It is clear that Marx confuses the economic and ethical categories. The doctrine of added value [surplus value], which is what brings to light the exploitation of workmen [*sic*] by capitalists, Marx considered a scientific economic doctrine. But in actual fact it is primarily an ethical doctrine.
>
> (*ORC*, p. 100)

There is no inkling of a recognition here that for Marx scientific facts could entail values. Nevertheless, it is clear that, while the philosophical underpinnings of Marx's economics may be in dispute, its political implications, at least on their negative side, are endorsed by Berdyaev. Marx has made a case against capitalism, and it is guilty as charged.

Opinion and interpretation of Marx's politics

While Marx's economic doctrine may justify socialist politics, for Berdyaev too Marx's own political account of the grounds for socialist revolution are caricatured and rejected. 'To [the proletariat] are ascribed messianic attributes, to it are transferred the attributes of the chosen people of God; it is the new Israel' (*ORC*, p. 98). Berdyaev does not consider the possibility that there might be good scientific reasons for thinking that the proletariat has unique liberatory potential. However, despite his obvious distance from this secular messianism in *ORC*, he does present his own version of 'proletarian messianism' in *DR*. After the passage about his rejection of Bogdanov and Lunacharsky's 'class truth', he writes:

> This idea provided the basis for my theory of the messianic calling of the proletariat; for the proletariat is free from the sin of exploitation, and its social and psychological condition enables it to receive and bear witness to the truth. I viewed the working-class as embodying, as it were, the proximity, or even the identity, of man's psychological condition with the transcendental consciousness. In my opinion this gave a much more adequate foundation for radical, revolutionary Marxism than the views of the other adherents of critical Marxism.
>
> (*DR*, p. 123)

Although Marx would not talk in terms of sin or transcendental consciousness, this is closer than, I think, Berdyaev realises to Marx's position and indeed to Lenin's: 'True ideas always serve the people, false ideas serve the enemies of the people'.

Berdyaev's own view that emerges from the pages 97–100 of *ORC* is that the real grounds for socialism are moral ones: 'Exploitation is not an economic phenomenon but primarily a phenomenon of the moral order, a morally evil relation of man to man' (p. 100). The morality concerned is presumably seen as an eternally true personalism, rather than a historical *sittlichkeit* as for Marx. There is, of course, a lot more to be said about the relation between historical moralities (emphasised by Marx) and the permanent values of which they may be found to be expressions. My only objection to Berdyaev here is that he did not consider the possibility that *Capital* might condemn capitalism not *in addition to* explaining it, but simply *by* explaining it.

Opinion and interpretation of Marx's philosophy

Although Berdyaev praises the early philosophical writings of Marx and their (real or imagined) echoes in the theory of fetishism and reification, his opinion of Marx as a philosopher, and even more of later Marxist philosophy, is much lower than that of Marxist economics. It is curious that one of his first disagreements with his fellow socialist exiles was about the concept of 'class-truth', which for Bogdanov and Lunacharsky was the only kind of truth. Berdyaev rejected this relativism – but then so did Lenin. What Berdyaev saw as crude materialism, Lenin saw as idealism (as, I think, would Marx). More significantly for politics, Berdyaev took the same non-class view of justice (see *DR*, pp. 122–23).

But elsewhere Berdyaev often attacks Marxism as 'crude materialism' and even as 'out of date' (that is, out of fashion: Marxism has been in and out of fashion several times since Berdyaev, and this proves nothing). This is abuse rather than argument. He nowhere tries to show that Marx's arguments are weak or his premises groundless, or that his materialism is crude in the sense of simplistic (as Marx tries to show of earlier materialists). It is 'crude' simply because it is not idealism. Berdyaev's review of Engels' *Anti-Dühring* in *Life's Questions*, No. 2 (quoted in Lowrie, *Christian Existentialism*, pp. 289–90), for instance, is completely contemptuous, yet remains at a much lower, 'cruder' level itself than Engels ever descended to. However, this is the furthest part of Marxist theory from politics.

The overall picture of Berdyaev's assessment of Marx is that he accepts Marx's critique of capitalism, but is not a Marxist in that he justifies socialism by means of a timeless personalist ethic rather than because of capitalism's historically specific contradictions; however, he accepts that there are such contradictions. The relation between contradictions and transhistorical features of humankind is a complex one, and neither Marx nor Berdyaev explores it fully. Such a full exploration would perhaps show the conflict to be more apparent than real. Finally, he rejects materialism and regards this as no problem from the point of view of his political commitment to the left. His account of his relations with his fellow exiles (in Chapter 5 of *DR*) shows their scandal at his combination of socialism with idealism and his insistence that there was no conflict between the two. Although I do not share Berdyaev's idealism, I do share his view that socialism is compatible with a wide range of philosophical positions. His acceptance of Marx's economics, rejection of his philosophy and sympathetic critique of his politics seem to me to make up a perfectly tenable socialist position.

Soviet Russia

Berdyaev's complex evaluation of Soviet Russia can be considered under six headings:

1   His belief in the inevitability of the Bolshevik Revolution (about which he was far from happy), and also in the futility and perniciousness of trying to reverse it.
2   His twofold judgement on the Revolution as at once a just judgement on the old regime, and also deeply oppressive and hostile to the things of the spirit.
3   His own surprising activism during the revolutionary period, and his recognition that early Bolshevism allowed considerable freedom as instanced by its toleration of this.
4   The beginnings of a state capitalist analysis of Stalin's Russia.
5   His intense dislike of the counter-revolutionary mentality of the *emigrés* and his dissociation from them.
6   His 'Soviet orientation' in the later years of his life, at the time of the anti-Fascist war and the cold war.

I will now look at each of these headings in turn and discuss them in more detail.

Bolshevism as the only non-utopian programme for Russia

Berdyaev expresses his belief in the inevitability of the Bolshevik Revolution as follows:

> I believe that the revolution in Russia was inevitable and richly deserved, but I never saw it in rosy hues.
>
> (*DR*, p. 222)

> I foresaw [in an article written in 1907] with considerable accuracy that when the real hour for revolution in Russia struck the Bolsheviks would win the day. I did not imagine, like so many others, that a successful Russian revolution would be accompanied by the triumph of freedom and humanitarianism.
>
> (*DR*, p. 137)

Here we see that, although Berdyaev thought that the Revolution was a just judgement on the old regime and a move towards a just society, and that Bolshevism was the unavoidable form of that revolution, he did not approve of Bolshevism – of its all-or-nothing mentality, its militant materialism, its over-readiness for violence (although he was not a pacifist), of its suppression of its ideological opponents. This led to a certain alienation of Berdyaev from revolutionary movements generally from the defeat of the 1905 revolution until his exile in 1922. He could not put his heart and soul into a movement which, however just and inevitable, was bound to have these other consequences. But this does not amount to a rejection of socialism, as we shall see:

> I remember how, about a month before the February revolution, I was discussing with two old friends of ours, a Menshevik and a Bolshevik, the chances for revolution and the overthrow of the monarchy in Russia. The Menshevik's view was that we would have to wait for another twenty-five years, whilst the Bolshevik maintained that fifty years must pass before it could happen. The Bolsheviks did not so much prepare the Revolution as make use of a moment when everything got out of hand. This is evidence of that fateful character of the Revolution, to which I have referred. And, even while acknowledging the truth of the Revolution, we must not forget that a large element in it was a fateful, negative outburst of elemental and, indeed, demonic forces.
>
> (*DR*, p. 223)

> I did not doubt the utter inevitability of Russia's experience of Bolshevism. 'Historical inevitability' is, admittedly, often a grand name by which people seek to fortify themselves and sometimes even to paralyse their antagonists: but this was a different inevitability, showing a decisive experience in the inner destiny of the Russian people and ushering Russia into a new world in which she was enabled to speak the full truth about herself. There is no return to what was before the Bolshevik Revolution, and all attempts at restoration, even of the principles of the February Revolution, appeared to me as both powerless and harmful.
>
> (*DR*, p. 226)

Powerless and harmful: here we have both a realistic appraisal of Bolshevism as the only way forward for Russia and a rejection of attempts at counter-revolution, even republican ones, as doing only harm. This does not mean, of course, that he thought that no better policy for Russia could be envisaged than the Bolshevik one. He had a hundred and one criticisms to make of it. But any attempt to overthrow it could only make matters worse, whether it succeeded or not. Bolshevism had to run its course and await a spiritual revival which would leaven Soviet society from within:

> In Russia it was not a communist revolution which turned out to be utopian, but a liberal bourgeois revolution.
>
> (*ORC*, p. 74)

> It was not revolutionary *narodnichestvo* [that is, the politics of the Narodniks], but orthodox totalitarian Marxism which succeeded in achieving the revolution, in which Russia skipped that stage of capitalist development which to the first Russian Marxists had appeared so unavoidable. And it was clear that this agreed with Russian tradition and the instincts of the people.
>
> (*ORC*, p. 106)

> the greatest paradox in Russian life and the Russian revolution lies in this, that liberal ideas, ideas of right as well as ideas of social reform, appeared, in Russia, to be utopian. Bolshevism on the other hand shewed itself to be much less utopian and much more realist, much more in accord with the whole complex situation in Russia in 1917, and much more faithful to certain primordial Russian traditions, to the Russian search for universal social justice, understood in a maximalizing sense, and to the Russian method of government and control by coercion.
>
> (*ORC*, pp. 112–13)

These quotes give a clue to Berdyaev's grounds for thinking Bolshevism inevitable. It is not the same as the Bolsheviks' case for this – namely, that the provisional government had no effective social base, but rested only on the strength of the workers' soviets combined with their initial reluctance to take power in their own name: ultimately, stable government could only come either from a reactionary military dictatorship or a revolutionary soviet dictatorship. Berdyaev's view has more to do with national traditions, not all of them admirable: Russia is a nation of extremes and a nation that has always been more effectively governed by those who 'combined progress and tyranny', like Peter the Great.

Berdyaev's twofold judgement on the Revolution

It is clear that Berdyaev sees both a good and a bad side to the Bolshevik Revolution. The two are asymmetrical in a peculiar way. In so far as he sees it as just and inevitable, and the alternatives as harmful, he seems to endorse it enough to justify shouldering a gun for it in the civil war. Yet his criticisms of its bad side are much more laden with emotion and show him as radically dissident.

The intelligentsia's disappointment with the Revolution and consequent disintegration:

> provided evidence for my own profound conviction that every political revolution is doomed and becomes stupefied by its own surfeit: the

subject of true revolution must be man, rather than the masses or the body politic; and only a personalistic revolution can be properly called 'revolution'.

(*DR*, p. 137)

I welcomed 'the Fall of the Holy Russian Tsardom' (the title of an article of mine published at the beginning of the Revolution): I regarded it as a just and ineluctable process of 'dis-incarnation', of the undoing of a series of historical symbols, which have been invested with a sacred meaning but, in the course of history, belied reality as it was, and not as the champions of the monarchy imagined it to be. This inevitable process of casting off false appearances and pretences, however, was not in itself a guarantee of the goodness of things to come.

(*DR*, pp. 222–23)

One of the most tangible and painful changes which came about as a result of the revolutionary upheaval was the astounding transformation in the appearance of many men and women. A new type of man seemed to have emerged. There was none of the tolerance and kindness in him so characteristic of the pre-revolutionary type of Russian; none of the pining for what is not; none of the anarchism which respects no rules; no doubts, no subjective reactions, no melancholy, no introspection. All this gave place to a buoyant and somewhat aggressive optimism and a readiness to conform to anybody and to do anything.

(*DR*, p. 227)

I recall a visit to an exhibition of Russian art of the revolutionary period, and the faces depicted bear this out disturbingly. They express a determination to achieve their ends at whatever cost to whoever; a lack of any openness to encounters that might require an unforeseen response; and, if not hatred itself, a readiness to hate rather than to love. They bear out Berdyaev's remark that:

Communists are fond of emphasising that they are opponents of Christian evangelical morality based on love, pity and sympathy, and that perhaps is the most dreadful thing in communism.

(*ORC*, p. 166)

Zamyatin's idea of fantasiectomy in his novel *We*, written in this period, expresses a similar worry about what was happening to the psychology of the Russian people.

Berdyaev records his open and continued opposition to the 'bad side' of Bolshevism:

I did not conceal my attitude to communism. Indeed, I waged an open war against its spirit, or rather against its hostility to the spirit. Least of all did I desire restoration. I was entirely convinced that the old world had come to an end and that a return to it was alike impossible and undesirable.

(DR, p. 228)

In Russian communism the will to power proved stronger than the will to freedom, and the element of power politics more decisive than that of genuine revolutionary socialism.

(DR, p. 229)

The worship of the collective is an unmistakably religious phenomenon – a form of idolatry, similar to that of nationalism, racialism, capitalism and the rest. As a critique and judgment upon proletarianized capitalist society, with its privileges and vested interests, however, communism seemed to me irrefutable, and I regarded all attempts at refuting communism which proceed from the assumptions on which that society is built as unconvincing, futile and stultifying.

(DR, p. 242)

Here we see Berdyaev's characteristic distinction between communism as a 'total world view', a secular religion, and communism as a programme for a classless society. He accepts the latter and believes that the former must be fought by spiritual weapons from within the latter:

Revolutionaries usually do not understand the meaning of revolution, for it is not covered by their rationalist ideal. But since they face the future, they may be instruments in the hands of the highest Tribunal of Judgment for making its meaning realized. Whereas counter-revolutionaries, as men who powerlessly and fruitlessly face the past, are those upon whom judgment is passed, impenitent, and, being in this condition, understand nothing.

(ORC, p. 130)

In revolution judgment is passed upon the evil forces which have brought about injustice, but the forces which judge, themselves create evil; in revolution good itself is realized by forces of evil, since forces of good were powerless to realize their good in history.

(ORC, p. 132)

Here, on the one hand, Berdyaev seems close to the pre-exilic Hebrew prophets, to Amos and Isaiah and Jeremiah: there is a divine judgement within history, a foretaste of the last judgement. Oppression brings disaster on the oppressors. But the disaster is not always a liberation for the oppressed. In ancient Israel it took the form of Babylonian invasion and captivity. Yet there is another theme here as well: good is realised by the Revolution; the workers and peasants of Russia were undoubtedly better off materially than before (once the hardships of the civil war were over) and had more opportunities for education and the realisation of their potentialities. But this has been realised by evil means, by civil war and dictatorship. Does Berdyaev think that they could have been realised by good means? The phrase about the forces of good being powerless suggests that they could not, and this suggests an attitude of the 'end justifying the means' in a sense which is far from Berdyaev's attitudes. Perhaps the forces of good were powerless but need not have been. If the church had practised Christianity when it had been powerful, things might have been different. It did not and brought Babylonish captivity upon itself – but this was not *mere* captivity, for it did good that the church should have done as well, but by evil means:

> Have Christians done very much for the realization of Christian justice in social life? Have they striven to realize the brotherhood of man without that hatred and violence of which they accuse the communists? The sins of Christians, the sins of historical churches, have been very great, and these sins bring with them their just punishment.
>
> (*ORC*, p. 171)

Berdyaev's activism

Given the feeling of aloofness and estrangement from the revolutionary process which comes through in even Berdyaev's most favourable judgements of it, it is surprising that he by no means retreated to private life during this period and frankly acknowledges that he had considerable freedom to express his views under the Bolsheviks. In between the two revolutions (February and October):

> As a result of a number of circumstances I found myself for a short time a member of the Council (*Soviet*) of the newly proclaimed Republic (pre-Parliament) – a position which, so far as I was concerned, seemed almost grotesque. But it was another opportunity for seeing at close quarters the currents and undercurrents in revolutionary Russia.
>
> (*DR*, p. 226)

He did not like what he saw:

> To see fighters for freedom become almost overnight upstarts and time-servers has been one of the most painful experiences of my life.
>
> (*DR*, p. 224)

> Kerensky and his associates made nonsense of [the first revolution] by their complete misapprehension of the situation and their inability to grapple with the inescapable problems.
>
> (*DR*, p. 224)

The summer of 1917 was like a nightmare. . . . I felt inwardly happier after the October Revolution, in the Soviet period, than during the preceding months.

(*DR*, pp. 224–25)

After the October Revolution:

I embarked upon an extensive educational plan: I gave lectures, read papers, wrote, discussed and took an active part in the All-Russian Union of Writers. I also founded the Free Academy of Moral Science [or Spiritual Culture – A.C.]. The possibility of engaging in such activities is an illustration of the degree of liberty which the ideological opponents of Bolshevism enjoyed in the first years after the October Revolution. Contrary to the general impression, the Soviet Government did not use methods of wholesale oppression until it was faced with the task of wrestling with half the world without and counter-revolutionary terror within.

(*DR*, p. 225)

It was not possible to remain inactive, and, despite the overwhelming pressure of events, nobody felt crushed or downhearted save those who were frightened out of their wits and dared not say their soul was their own. Even when labour conscription was introduced and I had to clear away snow or to march in the early mornings through the cold, dark streets to dig outside the town, I did not feel at all depressed and unhappy, despite the unaccustomed strain of the pick and shovel on my sedentary muscles and the feeling of dizziness when engaged in hard physical labour. I could not help realizing the justice of my predicament.

(*DR*, pp. 229–30)

Here we see the extent to which the Revolution passed through Berdyaev inwardly; it did not merely pass over him like a wave. He shares its excitement, the feeling of making all things new, even though he hates many of the new things.

And, considering the hardships of the times, he was not treated badly. Berdyaev was even one of those writers who, irrespective of ideological position, were allowed extra food rations:

In 1918 I took part in a church procession headed by the Patriarch, which became something of a demonstration on a large scale. People joined it in the face of possible victimization, although actually the government did not interfere.

(*DR*, p. 231)

> I actively participated in the All-Russian Union of Writers . . . and, for a year, was its acting president. Whenever there arose a need of interceding for the members of the Union, of obtaining their release from prison or averting eviction from their homes, I was, as a rule, asked to go and see Kamenev, the President of the Moscow City Soviet of Workers' Deputies.
>
> (*DR*, p. 231)

Although this clearly presupposes that persecution of writers was going on, it also shows that this was not yet policy or systematic practice. Berdyaev mentions the attitude of leading Bolshevik intellectuals:

> The Kremlin . . . was also inhabited by the representatives of the old Russian intelligentsia – Kamenev, Lunacharsky, Bukharin, Ryazanov and others. Their attitude to members of the intelligentsia who did not join forces with communism was unlike that of the Cheka. They were disposed to act as the generous enemy and were probably genuinely concerned by the persecution let loose on their former political associates.
>
> (*DR*, p. 231)

> In 1920 the Faculty elected me Professor of Philosophy at the University of Moscow, and, for a year, I gave lectures in which I openly and without any hindrance criticized Marxism.
>
> (*DR*, p. 232)

The anarchists had their own bookshops, clubs, etc. and were the only revolutionary group with whom Berdyaev maintained personal connections. On one occasion in the winter of 1918–19 they held a debate on Christ, attended by both atheistic and Tolstoyan anarchists, and also some Bolsheviks and Red Army soldiers. Berdyaev alone made a speech defending orthodox Christianity, which he later wrote up as a pamphlet 'On the Worth of Christianity and the Unworthiness of Christians'. He records that: 'With the very first words I felt as if I was seized by some power inspiring me and giving me strength and all the words appropriate for the occasion. Indeed, I do not think I have ever spoken better in my life than at this meeting' (*DR*, p. 233). The initially hostile audience ended by applauding him.

This is not the life of an 'internal exile', like the dissidents of the Brezhnev period. Indeed, but for the Revolution Berdyaev could never have held an academic position since he had been expelled from university when he had been arrested for socialist agitation under the tsars and had never finished his degree. Aside from the fact that at the time that the Revolution broke out there was a 'blasphemy' charge against him pending for criticising the Orthodox Church (of which he was a member) for using the force of law to suppress a spiritual movement within its own ranks, and had he been convicted he could have been exiled to Siberia for life. Naturally, the charge lapsed with the Revolution and Berdyaev comments: 'Had there been no revolution, I should have been exiled for life to Siberia instead of to Paris' (*DR*, p. 203).

Perhaps I should here mention in passing a statement in Donald Lowrie's biography of Berdyaev which, if true, would entirely alter this picture. He writes almost as an aside, clearly oblivious of the enormous consequences of what he is saying:

> Berdyaev and some of his friends . . . belonged to a secret group maintaining contact with the 'rebel' general Judenitch. A new member admitted to their small circle turned out to be a spy, which resulted in the arrest of all the men in the group.
>
> (*Rebellious Prophet*, p. 151)

If this were true, then in everything he said about opposing counterrevolution, Berdyaev would have been lying like an American president and we simply could not take him seriously at all. However, I feel sure that it is not true; not only because I don't think Berdyaev was a liar, but because if it were true, he would hardly have got away with exile to the West. Lowrie is a none-too-intelligent biographer, particularly about political matters, and I feel sure that he has got hold of the wrong end of the stick as usual.

State capitalism

We have seen that Berdyaev's judgements on the Revolution in its early years treat it as just and not yet totalitarian in the modern sense (though, as we shall see, Berdyaev uses that word in a slightly different sense in which he does apply it to Bolshevism under Lenin). However, it was violent (in spirit, as well as by necessity) and anti-Christian. But its Stalinist phase comes in for a different type of criticism, although even in this phase, as we shall see, Berdyaev was prepared to defend it from its enemies abroad:

> This new Soviet bureaucracy is more powerful than that of the Tsarist régime. It is a new privileged class which can exploit the masses pitilessly. This is happening. An ordinary workman very often receives 75 roubles a month, but a Soviet civil servant, a specialist, gets 1,600 roubles a month, and this portentous inequality exists in a communist state. Soviet Russia is a country of state capitalism which is capable of exploitation no less than private capitalism.
>
> (*ORC*, p. 128)

It is even possible that the bourgeois spirit in Russia will actually make its appearance after the communist revolution. The Russian people was never bourgeois; it had no bourgeois prejudices, nor reverence for bourgeois virtues and criteria, but the danger of becoming bourgeois is very great in Soviet Russia.

(ORC, p. 146)

Lenin did not reach dictatorship in the present-day sense of the word [mid-1930s]. Stalin is a leader–dictator in the contemporary fascist sense of the word.

(ORC, p. 147)

This is a new attitude on Berdyaev's part since it means that, even in terms of social justice, the Revolution has failed and as a result changes 'are unavoidable for the final realization of communism' (p. 128). I don't think these changes are now seen as limited to spiritual revolution and a revival of Christianity, but must be political and economic too. Yet, as we shall see, Berdyaev still rejects counter-revolutionary solutions and takes a defencist view of the Soviet state in world politics.

Berdyaev and the emigrés

Berdyaev did not wish to leave the Soviet Union:

> I never wanted to leave Russia and become an *emigré*, for I had faith in the possibility of the spiritual regeneration and liberation of communist Russia from within.

(DR, p. 236)

> My own banishment was based not on any political but on ideological grounds. When I heard of the decision, I was overcome with grief and bitterness: as I have said, I did not want to emigrate, and the prospect of merging with the *emigré* world filled me with something like horror.

(DR, p. 239)

Those who had chosen to leave as soon as the Revolution occurred were hostile to those who stayed until they were thrown out. So far as Berdyaev is concerned, he reciprocated this hostility:

> There is a widespread tendency among the Russian *emigrés* to regard the Bolshevik Revolution as something brought about by the powers of evil and perpetrated by a band of criminal maniacs, while they, the *emigrés*, dwelt in untarnished truth and light. I find this tendency quite abhorrent.

(DR, p. 222)

He contrasts this smugness with the Dostoevskian passion of an atheist Soviet worker: after Berdyaev had given a public lecture on science and religion, the worker:

approached me and began with great vehemence to attack God and religion. I asked him why he had stayed on and listened to my lecture, whereupon he said: 'I want my convictions and arguments against God and faith to be disproved. I want to see if I can stand up to God.' Nothing of this kind could ever have been said by the young Russian *emigrés*, who seem to have lost completely the searching mind and the intense spiritual disquietude characteristic of the Russian.

(*DR*, p. 234)

He describes the *emigrés* as 'blinded by rancour' (p. 241) and himself as having 'become a kind of permanent thorn in their flesh' (p. 242). He speaks of his first encounters with them – his 'first unpleasant experience in Germany', of their slander that he was a Soviet agent sent to demoralize them ('a task which the *emigrés* were already themselves successfully performing' (p. 245)) and of his loss of temper when they outlined their plans to overthrow Bolshevism:

I envisaged a wholly different way of saving Russia from the perils of Bolshevism: I believed in her regeneration from within, through a painful process of inner purification.

(*DR*, p. 245)

Later, in occupied France, he speaks of *emigrés* who collaborated with the Nazis or welcomed Hitler's invasion of Russia. He refused to meet them and regarded them as traitors (p. 317). He never became part of their community or even their church, since his affiliation was to that section of the Russian Orthodox Church in the West which adhered to the Patriarch of Moscow who had made his peace with the Soviet regime and whom the *emigré* church refused to acknowledge.

Berdyaev as defender of the Soviet state

Despite Berdyaev's recognition of the Stalinist state's similarity to Fascism and its economy's status as state capitalist, he remained a defender of the Soviet state in international politics. Just after the passage quoted above in which he compares Stalin to Fascist dictators, he says of the Soviet state 'but at the present moment it is the one power which provides some sort of defence for Russia against the dangers which threaten it' (*ORC*, p. 147). This comes out strongly in the epilogue to *DR* which deals with the period of the war and the beginnings of the cold war (1940–49). In the war he felt 'one with the successes and failures of the Red Army' and saw its strength as providential (*DR*, p. 317). His house in Clamart, near Paris 'became a kind of meeting-place for Russian patriots' (p. 318). He speaks of his 'Soviet orientation' in international relations and, while remaining a critic of repression in Russia:

continued to regard the Soviet government as the only representative national government, even though I did not approve of its policy in some respects. No true Russian can feel or believe the communist *régime* to be an alien occupation, or will accept the view that its foreign policy is in conflict with 'national interests'.

(*DR*, p. 320)

This was written of the post-war period, so it is not just a matter of tactics in the anti-Fascist alliance. This attitude determined his circle of friends: 'I met now almost exclusively Russians representing the 'Soviet orientation', young writers, journalists and churchmen belonging to the Patriarchal Church' (p. 321). Some commentators have presented this as a temporary attitude, soon changed by a recognition of the evils going on in the Soviet Union, but it is clear from this epilogue, written right at the end of Berdyaev's life, that he was throughout fully aware of the oppression that prevailed there, and condemned it in no uncertain terms, yet could still write:

My attitude to the ugly things that are going on in Soviet Russia is, however, complicated, though not cancelled, by the fact that in the present [postwar] international situation I feel bound to defend my country. I am prepared to stand firm by the principles which govern Soviet foreign policy *vis-à-vis* an increasingly hostile world, although I do not endorse all the methods which are used in their application.

(*DR*, p. 325)

This Soviet orientation was no doubt partly motivated by patriotism, but I think there is more to it than that. Most people who held a state capitalist analysis of Soviet society held a 'plague on both your houses' attitude to international affairs. Yet it is arguable that Soviet militarism was defensive, whereas Western militarism was aggressive, and that a socialised economic structure – albeit 'state capitalist' in that it exploited the workers – gave the Soviet bloc an objective interest in peace and the liberation of colonised countries, while the West had an economic interest in an arms race and imperialism; and that consequently the Soviet bloc was consistently closer to the interests of humankind in its foreign policy throughout the cold war period. Whether that was Berdyaev's view I don't know; anyway, I think it is true, and that his defencism was therefore justified.

It seems to me that Berdyaev's complex attitude to Soviet Russia is in all points at least within the spectrum of socialist opinion. His intense dislike of the violence and militant materialism of the Bolshevik regime often seems to outweigh his assessment of it as inevitable and just. This is quite biographically understandable: it cannot have been a nice time and place to live, especially for one with Christian commitments, not to say an erstwhile aristocratic lifestyle. But his criticisms do not amount to a rejection of socialism.

It is now time to turn to Berdyaev's statements about socialism itself. But first one last remark about his view of the prospects for Soviet Russia. The outcome that he wanted – a spiritual revival that would reverse the materialism of the Bolsheviks and restore freedom, but would build on their economic achievements and usher in a classless society – has not happened. The outcome that he feared – that the secularisation of Russia would presage its bourgeoisification and forestall the possibility of real communism – has happened:

> If it were granted that anti-religious propaganda were finally to destroy all traces of Christianity in the soul of the Russian people, and annihilate all religious feeling, then the actual realization of communism would become impossible, for no one would be willing to make sacrifices, no one would interpret life as service of a higher purpose, and the final victory would remain with the self-seeking type who thinks only of his own interests. This last type of person, even now, already plays no small part, and the growth of the bourgeois spirit is due to him.
>
> (*ORC*, p. 170)

Although Russian Christianity is far from dead, the post-Stalin bourgeoisie have triumphed and are making Russia in their own image, though less competently than the bourgeois of any other major country. The two true prophets of Russia's destiny have been Berdyaev and Trotsky. Both have offered two alternative outcomes to the contradictions of Soviet society, one good one (Trotsky: a political revolution against the bureaucracy leading to a workers' democracy; Berdyaev: a spiritual revolution leading to a classless Christian society), and a bad one (Trotsky: the bureaucracy transform themselves into a proprietorial bourgeoisie; Berdyaev: the communists breed a bourgeois cast of mind among themselves when they cut off their roots in religion and leave their millenarian enthusiasm behind). The outcome has been the combination of the bad outcomes foreseen by both.

Socialist proposals

Berdyaev's lifelong attitudes to Marx and to the Soviet regime were compatible with his remaining a socialist, but did he in fact remain one? His alienation from the Social Democrats (that is, organised Marxists), with whom he had had close contacts and among whom he had been an activist, took place during his exile in northern Russia, and was due entirely to his move towards idealism (not yet towards Christianity); Bogdanov thought this move a sign of incipient insanity (*DR*, p. 129). Berdyaev did not himself see it as a move away from socialism: 'politically I remained a Social-Democrat with strong leanings to the extreme left' (*DR*, p. 128). However, the hostility of other Social Democrats meant that he could no longer be an effective activist in that circle. He began to have some contact with the

Liberals, but this did not amount to a conversion from socialism to liberalism. He even found their superciliousness about his spiritual searchings more offensive than the Marxists' open hostility (*DR*, p. 134). But he did get involved with a predominantly Liberal movement for democracy called the League of Liberation. He attended two of its conferences 'held respectively in Schwarzwald and Schaffhausen, beside the Rhine waterfalls. To be frank, the beauty of the surrounding country was more to my liking than the conferences' (*DR*, p. 135). When the Cadet (constitutional democrat) party emerged from the League of Liberation, Berdyaev did not join it because it was 'too "bourgeois" for my liking. I continued to regard myself as a socialist' (*DR*, p. 135). In the face of the moral disintegration of the left intelligentsia after the defeat of the 1905 revolution, Berdyaev increasingly withdrew from active politics and devoted himself to 'the struggle of the spirit' (*DR*, p. 137). But he comments:

> social problems did not cease to exercise my conscience and imagination, and, from time to time, I threw myself into the social battle. Much later, as an *emigré* abroad, I reverted to some of the most radical social and political ideas of my youth, but then they rested on a new and firmer spiritual foundation.
>
> (*DR*, p. 137)

A time out of active politics does not necessarily mean a rejection of a political standpoint: Marx was out of active politics throughout the 1850s and until the 1st International was founded in 1864. But for Berdyaev, politics had clearly come to take a second place to first idealist and then Christian ideas about the life of the spirit (whereas Marx was writing *Capital* during his sabbatical decade). A second place, however, is not no place at all. Politics continued to have second place for Berdyaev later during his 'radical' years abroad. There is no evidence that the content of his ideas ceased to be socialist at this time.

What, then, of Berdyaev's renewed radicalism after his exile? When he was exiled, he was told by the communist President of the Academy of Arts: 'they hope in the Kremlin that when you find yourself in Western Europe you will understand on which side justice lies' (*DR*, p. 242). Berdyaev comments that he did not need to go to the West and that he had never failed to understand the injustice of capitalism. But he admits to having become 'more of a socialist' than he would have been had he remained in Russia, although he reasserts his opposition to totalitarianism whether East or West.

Berdyaev's statements on socialism

I will now discuss Berdyaev's explicit statements about socialism, under four headings:

1   his apparent attack on socialism in works written in Bolshevik Russia;
2   his commitment to socialism as an economic system;
3   his characterisation of the socialism he favours as personalistic and plural-
    istic; and
4   his attack on 'integral socialism' and defence of Christian socialism.

Berdyaev's apparent attack on socialism

Berdyaev was clearly a 'counter-suggestible' person – a trait I greatly sympathise with – and one would expect his least favourable comments about
socialism to date from his time living in Soviet Russia. Soon after the
Revolution, in the spring of 1918, Berdyaev wrote a book called *The
Philosophy of Inequality*, attacking egalitarianism. I have not read this book,
so cannot comment on it, except to say that in *DR* Berdyaev makes two
points about the book: that he now dislikes the book more than any other
he has written; and that it attacked spiritual, not social egalitarianism, and
defended the dignity and worth of the human person as the only basis of
true social equality. If he is defending qualitative differences between people
(which, by definition, cannot be quantified and therefore cannot be either
equal or unequal), no socialist should quarrel with him – Marx certainly
would not. Whether he is defending more than this, I don't know. He states
a similar case from clearly within socialism:

> Class inequality ought to be overcome in human society, but personal
> inequality would come out all the stronger for that. Man should be
> distinguished from man by his personal quality not by his social posi-
> tion, his class or his property. The qualitative, that is to say, the personal
> aristocratic principle, cannot disappear from human society. On the
> contrary, it will become all the clearer in a classless society, when classes
> no longer exist, for classes mask and conceal personal qualitative differ-
> ences among men and make them symbolic, not real.
>
> (*ORC*, p. 179)

Another book that comes from this period is his *Dostoevsky*. In this book
(based on a series of seminars he gave in Moscow with a Cheka agent
present) he sometimes seems to be attacking socialism outright. This gives
the anti-socialist Lowrie the opportunity to quote out-of-context gobbets
with headings (Lowrie's, of course) like 'Socialism Does Not Believe in God'
and 'Socialism Opposes Freedom' (see *Christian Existentialism: A Berdyaev
Anthology*, p. 286). It is not always clear which opinions Berdyaev is avowing
in his own person and which he is attributing to Dostoevsky, but he does
seem in the part of the book on socialism to be endorsing Dostoevsky's views.
He quotes Dostoevsky:

> Socialism is not only a problem of labour or of what is called the fourth
> class but is even more concerned with atheism, a modern incarnation of

godlessness, the tower of Babel built without God, not to raise earth to heaven but to bring heaven down to earth.

(*The Brothers Karamazov*, in *Dostoevsky*, pp. 137–38)

The quote is in connection with what Alyosha might have been had he not been a young monk – that is, he might have been a socialist.

Berdyaev comments:

In Russia revolutionary socialism has never been regarded as a passing form of the economic and political organization of society but as a definitive and absolute condition, a solution of the destinies of mankind and the beginning of the establishment of God's kingdom on earth.

(*Dostoevsky*, p. 138)

Socialism is a manifestation of the spirit. It claims to be concerned with nothing short of final things, it wants to be a new religion and to respond to man's religious needs.

(*Dostoevsky*, p. 139)

The idea is that socialism is a competitor, not with capitalism for economic organisation, but with Christianity for the human soul:

Dostoevsky went further and more deeply than the most understanding of the Marxists themselves in laying bare socialism's hidden nature, and at the heart of its revolutionary godless variety he discerned the very principle and spirit of Antichrist. Not that he looked at it from the viewpoint of bourgeois principles; on the contrary, he was more radically opposed to the bourgeois spirit than the socialists themselves, who are, fundamentally, led captive by it. He was indeed a socialist himself in a manner of speaking: an 'Orthodox Christian socialist'.

(*Dostoevsky*, pp. 140–41)

The socialist state, [Dostoevsky] said, was not a secular but a confessional state, like a country in which a church is 'established'.

(*Dostoevsky*, p. 147)

It should not be necessary to say that socialism is considered here as a new religion and not simply as a programme of social reforms or as an economic system, for in these it is possible that it may be justified.

(*Dostoevsky*, p. 201)

The position here is that socialism as a movement is not essentially defined by its economic programme, but is 'integral socialism', a total world view or secular religion. The possible justification of socialism as an economic system is conceded almost in an aside. To a Western socialist, this is odd:

socialism just is an economic system, and movements, whatever other aims they may have, are defined as socialist or non-socialist by their commitment to common ownership or lack of such commitment. But in Russia in 1921 it must have looked different (also, of course, to Dostoevsky – but he was only acquainted with French utopian socialism, not with Marxism). Lenin was to endorse the New Economic Policy with considerable concessions to capitalism, but so far from adopting a New Religious Policy, opening a dialogue with the Christian majority of the Russian people, the attitude to religion hardened, as instanced by Berdyaev's exile.

The question at issue here is whether socialism has to be an integral world view or whether it can be a view of economics, combinable with many different attitudes to religion – as also to art, science, the family, and so on. To this we will return under the heading, Berdyaev's opposition to 'integral socialism' (p. 124).

Socialism as an economic system

Berdyaev expresses his commitment to a socialist economy as follows:

> If I opposed communism, I did so solely on account of the freedom of the spirit. . . . I did not, however, oppose communism in so far as it deals with the limited sphere of social and economic organization and is based on a scientific analysis of certain aspects of social life. I believe that the organization of material resources for the benefit of all and the curtailment of economic individualism will make men not less but more aware of those final realities and values of human existence which are imperilled by communism and anti-communism alike. . . . If Marxism is in earnest about its avowed aim to liberate humanity from servitude to economics, then I am a Marxist.
>
> (*DR*, p. 241)

> In regard to economic life two contradictory principles may be postulated. One of them says: In economic life follow up your own personal interest and this will promote the economic development of the whole, it will be good for the community, for the nation, for the state. Such is the bourgeois ideology of economics. The other principle says: In economic life serve others, serve the whole community and then you will receive everything you need for your life. Communism asserts this second principle, and in that respect it is right.
>
> (*ORC*, pp. 185–86)

> I am a supporter of the classless society, that is to say, in that respect I am very near to communism.
>
> (*ORC*, p. 179)

Although Berdyaev couches these statements of commitment to a socialist economy in terms of morality rather than structural organisation, I think there is no doubt that he means them to be a full commitment to socialism as defined, for instance, by the pre-Blair Labour Party's Clause 4.

It should be said in passing that, when characterising the brand of socialism he favours, Berdyaev uses terms like personalist socialism and pluralistic socialism, but not democratic socialism. I think that this is partly because he is as worried about integral democracy as about integral socialism and strongly rejects democracy in spiritual matters; and partly because the sort of democracy that he does favour for the state and the economy is not the prevalent parliamentary democracy, but a sort of corporate democracy akin to the soviets before Russia became a one-party state or to guild socialism.

Berdyaev's socialism

The personalist moral basis and pluralist structure of Berdyaev's socialism can be found in the following:

> I am prepared to describe myself as a socialist, but my socialism is personalistic, not authoritarian: it precludes the primacy of society over the person, for it springs from a recognition of the supreme value of each individual human being made in the image of God and endowed with a free spirit.
>
> (*DR*, p. 241)

> I am a supporter of Christian personalism, certainly not of individualism which is hostile to the principle of personality. In a bourgeois capitalist community personality is levelled down and looked upon merely as an atom. Individualism is hostile to the Christian idea of the community of men, whereas the realization of personality presupposes the communion of men.
>
> (*ORC*, p. 179)

This personalism is the moral principle on the grounds of which Berdyaev prefers socialism to capitalism. But it also has consequences for the type of socialism advocated. It could be called libertarian socialism, and indeed Berdyaev sometimes shows a soft spot for anarchism. The anarchists, as already mentioned, were the only political group he was in close contact with in post-revolutionary Russia. When he met the French Catholic existentialist philosopher Gabriel Marcel, Berdyaev wrote that Marcel 'accused me of anarchism and similar crimes of which I happen to be rather proud' (*DR*, p. 318). Nevertheless, Berdyaev recognises the need for government and favours a mixed socialist economy, with state ownership, co-operatives and one-man businesses:

It is indisputable that a part of commerce, of commerce on the most considerable scale, ought to pass over to the state. But side by side with this one must recognise the co-operation of men, the labouring syndicate, and the separate man established by the organization of society in conditions which exclude the exploitation of one's neighbour; and the state will have controlling and mediating functions, such as will not permit the oppression of man by man.

(*ORC*, pp. 186–87)

Berdyaev's opposition to 'integral socialism'

Time and again Berdyaev attacks communism, not for its economic aims, but for claiming to be a total world view, with a line about everything – 'integral socialism'. 'Communism is integrated; it embraces the whole of life; its relations are with no special section of it' (*ORC*, p. 158). He also uses the word totalitarian in this connection. Lenin's Russia was not totalitarian in the sense that Stalin's Russia and Hitler's Germany were, but the Bolsheviks already had a total world view and the seeds of totalitarianism are in that. This is one of the differences from Western socialists:

The social democrats, while continuing to consider themselves Marxists, admitted people who were believing Christians to membership of the party, even ministers of religion and professors of theology. But this means that social democracy does not wish to be a 'world outlook'; it wishes to be only a political party, only a system of social reform. I am not speaking of English socialism, which is connected with Christianity far more than with Marxism.

(*ORC*, p. 165)

Berdyaev attributes the integral or totalitarian mentality to Russian revolutionary traditions, pre-existing Marxism, although he also (wrongly, in my opinion) regards Marx as having an 'integral socialist' world view. He refers to 'critical Marxists', presumably including himself in his period of Marxist activism, as dissenting from this:

One might criticize this or that side of the Marxist world view. Marxism in that case ceased to be an entire totalitarian doctrine; it became a method of cognition in social matters and of carrying on the social conflict. This is the opposite of revolutionary totalitarianism. Russian revolutionaries in the past, also, had always been totalitarian.

(*ORC*, p. 105)

It should be said that, although Berdyaev no doubt saw integral socialism all around him in the Russia of the 'war communism' period, Marx and

Engels were not really integral socialists, and Lenin and Trotsky were not consistently so. Marx opposed the exclusion of religious believers from the 1st International proposed by Bakunin, and he always regarded science as independent of ideology; Engels condemned Dühring for proposing a socialist state in which religion was illegal, and he preferred novels without political motivation to *tendenzromans*. Lenin and Trotsky both polemicised against the politicisation of art and science, against 'class art' and 'class science', although Berdyaev's old antagonists Lunacharsky and Bogdanov favoured them, and they were to have a new lease of life under Stalin. Lenin even coined the portmanteau word 'komchvanstvo' ('communist swagger') for the belief that one's communism gave one the licence to pronounce on all topics. Unfortunately, Lenin and Trotsky did not extend this tolerance to religion, although they were mercifully free from the idea that 'the personal is political'.

Indeed, it is arguable that, although many Marxists have seen themselves as integral Marxists, what they have been, in fact, is Marxists who have integrated attitudes derived from other world views with their Marxism, and presented the amalgam as through-and-through Marxist. Marx and Engels themselves combined their 'Marxism' – that is to say, their politics and economics – with attitudes derived from the French Enlightenment and Rousseau, and from the left Hegelians; Lenin combined Marxism with the heritage of the Russian revolutionary intelligentsia, as Berdyaev has shown; Lukacs, whom Berdyaev mentions as an integral Marxist, had a world view derived from a romantic reading of Hegel, into which he integrated his Marxism but which, as a whole, looks far from Marxist from the standpoint of, for example, Althusserian Marxism; and the latter derives most of its outlook from Spinoza, Freud and structuralism.

This raises the question whether Berdyaev is not throwing stones at integral world views from a glasshouse: if he was a socialist without being an integral Marxist, it might be said, that was not because he had no integral world view, but because his socialism was part of a different integral world view: Christianity. He certainly sees socialism as entailed by Christianity:

> In the Prophets, in the Gospels, in the Apostolic Epistles, in most of the Doctors of the Church, we find censure of the riches of the rich and repudiation of property, and the affirmation of the equality of all men before God. In Basil the Great, and especially in John Chrysostom, may be met judgments upon social injustice due to wealth and property, so sharp that Proudhon and Marx pale before them. The Doctors of the Church said that property is theft. St John Chrysostom was a complete communist, though of course his was not communism of the capitalist or the industrial period.
>
> (*ORC*, p. 171)

Is this Christian socialism not another integral world view? It seems it is:

> A communist society can profess to be totalitarian, but only the King-
> dom of God can be totalitarian; the kingdom of Caesar is always partial.
>
> (*ORC*, p. 154)

'Totalitarian' here means integral, of course. Is integral Christianity
(including socialism) any less likely to be totalitarian in the more usual sense
than integral socialism? I think Berdyaev's position could be defended like
this: socialism can be a part – the political and economic part – of a number
of different world views, and adherents of all those world views could in
principle co-operate in building and living in a socialist society. But socialism
itself cannot be the basis of an integral world view, only a part of one.
What is wrong with integral socialism is that it takes the part for the whole
and politicises (or economicises) all other areas of life – art, science, religion,
the family, psychology, and so on. An integral world view is acceptable
only if it gives all these different areas of life their own value as distinct parts
within the whole. What is wrong with integral socialism is neither that it
is socialism nor that it is an integral world view, but that it bases a whole
integral world view on an attitude that is appropriate to one part of life.
Christianity, on the other hand, can give all areas of life their due since God,
unlike 'Caesar', is the God of all things. This assumes, to use Paul Tillich's
distinction, that Christianity is committed to a 'theonomous' culture, not a
theocratically 'heteronomous' one, as in forms of fundamentalism which
derive 'science' from the first chapter of Genesis or reject medicine in favour
of reliance on miraculous cures.

It might be thought that integral socialism died with Stalin. But unfortunately it has had a new lease of life from two sources. In the first place,
the leftism of 1968 and its successors have been fiercely integral socialist,
politicising art, science and personal relations as surely as Zhdanov, Lysenko
or the Maoists of the cultural revolution did. I may say that one major
theme of my own philosophical writing has been to combat this politicisation of everything within the left, and I have been subjected to all sorts of
abuse from comrades because of this. But there is another source of this 'integral socialism', which is as different in style from Bolshevik integral socialism
as might be, yet is damaging in every sphere it touches. This is academic
integral socialism: many academics with left pretensions 'politicise' their
subject matter and believe as a result that their academic work is political
work. It is not, it is simply bad academic work. Every academic discipline
worth its salt has its own internal criteria, as does every other practice.
Subordinating these to political criteria always spoils the work, while providing a completely gratuitous sense of political rectitude to the academic
who has not brought human emancipation one day nearer by this work.

Whatever one thinks about Berdyaev's own world view, his stand against
integral socialism should be followed. If we want an integral world view, on
the Blakean principle that one must have a system or be enslaved by another
man's, let us think about each issue on its own terms and then see how they

might be integrated; that way one might find oneself, as I do, a Bhaskarian in theory of knowledge, a Spinozist in philosophy of mind, a Kleinian in psychology, an Augustinian in ethics, a Lutheran in theology, and an eco-Trotskyist in politics. Let us not arrive at a world view by reapplying one principle to all areas of life and thought, as postmodernists do.

Finally, there is in Berdyaev, as in those two giants of twentieth-century Protestant theology, Barth and Tillich, who were also socialists, a complex relation between his Christian commitment to the Kingdom of God and his espousal of socialism as the best order for the kingdom of Caesar. Socialism has relative truth: it is right as against feudalism and capitalism, it is the best way of organising sinful human beings. But it does not have absolute truth: it is the kingdom of Caesar, not the Kingdom of God. Some have seen this distinction of all human kingdoms from the Kingdom of God as so relativising human politics that it is inconsistent to continue to prefer one form of social organisation to another. But this is not so. There are objectively better and worse ways, from a Christian point of view, of organising sinful people:

> The argument that socialism is unrealizable because it presupposes a moral height to which the actual state of men and women does not correspond is completely bankrupt. It would be more true to say that socialism will be realized precisely because the moral level of men is not high enough, and an organization of society is needed which would make impossible the excessive oppression of man by man. . . . A socialist society is not a society of saints; it is just simply a society of sinful and imperfect men, the manifestation of human perfection is not to be expected of it.
>
> (*Slavery and Freedom*, p. 208)

Berdyaev refuses to see socialism as a perfect society or to idol-worship it. But then Engels is also on record as saying there can be no perfect society and Rosa Luxemburg as saying that we should not idol-worship socialism. Berdyaev is here taking a position which is not only common ground of the most eminent Christian socialists, but has nothing in it which should offend classical (non-totalitarian) Marxists.

However, this makes Berdyaev's position sound a little simpler than it is. It is not that, having postponed perfect society until after the last judgement, Berdyaev treats socialism as beyond criticism for the here and now while all are sinners. Rather, he sees socialism as having relative or 'negative' truth and rightness in that, as against other historic societies (for example, feudalism and capitalism), it is in the right; but it still contrasts with the Kingdom of God and can be seen by that contrast to fall short. For the Kingdom of God is not so much radically unlike all human political ideals as like one of them, which, however, (unlike socialism) cannot be realised while we are sinners – namely, anarchism:

> There is a certain amount of truth in anarchism. Anarchism is not applic-
> able to our sinful world which is under the law, and anarchic utopias
> are a snare and a delusion. But the perfect life, the Kingdom of God,
> can only be conceived in terms of anarchism.
>
> (*The Destiny of Man*, p. 197)

But the contrast between socialism and anarchism is clear enough: socialism
involves a state, anarchism does not. I think that Berdyaev's point is that,
while a state is made necessary by sin, it is also itself always sinful. Political
power may be necessary to prevent economic oppression, but it will itself
always tend to be oppressive: 'the state is devoid of grace and holiness and
has a non-Christian nature and origin' (ibid.). It cannot help but ignore the
personalistic values which for Berdyaev are all-important. It may be a necessary evil, but that clichéd phrase should by taken seriously: a necessary evil
is still an evil and one needs a long spoon to sup with it. For this reason
socialism, even though the best system available to us, is a sinful system.
This is a rather stronger reservation about socialism than saying that we
should not idol-worship it; we should not even treat it as a good system,
only as the best system out of a bad lot. But to say this is surely still to be
a socialist.

References

Berdyaev, Nicholas, *The Origin of Russian Communism*, Geoffrey Bles, London, 1937.
—— , *The Destiny of Man*, Geoffrey Bles, London, 1937.
—— , *Slavery and Freedom*, Geoffrey Bles, London, 1943.
—— , *Dream and Reality: An Essay in Autobiography*, Geoffrey Bles, London, 1950.
—— , *Dostoevsky*, Meridian Books, Cleveland and New York, 1957.
Lowrie, Donald, *Rebellious Prophet: A Life of Nicholas Berdyaev*, Gollancz, London, 1960.
—— , (ed.), *Christian Existentialism: A Berdyaev Anthology*, Allen & Unwin, London, 1965.

Part II

10　In defence of objectivity

This criticism, therefore, loses itself in a sad and pompous spiritualism. Consciousness or self-consciousness is considered to be the sole human quality. Love, for example, is rejected, because in it the beloved is only an 'object'. Down with objects!

(Marx, 'Letter to Feuerbach, 11th August 1844',
in *Early Texts*, p. 186)

The issue

§1 Defining objectivity

The problem and verbal preliminaries

In many contexts, objectivity is highly regarded, and to say that someone's judgement or analysis or description was very objective is to praise them. Why, then, does objectivity need defending? One reason is the frequent *misuse* of this word and the attacks that this misuse calls forth. When, for instance, it is said that something should be judged by objective criteria, it is often meant: criteria that can be spelt out in advance and possibly measured. But in fact criteria that cannot be measured or even spelt out in advance of a judgement of something may be perfectly objective. Suppose one is interviewing candidates for a post. It is precisely the qualities which the candidates in fact have, and which were not or even could not have been predicted in advance, which are the objective grounds for the selection of a candidate; criteria spelt out in advance reflect nothing but the interviewers' subjectivity. Moreover, there is no guarantee that something objective will be measurable, and trying to force the unquantifiable into a quantitative straitjacket is subjectivity in the worst sense.

However, my main task in this part of the book is to reply to two philosophical tendencies which, in their different ways, denigrate objectivity. The first is epistemological subjectivism, both in its early modern form of subjective idealism and in its more extreme recent forms of relativism and postmodernism. I shall criticise these views in the first part of this essay – implicitly in this section and explicitly in the next one – by looking at the questionable assumptions underlying their arguments. I shall do this for the most part without reference to specific texts. The second such tendency is existentialism, which is for the most part not epistemologically subjectivist, but which impugns objectivity in a number of different ways. My critique of these existentialist positions is much more sympathetic and, to an extent, is a set of immanent critiques of individual writers, all of whom, despite my criticisms, I have a high regard for as thinkers. This takes up the second part of the book. There are also philosophers who do not attack objectivity, but limit its application to certain discourses – to everyday knowledge but not to science or ethics, or to science but not to everyday knowledge or ethics. I want to defend objectivity in all these areas.

One task in defending objectivity is untangling various senses of the words 'objective' and 'subjective' and related words which have become ambiguous and even systematically confused in some usages. In part, this is a matter of serious philosophical confusions with instructive reasons behind them. But in part it can be resolved at the level of mere verbal usage and is a question of whether we let words get the better of us or not. The remainder of this section is devoted to these latter questions.

It has been pointed out by Elizabeth Anscombe that in some contexts the terms 'subjective' and 'objective' have swapped meanings between the Middle Ages and now:

> I might illustrate the double reversal by a true sentence constructed to accord with the *old* meanings: subjectively there must be some definite number of leaves on a spray that I see, but objectively there need not: that is, there need not be some number such that I *see* that number of leaves on the spray.
>
> ('The Intentionality of Sensation', in
> *Collected Philosophical Papers*, vol. 2, p. 3)

For the medievals, *object* was always the object *of* something (in this case, perception). The spray itself would be the subject of its predicates. It is reminiscent of the difficulty some people have in deciding which side of the cupboard is the left side; whereas most people mean the side which is on your left when you are facing it, some think of the side that would be your left if you were the cupboard. The change that Anscombe notes is not a mere accident; it bears witness to a philosophical shift: epistemologisation. Subject and object are read as subject and object of knowledge, not of possession of leaves – of which more later.

While the word 'object' still has the sense 'object of . . .', intentional object, as well as the sense 'material thing', the word 'objective' has, in everyday speech and most philosophical usage, totally lost its original connection with being the object of something (of some 'subject'). 'Objectivity' is now generally used to mean independence of any (knowing or valuing) subject. However, some philosophers – postmodernists and Heideggerians, for the most part – trade on this etymology, and when someone says that something is objective, read them as saying that it is correlative to a subject, when they are, in fact, saying the exact opposite. In this way, philosophers who are somewhat anthropocentric try to make philosophers who are less anthropocentric look as though they were more anthropocentric. But it is just a verbal trick.

'Subject' and 'object' can be merely grammatical terms, and one source of trouble is that this grammar is taken as reflecting real metaphysical distinctions. A subject of a verb is seen as the agent of an action, its object as the passive recipient – the 'patient' – of the action. The subject position is then seen as the desirable one: 'I'd rather be a hammer than a nail', as Simon and

Garfunkel sing. But verbs do not always denote actions in any strong, onto-logical sense – a verb is, as in German, a 'time-word', rather than, as taught in English schools, a doing-word. The grammatical subject–object distinc-tion does not match the ontological agent–patient distinction. Take the verb to see: is it the seer or the seen who is the agent? Philosophically, the Sartrean account of The Look makes the seer the agent, while the causal theory of perception (which must be true at some level, even if it is not the most important one), reverses this. The myth of the evil eye makes seeing an act of violence against the seen, but the myth of Medusa inverts this relation. A man who sees a woman undressing in a window can be prosecuted as a peep-ing tom, but a man who is seen undressing in a window by a woman can be prosecuted as an exhibitionist. And what is true of seeing is also true of knowing. To be the object of knowledge may be to be the subject of self-revelation. Failure to recognise this has sometimes led theologians into the absurdity of denying the knowledge of God since it would make God an 'object' (it seems to me that this is one of the several related things that is going on in Rudolf Bultmann's extraordinarily bad paper 'What Does it Mean to Speak of God' in *Faith and Understanding* – of which more later).

The moral of all this is that one should not pass thoughtlessly between the bland grammatical subject–object distinction and either the ontological agent–patient distinction or the epistemological knower–known distinction.

Nor should we confuse these last two. 'Subject' in modern philosophical usage most often has the sense of 'subject of knowledge'. Since the class of subjects of knowledge and the class of human beings are often deemed co-extensive, 'subject' becomes a synonym for human being. 'Object' has correspondingly (in ordinary usage even more than in philosophical) come to mean something subhuman. Subjects and objects come to mean 'people and things'. However, this has given rise to several problems. First, human beings are much else besides knowing subjects. Macmurray has pointed out that we are more fully understood as agents than as subjects, and are subjects only as an aspect of being agents. Hence the reduction of the ontological subject–object distinction (the agent–patient distinction) to the epistemo-logical one misrepresents our place in the world. Second, human beings can be both the objects of knowledge and the objects of action; neither of these 'objectifications' degrade us to the status of objects in the sense of subhuman things. This ought to be too obvious to need saying, but we shall see that it is not.

What objectivity is

The first and central use of the word 'objectivity' is to refer to what is true independently of any subject judging it to be true. To say that it is an objec-tive fact that the Earth is the third planet from the Sun is to say that this is so whether or not anyone knows or believes it, or even is able to formu-late the statement. To say that kindness is an objective value is to say that it is a value, whether or not anyone judges it to be a value; it would be a value even if the whole of society regarded it as a culpable weakness and it was only practised shamefacedly as a private foible. These two judgements – that facts are objective and that values are objective – which I have introduced as examples, in fact carry widely differing credence. The former is doubted by Feyerabend and by some postmodernists, but only ever by academics in their studies. It is generally accepted by plain men and women, and by academics when they are not posing as such. The second is doubted by virtually all twentieth-century thinkers and by non-academics as much as by academics. I hold both. But in this section, I am not so much concerned to defend them, as to make it clear what the position is that I shall later be defending. There are also senses of the word 'objectivity' in which it can be a quality of human judgements or attitudes, and I shall discuss these senses below. But this first sense makes no reference to human judgements or attitudes. Something is not objective because some subject judges it, but whether or not any subject judges it or even exists. Hence there need be no answer to the question 'Who is to say that it is objective?', a question that is consequently always a red herring. Maybe no one can say whether some particular fact or value is objective, but that does not impugn its objectivity. There are doubtless many objective facts – and even objective values – that we may never know to be such.

But although what is objective is independent of anyone judging it, it does not follow that every objective fact is independent of any human judgement, since it might be a fact *about* a human judgement. It is an objective fact that I make the judgement that it is an objective fact that the Earth is the third planet from the Sun. The former fact, unlike the latter, is dependent on *some* human judgement – namely, mine about the Earth, but not on the human judgement that it is true. It is important to get this straight because it is sometimes mistakenly said that all objective facts are independent of all human judgements; each is independent of the judgement that it is true, but not of any judgements that it may be about. It is also sometimes mistakenly said that human judgements are not themselves objective facts, which they clearly are.

This first use of 'objective' is central because the other two uses depend on it and are derivative from it. However, it is not a very common use. We do not usually talk about objective facts and values because, in the case of facts, we generally assume that they are objective without needing to say so, and, in the case of values, most people assume that they are not objective without feeling the need to say so.

The second sense of objectivity is that in which human judgements are said to be objective. I think this notion is a causal one: in calling a judgement objective one is saying at least that it is caused by its object, not by some feature of its subject other than that subject's openness to the effects of the object. If my judgement that the Earth is the third planet from the Sun is objective – then it is not due to my desire to believe it or some dream that I have had, but because the Earth *is* the third planet from the Sun – and this has been registered in the results of some scientific experiments and passed on to me by lines of communication which, because of the objective attitude of the scientific community (of which more later), are themselves free from subjective interference.

An experiment is the classic case of deliberately making a judgement objective: an experiment is so set up that what is objectively true will determine its outcome. Thus, if you want to discover whether one substance is heavier than another, you will make sure that your scales are accurate and that you have got the same volume of the two substances, so that the only thing that will make one side of the scales fall and the other rise is the first side's being heavier. Outside experimental situations we test objectivity by practice ('the proof of the pudding is in the eating'), we acquire objective knowledge of other people by listening to them rather than projecting our fantasies upon them, and we acquire an objective though non-scientific knowledge of nature by (metaphorically) 'listening to' nature. This is not meant to be an exhaustive list, but an indication of the ways that human judgements can be the outcome of objective facts rather than subjective dispositions. Subjective dispositions are, of course, also objective facts, but they are facts about the person whose dispositions they are; it is when they determine that person's judgement about other matters that those judgements become 'merely subjective'. The sense of subjectivity that contrasts with objectivity in this second sense is the determination of belief about objects, not by those objects, but by such phenomena as wishful thinking, projection (in the Freudian sense), forgetfulness, an over-optimistic or over-pessimistic disposition, and so on. Many of those who, in other senses, praise subjectivity and attack objectivity, recognise this as the 'bad sense' of subjectivity. We shall see that this is true of Berdyaev. However, there are some who will defend subjectivity even in this sense *in some contexts* – Pascal and William James on religious belief, for instance. Furthermore, the general devaluation of objectivity as an attitude allows this kind of subjectivity to prevail in practice by default. Of course, not any old causal chain linking object to judgement will make the judgement objective. There is a dual relation of judgement to object, a relation of intentionality – the judgement is *about* the object, and a relation of causality. The causality must be such that it makes the judgement evidence for its own truth. Thus the fact that I judge now that there is a picture of my parents on top of my computer, which I am sitting in front of in broad daylight, is evidence for the truth of that judgement. That is because what one has before one's eyes in broad daylight causes one to see it. Whether this constitutes a 'causal theory of perception' I leave others to judge; the point is simply that there is a causal process, known to the science of optics, linking object to perception of it, and the process is of such a nature as to produce a perception which is precisely the perception *of it*. This is the feature of our knowledge[1] of the world that has led some philosophers (Lenin, for instance) to talk of knowledge as a *reflection* of its object. The metaphor of reflection is helpful in so far as it indicates that the causal chain from object to knowledge of it explains the aboutness of the knowledge, as is present in a mirror or a camera; it is unhelpful in so far as it suggests both pure passivity in perception and a representational theory of aboutness. Later in this book, an analysis of the nature of experiment in science will help to clarify the causal nature of objectivity in contexts where knowledge is being actively pursued.

I now come to the third sense of objectivity: as a human attitude. This is an attitude of trying to make one's judgements objective in the second sense; trying to make one's beliefs and values conditional upon what is objectively true and valuable – objective in the first sense. The objective attitude is an important part of the scientific attitude and, while some parts of the scientific attitude are open to criticism (the tendency to inappropriate quantification, for example), this one cannot really be objected to on any grounds other than the desire to deceive oneself by wishful thinking. It is this attitude that gives rise to experiment and careful observation. But it also has other manifestations: attempts to escape from the bias of one's own subjectivity and one's own historical place. To this end one can carefully examine one's own presuppositions and make a critique of them; one can pay particular attention to positions radically different from one's own; one can analyse one's own mistakes; one can deliberately choose to learn from the most unfashionable sources. There is real wisdom here in C.S. Lewis' advice that, when one has read a modern book, one should never read another until one has read a book from a past age; this way one learns presuppositions other than those of the present age and, since we have no access to the books of the future, that is the only way available to us for doing so.

Objectivity as an attitude means openness to refutation by data derived from the real objects with which we are concerned; the alternative is to be shut up in one's own subjectivity.

The attitude of objectivity involves recognising the primacy of the object, or what Aurel Kolnai calls 'the sovereignty of the object'[2]. Kolnai argues that, in discussions, not only about the objects of science and everyday knowledge, but also of metaphysical questions like free will and determinism, the existence of God, the nature of the self and society, and so on, we are concerned not just to express ourselves, but to find out the truth; our thinking is governed by the object that we seek truth about, not by considerations that are subjective in the sense of not themselves being determined by reference to the object. Of course, the power of wishful thinking may be especially great in these matters, since our emotions are engaged and there is no easy way to verify or falsify positions by observation or experiment. But wishful thinking is still an error that we try to avoid; it is not a process that we can accept with a good conscience. This is so because even the phenomena of which human subjectivity is composed – experience, emotion, practice, language, value judgements, beliefs – are all object-centred and defined by their objects. 'Experience' is simply the nominalisation of a transitive verb:

experiencing something. There is no experience that is not an act of experiencing something and each experience is defined by the something that is experienced. Experience is therefore essentially fallible: it can be right or wrong about what is experienced, but either way it remains about just that. As we shall see, it is failure to recognise this essential reference of experience to its object – the error of believing that experience is an object that we can inspect without reference to its objects – that makes subjectivism or idealism possible. The same is true of emotions: they are about something and they can be based on a true or false conception of that something. Othello's emotion of jealousy is about Desdemona's adultery, but Desdemona has not committed adultery. Emotions, like other experiences of the world, are judged by their truth or falsity to their objects. Practice likewise cannot be inspected aside from its objects and then made the criterion for the reality of its objects, as in pragmatism. Practice is always work upon its object and defined by its object: riding *a bike*, hammering in *a nail*, cooking *a moussaka*. Language too is only possible because there is a pre-existing public world of objects that we can refer to by language. And when we value something – say, the New Forest – that valuing is a judgement about the New Forest – that it has value – not about some mental process of ours that could be inspected in isolation from the New Forest. One discovers the value of the New Forest by going to the New Forest, not by describing a set of human preferences. This essential other-directedness of human mental acts and processes not only makes it possible for them to be determined by their objects; it means that they are defined by their attempt to be determined by their objects. A non-objective experience, emotion or belief is a *failed* experience, emotion or belief.

This objective reference should be especially clear in the case of beliefs. What makes something a belief and not an image or an itch or a tapeworm is that it is a claim that a particular state of affairs holds. It is therefore very strange that some people can say that certain statements – for example, the Christian creeds – 'don't make claims about what is objectively so, they express beliefs'. Normally, to express a belief *is* to make a claim about what is objectively so. A comparison with the case of expressing emotions may clarify this, and give some idea of what such people are saying and why they are wrong. One can express an emotion in a number of ways: by a facial expression or a bodily movement or a non-verbal noise or a non-propositional use of language – or by a statement. I can express my anger at a politician by swearing about him or by banging my fist on the table when his name is mentioned, or by saying 'He is a cynical liar'. The anger and any of these expressions of it may be appropriate or inappropriate. But the last one can also be true or false and is appropriate only if it is true. Of course, other things than his being a cynical liar may make anger with him appropriate: I may be rightly angered by his policies, even though he pursues them with due regard for truthfulness. But if I say 'He is a cynical liar' and, when asked what lies he has told, say 'None as far as I know, I was just expressing anger at him', then it is me who is the liar.

Now those who contrast 'expressing belief' with 'claiming something is objectively so' may be assimilating belief to emotion. But if even an emotion is expressed by a statement, the statement must still be believed true for the expression to be an appropriate one. If someone says in the Creed that God created the Earth and that Jesus died for us, they may be expressing the emotion of trust in God; if they trust God because they believe that he created the Earth and that Jesus died for us, this is a wholly appropriate expression of that trust. But if they believe nothing of the kind but still trust God and wish to express that trust, they should find other words to express it, just as I should express my anger at the politician by saying 'He has iniquitous policies' rather than 'He is a cynical liar', if that is what I believe. There is no place in the inventory of mental acts for 'a belief that makes no truth claims', any more than for 'a pain that does not hurt'. (The fact that some statements in the Creed are metaphorical is irrelevant to this discussion: metaphors can be true or false like any other statements.)

What objectivity is not

It is at least as important to dispel a number of false notions about objectivity as to characterise what it is, for it is true both that a number of quite inappropriate attitudes are often recommended in the name of objectivity and that objectivity is often disparaged because these attitudes are inappropriate. In the first place, objectivity is not neutrality. There may be objective grounds for deciding one way or the other between competing positions, and if there are, neutrality can only be subjective in the bad sense – that is, a position about an object is maintained because of features of the judging subject rather than because of features of the object. As has been pointed out before, if you take a series of descriptions of an event – millions of people died; millions of people were killed; millions of innocent civilians were massacred – then assuming all are true, each is both more objective and less neutral than the last. It is more objective because it gives a fuller account of what occurred, excluding more misconceptions; and it is less neutral because it paints what occurred in a more gruesome light.

Objectivity is often thought to entail neutrality because neutrality is confused with lack of bias and, properly speaking, the objective person is unbiased. But unbiasedness is itself not the same as neutrality. If you believe the prisoner to be guilty because you don't like the look of him, you are biased; but if you believe the prisoner to be guilty because several reliable independent witnesses report seeing him commit the crime, you are not biased; but neither are you neutral: you have objective grounds for taking one side rather than another in a dispute. People are often accused of bias because they have strong partisan opinions, but this is a misuse of the term. If there are good grounds for strong partisan opinions, they may be unbiased and objective. Marx's *Capital* is a book as noteworthy for its object-ivity as for its partisanship. Hence objectivity is not dispassionateness. In the example of the massacre quoted above, if 'millions of innocent civilians were massacred' is true, then it is objectively true that the people who did the massacring were a bunch of brutal mass-murderers, and the emotion of intense indignation against them is objectively appropriate. One's emotions would be lacking in objectivity if one felt anything less. One of the unargued assumptions of several existentialist thinkers is that objective considerations cannot rouse our passions or be of existential concern for us, so that to focus on the objective is to *evade* passion and concern. Nothing could be more antagonistic to the true mission of philosophy which, as exemplified by Socrates and Spinoza, is precisely to be objective about the things that we are and ought to be passionately concerned about.

Of course, there are philosophical positions according to which values are not objective and, if these were true, objective judgements would indeed be value neutral. However, these positions cannot be assumed; they are con-tentious (and I shall argue that they are false). To treat 'objective' as if it *meant* value-neutral is to assume their truth. It has to be argued for (or against) that objectivity *implies* value-neutrality.

The next thing that objectivity is not is *infallibility*. There is a curious confusion about this, in that it is widely held that belief in objectivity is a claim to infallibility, which is not just false but the precise opposite of the truth: belief in objectivity entails, and is entailed by, the fallibility of our judgements. For one's belief cannot be fallible unless there is something independent of the believing of it that would make it true and some-thing that would make it false. If beliefs refer to nothing outside themselves, they are all infallible, for nothing could refute them. They could not even be contradicted by another belief, for what it is for one belief to contradict another is for it to be impossible that both are true. On the other hand, if a belief claims objectivity, it gives hostages to fortune: one knows where to look to show it to be false. For instance, the world of religious belief as described by Wittgenstein is a world in which one belief cannot contradict another because neither is about anything. For beliefs to contradict there has to be something for them to contradict about. Wittgenstein's theory makes the believer uncriticisable, unfaultable, and in that sense infallible. Of course, it does the same for the unbeliever. It is a marvellous philosophy for one whose cherished beliefs feel threatened and who wants to hang on to them at any cost; it is a philosophy of despair for one who wants to argue for their beliefs and convince others.

The accusation that objectivity means infallibility gains its credence from a sort of urban legend about realists that has gone the round of non-realist circles. This is the legend that realists believe in a complete and final account of what is true, that could in principle be possessed by us; in some versions, realists are even made out to claim to possess it. It is often said to be a 'God's eye view' of reality. A word is necessary about this. Some realists believe in

God and some do not. Those who do, believe that God has a God's eye view of reality. But they agree with those who do not believe in God, that no one else could conceivably ever have such a view. So the issue of God's existence or non-existence can be bracketed off here.

One form of the legend says that the realist claim to objectivity is a way of closing debate by saying 'This is the objective truth and there is nothing more to be said'. No realist ever claims anything of the sort. Rather, they claim that beliefs are attempts, more or less successful, at objectivity, and are to be judged by the extent to which they achieve it. If anyone has anything to say against the objectivity of a given set of beliefs, they can say it, and thus debate is opened up. If, on the other hand, beliefs are just a set of subjective opinions, there is nothing to be said against them and debate really is closed.

The more moderate form of the legend attributes to realists the idea of objective truth as an ideal which we can approach asymptotically. There is, in fact, one version of this idea that is acceptable and even tautological – namely, that the more truths we find out the more of the total truths possible to be known are in fact known. But to call this approaching absolute truth asymptotically is about as true and as relevant as the claim my grandmother made as a young girl that it was warmer sitting on the farmer's gate than standing on the ground because 'It's nearer the sun, you see'. Realists do not typically make any claims about any final states. They claim that each particular belief is a claim to truth about its object – a fallible claim, of course, but something that cannot be understood as the belief that it is unless it is understood as a truth claim about its particular object.

Another thing that objectivity is not is explicit knowledge as distinct from tacit knowledge. Since practice and emotion are object-centred, the unspelt-out knowledge that they include is potentially, and often actually, as objective as any theoretical knowledge. When bureaucrats ask for 'objective criteria', meaning explicit criteria, they are misusing language and engaging in a rhetoric that is very harmful to good management, since the latter requires much more reliance on tacit than on explicit knowledge. This misuse of language may also explain some of the hostility to objectivity among those (including both some existentialists and some postmodernists) who quite rightly stress the value of tacit knowledge.

Related to this misuse is the tendency to regard what can be quantified as more objective than what cannot. For example, the sort of questionnaire that asks people to rate something on a scale from one to ten, which ratings are then averaged, is regarded as an objective measurement. Yet the ratings are purely subjective. Qualitative ratings, on the other hand, in which people say why they judge something as they do, can give objective, though non-quantifiable, information. Again, the most mathematical of the social sciences, economics, is also the most subjective, both because it reduces values to purely subjective preferences and because it prefers arbitrary mathematical models to realistic non-quantitative ones.

Finally, objectivity does not imply physicalism or any other kind of reductionist programme. One finds among existentialists statements like 'Objectively, there are no intentions', but this does not follow from the notion of objectivity as characterised in this section. Of course, there are philosophical positions – for example, physicalism and behaviourism – that argue that objectively there are no intentions. But this requires a separate argument; it does not follow from the definition of objectivity. That is, objective which is independent of our judgement about it. Your intention exists independently of my judgement that you have that intention, hence it exists objectively. So do your thoughts, beliefs, emotions, pleasures, pains, virtues, vices. So, I will argue, do values – not just our value judgements, but the value of human life, the value of diversity in nature, the value of truth and beauty. This is a very luxuriant ontology – an ontology of the rain forest, not of Quine's desert landscapes.

Subjectivism, on the other hand, is deeply reductive: it reduces values to value-judgements, physical objects to sense data or discourse, beauty to something in the eye of the beholder, the entities discovered by science to constructions made by us, God to religious experience.

All forms of reductionism, whether subjectivistic or physicalistic, have their roots in Descartes' dualism: Descartes reduces everything to human consciousness on the one hand and extended matter on the other. Subjective idealism is Cartesianism with the material pole suppressed, physicalism is Cartesianism with the subjective pole suppressed. Cartesianism itself I shall criticise in the following section.

Notes

1   I am enough of a Spinozist to regard perception as a kind of knowledge, carrying judgement with it.
2   See Kolnai's paper 'On the Sovereignty of the Object' in his book *Ethics, Value and Reality*.

§2 The origins of modern subjectivism

Philosophical

Philosophy's most fundamental step in the direction of the modern retreat from objectivity was made by Descartes when he duplicated the world with the world of ideas: on the one hand, there are bodies whose essence is extension; on the other hand, there is a world of ideas which (or some of which) are of or about these bodies. Descartes' successors all take this 'new way of ideas' as their starting point. For Spinoza, an idea and the body that it is of, are in some sense identical (transattributively identical), a tricky theory that he nevertheless used with such genius as to come as near as anyone between Descartes and Marx to escaping the adverse consequences of Descartes' theories. For Locke, ideas could resemble their objects, although not all did. For Berkeley, an idea could resemble nothing but another idea, and anything of which ideas are ideas disappears from the scene. Once you have taken Descartes' step and rejected Spinoza's, this conclusion is very difficult to avoid, even though, as we shall see, it undermines its own starting point.

The Berkeleian conclusion can be arrived at from the Cartesian premiss in this way: we start with the apparently innocent premiss that to know anything is to have an idea of that thing. So there is no knowledge of bodies except by having ideas of those bodies. The empiricists tended to understand such ideas as in the first place images. Later philosophers have tended to see them as linguistic or quasi-linguistic entities, words or concepts or discourses. But nothing is altered about the structure and logic of the argument, its strengths and weaknesses, by this shift. Berkeley and Derrida stand or fall together.

If there is no knowledge of bodies without having ideas of those bodies, it is easy to present the knowledge of bodies as indirect: the step is taken (for instance in Locke) from the near-tautology 'To know a body is to have an idea' to the falsehood 'To know a body is to know an idea and infer a body'. Ideas come to be seen as the only direct object of knowledge and as, in a sense, obvious and unproblematic: anything else becomes problematic – arguments are needed to prove its existence.

The question then arises: how do we check the veracity of our ideas; how do we ensure that they really do tell us something about their objects? One might think that this has to be done by comparing the idea with its object, as one can compare a picture with what it is a picture of. Suppose I have a remembered image of the Tudor Merchants' Hall in Southampton. Then I go and look at the hall and compare the remembered image with it to check whether it is a true image. But the adherent of the 'way of ideas' will object: what you compare the remembered image with is not the Tudor Merchants' Hall but your perception of the Tudor Merchants' Hall, and that is as much an idea as is the remembered image. So checking one's knowledge comes to be seen as comparing ideas. Epistemology loses its reference to what ideas are about and comes to be a matter of coherence between ideas. This gives us the clue to Berkeley's dictum that an idea can be like nothing but another idea. On the face of it, it is an unhelpful half-truth, much as if one were to say that a photograph cannot be like anything but another photograph. In one way, of course, a photograph of the Tudor Merchants' Hall is more like a photograph of a duck-billed platypus than it is like the Tudor Merchants' Hall; but in another way it is not, and when one signs the back of a passport photograph stating 'This is a true likeness of Jenny Jones', one is not a priori perjuring oneself. Likewise, with *some* ideas. However, the relation that we need to establish between ideas and their objects is not necessarily one of likeness, but one of aboutness.

But Berkeley's case does not rest on the sort of unlikeness that subsists between the image of the Tudor Merchants' Hall and the hall itself. The point is rather that likeness (and presumably other forms of aboutness too) involves comparison, and comparison can allegedly only take place between ideas, since in order to compare one must perceive or conceive or imagine two comparables, and a percept or concept or image is an idea.

But now the objects of ideas have dropped out of the picture altogether. Berkeley's final step is to say that ideas have no objects, they are not of or about anything. They are not about the world, they are the world. And since ideas are by definition in the mind, there is nothing outside the mind – or, in Berkeley's modern reprise, there is nothing outside of discourse.

It might be useful to ask at this point what happens if we refuse to start this series of steps; if we become anidealists – people who do not believe in ideas. We could say: we know lots of things – people and oak trees and squirrels and violets – but where are these *ideas*? Knowledge is a relation between people and the world; ideas don't come into it. The idealist might reply by giving instances of ideas: beliefs, images, sensations, concepts. The anidealist will be hard put to say much without alluding to such things, but might well say: these are features of the way we relate to the world, but what makes them ideas? Eventually, anyone who is going to say that there is anything special about these phenomena that justifies our grouping them together as ideas and distinguishing them from things that are not ideas, is going to have to say: they are ideas because they are about something. This is Brentano's concept of intentionality, but it is implicit in any plausible talk about ideas. And with it goes another feature of ideas: they are fallible. My idea of something may be mistaken about that something. And the path from the 'way of ideas' to idealism goes through this assumption of fallibility, because it was this fallibility that gave rise to the project of checking them and the conclusion that this can only be done by comparing them with other ideas. Yet the idealist conclusion undermines its premises by removing this defining feature of ideas, their aboutness. In doing so, it makes them in a sense infallible, since there is nothing for them to be false about. Indeed, the phenomenalism that takes its rise from Berkeley typically regards sense data as 'incorrigible'. Of course, mature idealism has its own account of truth and error in terms of coherence. But while coherence in the sense of resemblance between a series of ideas might do as an idealist definition of non-illusion, coherence of propositions will not do as a definition of truth because it can only mean non-contradiction between the propositions, and contradiction is a notion that presupposes truth, making the whole coherence account circular. The real importance of coherence as a *criterion* (not definition) of truth rests on the fact that, when ideas are true (in the sense of corresponding to their objects), they cohere, while contradictory ideas can have nothing to correspond to.

To refute an anidealist position, therefore, one must postulate ideas as about their objects and fallible about them, and thus reject idealism too. But something remains from the anidealist account: we may know ideas, but not until we have a fairly sophisticated knowledge of the world which is not composed of ideas. Ideas, in the modern sense, were only postulated after two thousand years of the history of philosophy and science; no individual could acquire the concept of an idea until they already had a sufficient knowledge of the world to understand what fallibility is – to understand that what we think is true of something may be 'only our idea of it'. So the world is not only ontologically prior to ideas – it existed for millions of years before ideating beings evolved; it is also epistemologically prior, in that there can be no knowledge of ideas without prior knowledge of the world. And the world is logically prior to ideas, in that we can only define an idea in terms of what in the world it is about.

I hope to have shown that the 'way of ideas' was led historically by a series of plausible steps to a self-undermining idealism. Where did it go wrong? The first clue comes from Marx's *Theses on Feuerbach* which suggests that it is the neglect of practice that leads theory astray. Marx never worked this out in detail, but John Macmurray, who was deeply influenced by Marx's text, has this to say, referring to the argument for idealism from the inability to compare ideas with anything but other ideas:

> Now, this argument for idealism is only difficult to meet, indeed it only seems reasonable, provided we confine ourselves to a purely theoretical attitude. . . . there is something else, besides 'the thing' which we

> contrast with thought, and that is action. When we are thinking we are
> not doing anything. We are immersed in ideas. But the moment we
> begin to act we find ourselves in contact with things, not with ideas.
>
> (*The Philosophy of Communism*, p. 24)

This indicates where Descartes went wrong. He made contemplative experience the paradigm case of experience, rather than practical experience.
If practical experience were foregrounded, idealism would be avoided because
a reality that is independent of our ideas is intrinsic to practice in a way that
it is not intrinsic to contemplation. One can, if one is weird enough, wonder
whether the bike one sees is real or a hallucination; one cannot do the same
with the bike one rides. This is also implicit in Heidegger's critique of the
Cartesian heritage in philosophy: not 'I am conscious therefore I am' but, in
effect, 'I fix a shutter with a hammer, therefore the world is'.

This is not pragmatism: pragmatism is what happens when one comes to
regard practice as epistemologically crucial *having already accepted idealism*.
One then gives a pragmatic account of the world of ideas, without that world
referring to the real world as it is independent of our experience of it. The
point of the centrality of practice is to avoid idealism in the first place, since
in practice one encounters a world that is independent of one's ideas and is
pulled up short by it.

But doesn't the idealist conclusion follow from the plausible premiss
that knowing something involves having an idea of it? No, it does not. Two
things need saying here. The first is that to say 'Knowing something involves
having an idea of it' is not the same thing as to say 'Knowing something is
really just knowing an idea of it.' If I know the footpath from Fritham
to Linwood, then I have an idea of that footpath, but my knowledge is not of
that idea but of the footpath. This will be made clearer by the second
point: talk about 'having an idea' is misleading in its form. It would be
better to talk about 'ideating something'. The transitive verb refers us immediately to its object, but the phrase 'having an idea' suggests that an idea is an
entity rather than an act, and an entity that can be inspected for what it is
in itself rather than as an appearance of its object. Of course, it *is* possible to
reflect on our ideatings, even to bracket off their objects for certain special
purposes, while we ask questions about our ideatings themselves. But even
while we do this, we can only understand what our ideatings are by what they
are ideatings of and we will not find it useful for long to keep the brackets
round the objects. I shall discuss this at more length under the heading of
reflexive objectivity and intentional objectivity in Section 5.

Ideological

Philosophy is essentially a polemical and divided discipline, so philosophers
cannot all be right. Nevertheless, when, for a whole epoch, most philosophers go wrong in the same way, it is worth asking if there are non-

philosophical reasons why they do so. This is not a reductive programme. All philosophers worth the name were wrestling with real problems and wrestling to find the truth about them. But all philosophers – like the rest of humankind – have had their presuppositions formed by their particular time and place in human culture. I am enough of a Marxist to think that class position has the dominant role here, so it may be worthwhile asking if the retreat from the objectivity of modern philosophy has its roots in the class structure of modern society.

There are two issues to be looked at here. In the first place, the whole history of Western philosophy (not just Western, of course, but that is my concern here) from the presocratics to the present day, has taken place in societies based on the exploitation of one class by another. The vast majority of philosophers come from, and represent the standpoint of, the ruling classes. Before the twentieth century, I can think only of Socrates, Spinoza and Rousseau as philosophers *from* other classes, and only Wyclif and Marx as philosophers *for* other classes. In the second place, the modern period, in which alone subjectivism is the norm, has been the era in which exploiting and exploited classes have been assigned to their respective positions by the market. Let us take these two points in turn.

Philosophy in the modern sense starts with Socrates, which means that, in its written form, it starts with Plato. It is a well-known saying that Western philosophy can be regarded as a series of footnotes to Plato. Plato came from the slave-owning class in a slave-owning society. There is some dispute, even among Marxist historians, about the extent of slavery in ancient Athens. George Thomson regards it as a slave-based economy, whereas Ellen Wood makes out a plausible case for Athens' being an economy of free peasants and artisans, with slavery existing on the fringes, on the estates of aristocrats and in the silver mines. But however the institution of slavery affected society as a whole, it certainly affected the ideology of the aristocrats, including Plato. And, arguably, the dualism that enters philosophy with Plato derives from this: physical work is despised as slavish; contemplation, free from practical aims, is seen as the source of knowledge; the body in general is devalued and the soul alone is regarded as immortal. It is instructive to contrast this dualist ideology with the non-dualism of the ancient Hebrew kingdoms. Under Hebrew law, although you could sell yourself into slavery, you would be released after seven years (or if your master injured you). Likewise, if you got into debt and had to sell your land, it would be restored to you or your heirs after forty-nine years. This jubilee law (so long as it was kept) meant that permanent classes of slaves and landless peasants could not arise. And although it was clearly not always kept – the prophets were always denouncing nascent class relations – it is significant that those prophets, the outstanding spokesmen of Hebrew culture, did denounce class exploitation. It is significant too that Hebrew scholars in later years would have manual trades in addition to their scholarship. And the non-dualism of Hebrew ideology reflects this. Not only the political ideology of the prophets with their ideal of a king who defended the poor and was a rod of iron to the oppressors, but also their metaphysics. When the idea of life-after-death entered the Hebrew culture, it did so in the form of a belief in the resurrection of the body, not the immortality of the soul. Even knowledge – and ignorance – of God is seen as essentially practical; Jeremiah warns King Jehoiakim:

> Doom for the man who founds his palace on anything but
>   integrity,
> his upstairs rooms on anything but honesty,
> who makes his fellow man work for nothing,
> without paying him his wages,
> who says, 'I will build myself an imposing palace
> with spacious rooms upstairs',
> who pierces lights in it,
> panels it with cedar, and paints it vermilion.
> Are you more of a king
> for outrivalling others with cedar?
> Your father ate and drank like you,
> but he practised honesty and integrity,
> so all went well for him.
> He used to examine the cases of poor and needy, then all went
>   well.
> Is not that what it means to know me? – it is Yahweh who speaks.
>   (*Jerusalem Bible*, Jeremiah 22: 13–16)

The dualistic separation of sacred from secular is also denounced: after their defence of the poor, the chief bone of contention of many of the prophets is religion as a separate activity from life: trampling the Lord's courts (Isaiah 1) and bowing your head like a bulrush (Isaiah 58) instead of freeing the oppressed and sharing your goods with the poor.

Hebrew and Greek culture have both flowed into Christian and modern Europe, yet it is the dualism that has prevailed. Why? Although medieval and modern European societies have not been based on slavery (with the exception of parts of the American continent before abolition), they have been class societies which consequently devalued manual labour and found Plato's dualism more congenial than Hebrew monism. Consider the extent to which Christians have come to believe in the unbiblical doctrine of the immortality of the soul. And this has affected epistemology throughout its history. Contemplation, whether in the form of 'just thinking' or 'just staring' has been seen as the source of knowledge and the cognitive fruitfulness of practice has been devalued. This is particularly clear in the empiricist concep-tion of experience. In non-philosophical English, some important senses of experience are practice-oriented. When we call someone an experienced builder or lover or musician we don't mean that they have been spectators of many scenes of building or love-making or music-making, but that they have built or loved or made music. But empiricist 'experience' is a spectator sport. This is nowhere clearer than in Hume's absurd view that we do not experience causality. I experience causality every time I open a door because when I open a door it is necessarily true that at the end of the process the door is open and that the cause of its being open is that I opened it.

We have already seen that it is the neglect of practice that makes it possible for modern philosophy to arrive at the conclusion that all we know is our own ideas. But the question remains why only *modern* philosophy arrived at that conclusion when the neglect of practice by epistemology, and its class basis, was already two thousand years old when modern philosophy emerged. To explain this we need to look at the other feature of society mentioned earlier, the commercial nature of *modern* society. The philosophy of Socrates, Plato and Aristotle, and medieval philosophy after them, is that of a society that produces primarily for use rather than for sale, and exchanges for use rather than for resale. Commerce and commercial ideology did make their appearance in ancient Greece and are represented in philosophy by the sophists, but not until the seventeenth century did the commercial paradigm come to dominate philosophy's way of seeing things.

Consider two of the controversies between the Platonic Socrates and the sophists. Callicles' image of the happy man is of one who maximises both desires and their satisfaction; Socrates replies by asking whether an itchy man with abundant opportunity for scratching will be happy (Plato, *Gorgias*, p. 64). Implicit in Socrates' view is the conception of happiness such as finds a fuller description in Aristotle: doing well and living well, such that one has no need that is not supplied. Implicit in Callicles' view is the idea of human desires as unlimited and happiness consisting in the succession of their particular satisfactions, each of which leaves us wanting something more. This view is fully worked out in the seventeenth century by Hobbes. These conceptions of happiness have their roots in two different economic systems: while we think of goods as 'use-values' in Marx's phrase, we know that enough is enough; we can only eat so many apples, live in one house at a time, wear one pair of shoes at a time. When the goal of striving becomes money, these limits are removed and the ideal of the Calliclean or Hobbesian itcher–scratcher becomes the common sense of the age.

The other controversy is with Thrasymachus in the *Republic*. According to Socrates, a shepherd is one who looks after sheep, a doctor is one who cures illnesses; a good shepherd is one who looks after sheep well, a good doctor is one who cures illnesses well; the best judge of the worth of a shepherd is another shepherd, the best judge of the worth of a doctor is another doctor. According to Thrasymachus, a shepherd is one who makes money by looking after sheep, a doctor is one who makes money by curing illnesses; a good shepherd is one who makes a lot of money, a good doctor is one who makes a lot of money; the best judge of the worth of anyone is presumably their bank manager. For Socrates the goal of any activity is internal to that activity, for Thrasymachus it is external. For Socrates the worth of anything is internal to it, for Thrasymachus it is external.

It is easy to see how the victory of commerce, and thereby of Callicles and Thrasymachus, in seventeenth-century Europe affected ethics: human activities lose their intrinsic worth and become a means to pleasure, as work becomes a means to money. So utilitarianism is born. Values become qualities bestowed by us rather than qualities possessed by things, and so ethical subjectivism is born. Unlimited desire ceases to be the sin of covetousness (*pleonexia*) and becomes economic rationality. But it is not only ethics that is affected: epistemology is transformed too, although this works through a homology. Just as the world of wealth comes to be represented by money, a human artifice, and loses its value except in so far as it is represented by money, so the world of objects comes to be represented by ideas, a human artifice, and loses its being except in so far as it is represented by ideas.

Furthermore, money secretes an ideology of atomism. It does this in two ways. Because value acquires a numerical representation, it comes to be divisible into tiny units. Real values are not, of course, divisible: a dog is an animal, half a dog is a lump of carrion; a cricket match is a game, half a cricket match (rain stopped play) is a disappointment. But half a grand is worth exactly half what one grand is worth. This facilitates the illusion that one can understand things by breaking them down into their smallest bits: methodological atomism. The second way is that money gives the illusion of autonomy to individual human beings. A lord and serf know that they are not independent, as the serf can be bossed around by the lord and the lord relies for his food on the serf's labour. But although money is in essence the power to dispose of the labour of other people, as Marx and Ruskin have pointed out, it looks like a property rather than a relation, so the rich man and the poor man can maintain the illusion that they are independent, even though the poor man has to allow the rich man to boss him around if he wants a wage, and the rich man's wealth would be no use to him unless there were poor men that it enabled him to boss around. Hence, social atomism makes its appearance with commercial society and is rampant in Hobbes and Locke.

Atomism feeds into subjectivism in two ways. First of all, the idea that we are autonomous individuals has its epistemic side in the idea that our minds are all blank sheets prior to autonomous individual experience and that we owe nothing to others for our capacity to know the world. In fact, of course, we all learn to explore the world with the help of our mums and dads, and if we want to go beyond that informal exploring and acquire scientific knowledge, we need a prolonged training in a university. And this training, informal or formal, teaches us what is significant in our experience for the purposes of acquiring objective knowledge and what is not; which of our ideas tell us about reality and which do not. The suppression of the facts that cognitive capacity is partly learnt and part of what is learnt is also taught, eases the way to the doctrine that 'the world is my idea'.

The second way that atomism feeds into subjectivism is that ideas themselves are seen as atomic: complex ideas are supposed to be reducible to simple ideas, and it is supposed to be these that we originally acquire and process to form our knowledge. Simple ideas might be things like 'sense data' whose ambiguous status between ideas and aspects of objects eases the path of idealism. But in reality, all our ideas of objects are complex ideas of complex objects and can be reduced in thought to simple ideas only afterwards by a process of abstraction.

Finally, the market and commercial ideology give rise to idealism and subjectivism by inducing an anthropocentric view of the world. This might seem strange for, after all, the medievals had supposedly thought of the Earth as the centre of the universe and seventeenth-century thought rejected this. But, in fact, the medievals never thought of the Earth as the centre of the universe in the modern sense of 'centre' (assuming that the much overused word 'centre' still has a sense). They believed that the Earth was the *middle* of the universe (they were quite aware that it is round and that people in the southern hemisphere would not drop off or seem to be upside down). But there was nothing special about being in the middle. To be at the *top* of the universe, where the angels supposedly lived – that would have been special. Modern thought is much more anthropocentric than medieval thought because it is epistemocentric or ideocentric. However, that is what I am trying to explain: my claim is that commercial ideology prepared the way for ideocentrism by making us think that the world was ours to do what we please with. Heidegger was right to see one of the features of modernity as being the idea of all nature, including ourselves, as a stockpile or 'standing reserve' to be used for the production of commodities. He was wrong to attribute this attitude to a technological world outlook – as he himself notes, it predated technology by about two hundred years. It is the ideology of commerce. There is a homology between idealism, particularly in its Kantian form, and the idea that 'the world is my raw material'. Of course, a homology is not an argument; but in the history of ideas it is often an explanation.

I am suggesting that the various subjectivisms, idealisms, sensationalisms and discoursisms, which have uniquely been features of the thought of the last four centuries, form the central type of philosophical ideology of one type of society: exploitive society in which the exploiters and exploited are assigned their positions, not by war or authority or tradition, but by the market – in short, capitalist society. This is emphatically true of postmodernism, which is not a reaction against aspects of modernism like atomism and subjectivism, but a taking of them to their extremes. Global capitalism breaks the internal link between humankind and nature, disguises the dependence of the individual on the whole, markets ideas without reference to reality or truth, and destroys the integrity of the individual by recasting him or her as merely a unit of more or less effective demand; and postmodernism makes all these violations look like the unalterable human condition.

Existentialist images of objectivity

§3 Preliminary remarks about Kierkegaard

Many existentialists defend subjectivity, but not always in the same sense. We will see the different things they mean in the course of looking at different existentialists. For the most part they are *not* defending epistemological subjectivism, although at least one – Sartre – is defending a sophisticated form of moral subjectivism.

But in the case of most existentialists I find it much easier to understand what they are defending and what they are not than is the case with the founding father of existentialism, Kierkegaard. For this reason this section will be shorter and less unified than I intended. I restrict myself to considering a few positions that Kierkegaard held or may have held. I should say before I start, since some of my comments will be so adverse, that I am far from dismissing Kierkegaard in general. He was a perceptive cultural critic and a brilliant psychologist. *The Sickness unto Death* and *The Concept of Dread* are among the great works of existential psychology. But, returning to *Concluding Unscientific Postscript* (hereafter *CUP*), which I read in my youth but have left on the shelf ever since, I feel unimpressed.

The first position, unlike the next two that I shall comment on, has implications that are for wider areas than the philosophy of religion, although, like all Kierkegaard's polemics for subjectivity and against objectivity, it originates in that area. This is the view that whatever could be objective could not be a matter of passionate concern. Kierkegaard does not argue for this; he takes it for granted. It is an odd mirror image of the positivist idea that only uncharged facts could be objective, while ethics, religion, aesthetics and politics were 'merely subjective'; Kierkegaard accepts this division of the world, but inverts the value judgement: whatever is objective is 'merely objective' and not worth making a fuss about. It is odd that Kierkegaard should take this view in the light of his attitude both to Socrates and to the New Testament. For nothing is more characteristic of his hero Socrates than his passionate devotion to objectivity, his willingness to think objectively about issues of passionate concern, however painful that thinking might be, and his desire to base his life on what is objectively true. I have already referred to this feature, which is shared by Spinoza and is the mark of any philosophy worthy of the name; the divorce of passionate concern from

objective knowledge is the worst legacy of Kierkegaard to later existentialists, and when they are true philosophers, they are so in spite of it. It would
also have been very surprising to St Paul who opens Chapter 15 of
1 Corinthians with what he regards as conclusive objective evidence of the
resurrection of Christ (the multitude of surviving witnesses) and concludes
'if Christ was not raised, your faith has nothing in it' (*NEB* 1 Corinthians
15: 16).

The second position is Kierkegaard's definition of faith as 'the contradiction between the infinite passion of the individual's inwardness and the
objective uncertainty' (*CUP*, p. 182). While this is not what Christians have
meant by faith throughout the ages – not what St Paul or Thomas Aquinas
or Luther or C.S. Lewis meant by faith – it is something like what most lay
people, particularly but not only unbelievers, mean by it today. But there
are two possible readings of what Kierkegaard himself means by it, one of
which (the 'Kantian reading') is a courageous and honourable position, the
other (the Tertullianite reading) a cowardly and dishonest one. Kierkegaard
gives the example of Socrates, who:

> puts the question objectively in a problematic manner: *if* there is an
> immortality. He must therefore be accounted a doubter in comparison
> with our modern thinkers with the three proofs? By no means. On this
> 'if' he risks his entire life, he has the courage to meet death, and he has
> with the passion of the infinite so determined the pattern of his life that
> it must be found acceptable – *if* there is an immortality.
>
> (*CUP*, p. 180)

On one reading of this, Socrates remains, cognitively speaking, an agnostic,
but lives and dies *as if* there is immortality. Most people who call themselves agnostics, while they regard the evidence as uncertain either way, act
as if there is no God or immortality – that is, are practically indistinguish-
able from atheists; but it is just as rational to be an agnostic and bet on the
religious possibility, and that is what Socrates, as described by Kierkegaard,
does. (As described by Plato, of course, he does attempt proofs of immortality, although he recognises that they are inconclusive.) This is essentially
the same position as Kant's: we cannot prove either the existence or the
non-existence of God, freedom and immortality, but we will live better if
we base our lives on the possibility that they do exist. There is absolute
intellectual honesty here: there is no attempt to convince oneself that the
possibility one bets on is also certainly true. And in support of this reading
of Kierkegaard, he also says:

> If I wish to preserve myself in faith I must constantly be intent upon
> holding fast the objective uncertainty, so as to remain out upon the deep,
> over seventy thousand fathoms of water, still preserving my faith.
>
> (*CUP*, p. 182)

The objective uncertainty is not abandoned, as it is by Pascal who urges you to convince yourself by going to mass. Kierkegaard clearly relishes the uncomfortableness of this position: one has neither the comfort of the believer's assurance, nor the comfort of the unbeliever's unconcern. No one can accuse him, on *this* reading, of wishful thinking. It is noteworthy that this position is not, as Kierkegaard seems to think it is, what faith has always meant. The religious agnostic could in all sincerity go to church, but could not in all sincerity say the Creed. But it is a position worthy of respect.

On the other hand, this reading implies that Socrates and religious agnostics in general *are doubters*. Yet Kierkegaard asks if Socrates is a doubter and replies 'by no means'. This suggests the other reading: that one recognises that the evidence is inconclusive, but nevertheless believes – even is certain about – the inadequately supported religious conclusion. There is much in Kierkegaard that suggests that this is what he actually recommends, and worse, that he even thinks the evidence is overwhelmingly against Christianity, that to believe it is against reason, yet that we should believe that it is true. Here we are close to Tertullian's 'I believe because it is absurd, it is certain because it is impossible.' This position is not really belief at all: it is pretending to believe, seeking to deceive first oneself and then others; for one can no more truly say 'I believe it although all the evidence is against it' than 'I believe it although it isn't true.' On this reading 'truth is subjectivity' is just a pretentious way of saying 'Don't bother about truth, believe what you like.' It is a prescription for epistemic amoralism. To understand its motive one has to imagine a fear of hell so intense as to make a person accept what he believes to be false rather than take the slightest risk of what may happen if it turns out to be true and one has not taken precautions.

There remains one example from the same chapter of *CUP* that has a certain plausibility – indeed, I used to think that here, although nowhere else, a real sense could be given to the saying 'truth is subjectivity'. Consider the following passage:

> If one who lives in the midst of Christendom goes up to the house of God, the house of the true God, with the true conception of God in his knowledge, and prays, but prays in a false spirit; and one who lives in an idolatrous community prays with the entire passion of the infinite, though his eyes rest on the image of an idol: where is the most truth? The one prays in truth to God though he worships an idol; the other prays falsely to the true God, and hence worships in fact an idol.
>
> (*CUP*, pp. 179–80)

To fill out the example of the true idol-worshipper, one could refer to the confrontation of Aslan and Emeth in C.S. Lewis' story *The Last Battle*. Emeth has all his life been a devout and sincere worshipper of the idol Tash, but when he meets the true god Aslan in heaven, Aslan addresses him as 'Son' and explains:

no service which is vile can be done to me, and none which is not vile can be done to [Tash]. Therefore if any man swear by Tash and keep his oath for the oath's sake, it is by me that he has truly sworn, though he know it not, and it is I who reward him. And if any man do a cruelty in my name, then, though he says the name Aslan, it is Tash whom he serves and by Tash his deed is accepted.

(The Last Battle, p. 155)

But it should be noted here that something is brought in that Kierkegaard had passed over in silence: it is not just a matter of how much passion you worship with, but what conduct that worship leads to. Tash is the god of a slave-based society and is worshipped by human sacrifices. One assumes, although Lewis does not tell us, that Emeth has not mistreated slaves or procured sacrificial victims, although that is what one might expect from a Tash-worshipper. And certainly Kierkegaard's privileging of the 'how' over the 'what' (*CUP*, p. 181) is not plausible in *secular* contexts. It is better to pursue an ideal with integrity rather than corruptly; yet consider these two instances: it is told of Himmler that on one occasion he was invited to a dinner party. On arriving he found the table laden with delicacies that could only have been obtained on the black market. He seized the tablecloth and tipped everything on to the floor and stormed out. Compare this with the corruption of New Labour, selling seats at table next to Cabinet ministers to businessmen who were prepared to contribute to party funds. Yet it is far better to be a corrupt servant of Tony Blair than an incorruptible servant of Adolf Hitler. Is there anything special about *religious* commitment which makes it different from this?

I used to think that there was a difference for the following reason. The idol-worshipper with infinite passion will express that passion by attributing more and more perfections to the idol. In the end, he will conceive of the idol as having 'all possible perfections', being 'that than which a greater cannot be conceived', like the god of the ontological argument. But if that is the true description of the true god, has the worshipper not ceased to worship an idol and will he not soon come to recognise that 'this wooden statue does not have all possible perfections; it can't actually *be* the true god, only a symbol'. On the other hand, the Christian who worships with finite passion will come to worship a finite god, an idol. It is not a case of the subjective passion being itself the truth, but of its leading one to postulate the objective truth.

However, it is not as simple as that. Suppose the worshipper of Tash has infinite passion, but that passion is one of self-abasement before naked power, or hatred towards enemies whom Tash is called upon to destroy. Their conception of Tash will correspondingly be of an infinite but evil being. It is, alas, all too natural for human beings to worship in this spirit, whether it is the ancient worship of Moloch or the modern worship of the state or money. Such infinite passion will never lead one to the truth. In short, before praising infinite passion, one should ask 'which passion?'. Perhaps infinite love would lead one to the truth, but infinite greed or hatred or self-abasement will not. And one will only worship God with an infinite passion of love if one already conceives of God as a god of love. In other words, one is referred back again to the object, the 'what' of passion. Needless to say, this does not mean that any one religion has a monopoly of true worshippers.

One more point from Kierkegaard: in *The Present Age* (hereafter *PA*) he discusses the difference between an age of reflection (like his own) and an age of passion (like the preceding revolutionary age). The age of reflection:

> leaves everything standing but cunningly empties it of significance. Instead of culminating in a rebellion it reduces the inward reality of all relationships by means of a reflective tension which leaves everything standing but makes the whole of life ambiguous.
>
> (*PA*, p. 15)

> A subject no longers freely honours his king or is angered at his ambition. To be a subject has come to mean something quite different; it means to be a *third party*.
>
> (*PA*, p. 17)

> A disobedient youth is no longer in fear of his schoolmaster – the relation is rather one of indifference in which schoolmaster and pupil discuss how a good school should be run. To go to school no longer means to be in fear of the master, or merely to learn, but rather implies being interested in the problem of education.
>
> (*PA*, p. 18)

Although objectivity and subjectivity as such are not mentioned here, several topics often discussed in those terms are raised. I think Kierkegaard is seeing everything in terms of the passion/reflection dichotomy, whereas there seem to me to be several different issues at stake here.

First, the description of a 'revolution' that is all in the mind and leaves structures intact must ring a bell with anyone who lived through the revolutionary outbreaks of 1968. I recall some years later an American telling me that 'everything was different' since 1968. It seemed to me that capitalism had gone on much as before. He replied that no one took any notice of the President any more. As Kierkegaard might have put it, no one freely honoured his president or was angered by his ambition; but presidents had just the same powers and used them just as badly as before. The description is recognisable, but the diagnosis is doubtful. Is this due to 'reflection' or simply to the impotence of the citizen to change the state? Is it the cause or the effect of the fact that the presidents who have been elected have been quite difficult to take seriously?

A second distinction might be between personal relations of power and relations regulated by something objective and law-like. The teacher–pupil relation (and elsewhere Kierkegaard says something similar about the father–son relation) is seen as being in truth one of personal authority; to resolve it into authority established by a rule which can be discussed is seen as a degradation of the relationship. One might argue that it is part of growing up to come to submit to or resist authority on the basis of under-standing its rationale rather than as simply submission to or rebellion against a personal authority figure, and whatever age might be thought appropriate for this in the family and school, in the state a constitution is necessary for a free people.

A third point concerns the retreat from the first order to the second order: not learning, but being interested in education. This is part of what Kierkegaard means by reflection, and this issue will re-emerge in my discussion of intentional and reflexive objectivity in Section 5.

This section has by no means been a full discussion of Kierkegaard's defence of subjectivity. But I hope it has set the scene for a discussion of later existentialist accounts of subjectivity and objectivity.

§4 Macmurray on objectivity

John Macmurray is not usually included in lists of existentialists, over-extended as such lists often are. But, as I have pointed out elsewhere (see my *Being and Worth*), he has a number of striking similarities to the three main existentialists, Kierkegaard, Heidegger and Sartre. I have also been told by someone who knew him in his old age that he privately accepted the title 'existentialist'. One similarity is his denigration of 'mere objectivity', but in the case of Macmurray this is ambiguous, for he also gives objectivity a central place in his account of what it is to be human, what it is to be rational and what it is to be moral. Is this simply an ambiguity in Macmurray's use of the word 'objective' or is there a real tension in his work between his two sets of statements about objectivity?

Objectivity and rationality

Macmurray's favourable remarks about objectivity come in his account of what it is to be a person: a person is a rational being, a being with reason. Here Macmurray affiliates himself to the long tradition that goes back to Aristotle: 'humankind is a rational animal'. Not all existentialists like this definition and it has certainly been used in the past to support the disparagement of emotions in favour of a supposedly separate faculty of reason, and of practical knowledge in favour of pure theory. Macmurray, as much as any existentialist, rejects this dualistic account of reason. But what, then, is reason?

> Reason is the capacity to behave consciously in terms of the nature of what is not ourselves. We can express this briefly by saying that reason is the capacity to behave in terms of the nature of the object, that is to say, to behave objectively. Reason is thus our capacity for objectivity.
> (*Reason and Emotion*, p. 19)

> Reason is the capacity to behave, not in terms of our own nature, but in terms of our knowledge of the nature of the world outside.
> (ibid., p. 20)

By the capacity for objectivity, I mean the capacity to stand in conscious relation to that which is recognised as not ourselves.

(Interpreting the Universe, p. 128)

an objective consciousness or a rational consciousness – the two phrases have the same meaning – is a consciousness of what is recognized in the consciousness itself as an object independent of the subject.

(ibid., p. 131)

Emotions, as much as thought, can be objective in this sense, so reason is not contrasted with emotions, but is seen as more or less characteristic of emotions – that is to say, emotions can be more objective or less objective, so that any given emotion can be rational to a greater or a lesser degree. An emotion towards another person, for example, may involve a true perception of that person's being, in which case it is objective and rational, or it may be the result of 'projection' (in the psychoanalytical sense) or wishful thinking, and hence be subjective and irrational. Emotions motivate behaviour, which can therefore also be based on objective or subjective accounts of others and of the world generally, and this is what makes it rational or irrational. A great deal of moral goodness consists in acting in the light of the real needs and feelings of others, as opposed to our egocentric illusions about them.

Rationality in this sense is both a defining characteristic of persons, since persons uniquely do relate to the nature of things independent of them, and also a norm that can be more or less attained, since we can be right or wrong about the nature of things. All human behaviour is 'rational' in the descriptive sense of being based on ideas of the world outside the agent, but it may be, in the normative sense, rational or irrational according to whether those ideas are true or false.

I think that Macmurray is absolutely right about these points: the distinctive feature of human beings, as characteristic of our emotions as of our thoughts, is our capacity to relate to the nature of things that are independent of us – our capacity to be ontocentric rather than anthropocentric (although Macmurray does not use these words). We can have a truer or less true understanding of the nature of things that are independent of us, and our destiny lies in having a truer one, both in our thought and in our emotions, and therefore in our actions. In view of this high place of objectivity in human life according to Macmurray, it is strange that he should also be one of those who talk about 'mere objectivity', but he is, as we shall see. For the objectivity in terms of which he defines human rationality is not the impoverished thing that existentialist polemic makes it out to be. It is not unemotional or abstract or related to emotions as means to ends. It is indeed a very fine thing. It means escaping from the prison of one's egocentric illusions and cultural prejudices, and understanding the nature of other people as they are independently of oneself, and other things in general as they are independently of humankind in general. That we can do this is one of the chief glories of the human mind. It is not always easy, and may cost painstaking effort and lead to unwelcome results, but it is always like a fresh breeze after the fug of self-referential discourse. It is politically important too to those committed, as Macmurray was, to human emancipation, because egocentric illusions always serve to prolong oppression, while objective knowledge clears the pathway for liberation. And environmental concern would hardly make sense without it, for it is precisely the value of things that are independent of us that is dear to it. If Kant were right – and everything we know is constructed by us out of data from unknowable noumena – we could hardly get emotional about preserving the wilderness or promoting the survival of endangered species.

'Mere objectivity'

In the first chapter of *Persons in Relation* (hereafter *PR*), Macmurray distinguishes his viewpoint in which persons are agents from the philosophical dualism of subject and object. According to this dualist view, for which 'subject' means the subject of thought, not of action, and is therefore contrasted with Macmurray's own view of persons as pre-eminently agents, philosophy accounts for the self as subject, and science – that is, 'anthropology' in the sense of a science of people – accounts for the self as object; but 'Anthropology is a science, and a scientific enquiry is merely objective; and an objective account is necessarily impersonal' (*PR*, p. 27). He thinks that, from his own standpoint, it is still philosophy that accounts for persons as agents (not as mere subjects of thought), but 'we still look to science for an objective account of man. . . . The change of standpoint makes no difference to science, but it does make a difference to philosophy and, in consequence, to the philosophical account of science' (*PR*, pp. 27–28). What makes the objectivity of this science '*mere* objectivity'? Macmurray tells us that 'a purely objective attitude reduces action to behaviour and represents it as a matter of fact, not a matter of intention' (*PR*, p. 28).

But this is not so. Once we have abandoned the philosophical dualism of subject and object for a conception of the person as essentially an agent, the science of people too, if it is to be objective, must take cognizance of the nature of its objects as agents. This is so, that is, if agency *really is* a property of the person studied, not merely something to do with the attitude someone else takes to them. It is about this last point that Macmurray seems to me to be confused:

> Formally, such knowledge is knowledge of the 'You', that is, of the other person; but not of the other person in personal relation to the knower, but as object in the world. I can know the other person *as a person* only by entering into personal relation with him. Without this I can know him only by observation and inference; only objectively. The knowledge

which I can obtain in this way is valid knowledge; my conclusions from observations can be true or false, they can be verified or falsified by further observation or by experiment. But it is abstract knowledge, since it constructs its object by limitation of attention to what can be known about other persons without entering into personal relations with them.

(*PR*, pp. 28–29)

Objectivity is here seen as an impersonal relation between persons. It can be justified only 'by a relation to a personal intention which includes it' (*PR*, p. 29). But it is important to get clear just what an objective scientific knowledge of one person by another does and does not exclude. It does not exclude any fact about the 'object' and hence includes their relations (intentional and otherwise) to others, including the investigator. In order to make sense of these relations, the investigator's intentional acts may also have to be included in the investigation, in the interests of fuller objectivity. This should be clear from the example of psychoanalysis, a discipline that Macmurray took seriously.

Now let us look at Macmurray's own example:

> Let us suppose that a teacher of psychology is visited by a pupil who wishes to consult him about the progress of his work. The interview begins as a simple personal conversation between them, and the teacher's attitude to the pupil is a normal personal attitude. As it proceeds, however, it becomes evident that something is wrong with the pupil. He is in an abnormal state of mind, and the psychologist recognizes clear symptoms of hysteria. At once the attitude of the teacher changes. He becomes a professional psychologist, observing and dealing with a classifiable case of mental disorder. From his side the relation has changed from a personal to an impersonal one; he adopts an *objective* attitude, and the pupil takes on the character of an object to be studied, with the purpose of determining the causation of his behaviour. There may be no outward sign of this change; indeed the teacher may deliberately conceal it and pursue the conversation as before. But what he now says is governed by a different intention, a theoretical intention to discover what is the matter with his pupil and what has brought it about.

(*PR*, pp. 29–30)

The teacher's investigation is moved by concern for the pupil. It is not 'impersonal' in any bad sense. What is new is that it has the *aim* of knowledge, instead of acquiring knowledge in the course of relating to the pupil in ways that have other aims. But it is quite unclear why the cognitive aim impersonalises the relationship. Can the project of knowing someone not be itself a personal relationship to them? Is it not part of any normal personal relationship? When one is getting to know a new friend, part at least of what one is getting to know is perfectly objective facts about the person:

what they like doing, what they believe in, what they hold dear, what their intentions are. Surely it is only if the cognitive aim is itself restricted to some functional aspect of the person studied, with aims indifferent to theirs, that we call it impersonal – as when a salesperson is considering what will make that person buy their product. To return to Macmurray's example: certainly a change has come about in the teacher's relation to the pupil, but there are many different attitudes that can all be part of a personal relation, the cognitive attitude among them. Even at the outset of the example, the relation was not a 'simple' personal one but a particular, functionally speci-fied, personal one – that is, a teacher–pupil relation. It is not clear why that is more personal than a (clinical) psychologist–patient relation. Other relations would be possible, equally different and equally personal: the pupil might want not academic advice, but emotional support, which the teacher might or might not give; one or both might get angry with the other; one or both might be sexually attracted to the other, and so on.

Macmurray goes on to contrast personal and objective attitudes to people and claim that they are incompatible (*PR*, p. 30). Yet he has just said that the objective attitude is justified if, and only if, it is included in a personal one (p. 29), so they cannot be incompatible. He argues further that both attitudes are emotionally motivated, so absence of emotion cannot be the defining attribute of the objective attitude. However, another difference makes its appearance in the following passage:

> If one person treats another person impersonally, he treats him as if he were an object and not a person. He negates the personal character of the other, then, that is to say, his freedom as an agent; and treats him as completely conditioned in his behaviour, as if he were not free but determined.
>
> (*PR*, pp. 33–34)

One problem here is a persistent one in the existentialist philosophy of inter-personal relations – the ambiguity of the word 'object' and its derivatives (Sartre is a good example of this) . It can mean object in the sense of inten-tional object or even grammatical object. In this sense the known person is the 'object of knowledge' by definition. But then there is no implication of impersonality. Or it can mean a being who is less than personal, is not an agent. The equivocation between these senses of object can make any human relations look degrading, as Marx noted long ago in the passage I used as the head-quote to Part II, in which he complains that, among the Young Hegelians of Berlin 'Love, for example, is rejected, because in it the beloved is only an 'object'. Down with objects!' ('Letter to Feuerbach, 11th August 1844', in *Early Texts*, p. 186).

The other aspect of the last quote from Macmurray is that the other person is said to be treated as subject to determinism, not as free. But freedom does not mean escaping causal explanation; it means causal explanation through reasons. And this sort of cause (reasons for action) can be known as objectively as mechanical or organic causes can.

The conclusion should be that, if the person is not reducible to the mechanical or the organic, a science of people that was adequate to its object must recognise the specific nature of personal being as distinct from organic or mechanical being. Such a science would be at once objective and personal in its subject matter.

Macmurray goes on to extend the example of the psychologist and his pupil, and asks what if the psychologist, instead of being concerned to cure the pupil, comes to think that the scientific interest of the case justifies his making the pupil's illness worse in order to discover something about hysteria. In that case, we *would* say that he was treating him impersonally in the bad sense. But it would be the abuse of science, not the science itself, that was impersonalising.

Intellect and objectivity

Macmurray's depreciation of 'mere objectivity' is associated with his depreciation of the intellect as, so to speak, the mental faculty of mere objectivity. It seems to me that the intellect is something of a bogey for Macmurray, as can be seen from reading the first four chapters of *Reason and Emotion*. By 'bogey' I mean that he sees it as a potent source of ills, yet this source as he describes it is entirely fictional, although some of its functions could be attributed to something called the intellect which, however, would lack other features that he attributes to it. To anticipate, the functions of thinking and of actively seeking knowledge could be called activities of the intellect, but the intellect in this sense is not, as Macmurray suggests, purely instrumental, nor is it an enemy of the emotions. Rather it is their growing point.

I need to make two preliminary points in order to avoid presenting Macmurray as an irrationalist, which he most certainly is not. First, like most others who fulminate against the intellect, he thinks that it has a legitimate place and is a good thing as long as it keeps its place. However, the place is limited and as soon as the intellect crosses its frontiers, it comes in for strictures. Second, the polemic against the intellect is not a polemic against reason, since reason inhabits the emotions as well and is an entirely beneficent capacity within them.

What is the 'place' of the intellect? Macmurray seems to have two answers: first, it steps in to solve problems when the ordinary knowledge that is implicit in practice runs aground. This is reminiscent of Heidegger's account of the origin of knowledge in the breakdown of practice. The difference between these two philosophers on this matter, apart from terminology, is that for Heidegger what we typically do when practice breaks down is stop and stare, whereas for Macmurray we stop and think. But in both cases, the result of this stopping is a special kind of objective, intellectual knowledge, distinct from, and in some ways poorer than, the tacit knowledge that was already implicit in the practice before it broke down. Incidentally, I have not been able to find out whether Macmurray was acquainted with Heidegger's *Being and Time*, perhaps the work of continental philosophy that comes closest to Macmurray's own position.

Second, intellect for Macmurray has an instrumental role: it is the Humean reason that is a slave of the passions, working out the best way to secure ends set by the emotions. But intellect is further seen as being itself emotionless (although always emotionally motivated), abstract and incapable of taking cognizance of the concrete; and capable of thinking only in mechanical, not in organic or personal terms. Yet the whole of science is seen as its work. It is further seen as having something of the role of Freud's superego, repressing emotions:

> All motives of action are necessarily emotional, but the intellect can use the emotion of fear to paralyse the positive emotions leaving only that one free to determine action which corresponds to the planned purpose.
> (*Reason and Emotion*, p. 45)

How the intellect can do this since it 'cannot be a source of action' (as he says on the same page) is unclear.

Now it seems to me that there is no such faculty as is here described. 'Nothing can drive out an emotion except another emotion', as Spinoza says (and as much that Macmurray says confirms). The superego is a complex of emotions, not intellect. Theoretical knowledge does take cognizance of the organic and the personal as well as of the mechanical, otherwise there could be no biological, social or psychological sciences. Sciences can be concrete as well as abstract – for example, geography – and can study intentions and emotions as well as structures and behaviour. Of course, sciences and much other knowledge is the product of systematically knowledge-seeking activity, as distinct from the tacit knowledge that precedes thought and results from practices whose aim is not knowledge. This activity could be called intellect. But since emotions themselves involve relating to the nature of objects outside ourselves, the discoveries of intellect in this sense about the objective world (including the emotions and intentions of others) can do more than guide the emotions instrumentally towards their ends. It can transform them from within by informing them about their objects, and so give them new ends. It can, in effect, do the same kinds of thing that Macmurray says that sensitiveness or 'the improvement of sensual enjoyment' (Blake) can do. Not the same things: some knowledge can only come from sensitiveness and some can only come from intellect. But it is objective knowledge, including knowledge acquired by the intellect, that educates the emotions by showing them the true nature of things outside them. For instance, intellectual knowledge of the ethology and ecology of a species may evoke an emotional commitment to its survival; or again, a heterosexual who was previously homophobic may change their emotional response to homosexuals as a result of purely intellectually acquired knowledge about the nature of homosexual orientation and love; and a person may become convinced of the injustice and inhumanity of capitalism by statistical knowledge of its effects or theoretical knowledge of its structure by reading the Brandt Report or Marx's *Capital*.

The conclusions so far are that we should accept Macmurray's account of the role of objectivity in human life as defining the rationality of human thought and emotions, and reject his disparagement of 'mere objectivity' and the intellect as misdescriptions of objectivity and intellect. Is this all that needs to be said for and against Macmurray on objectivity? I am afraid that it is not. For we should conclude from the notion of the rationality that defines humanity as objectivity – the capacity to relate to the nature of things that are independent of us – that it is the unique glory of our human race to be a non-self-centred race, a race that acknowledges the being and value of things other than our own interests. This freedom from self-centredness is not just a virtue in an individual – loving one's neighbour as oneself – but also in the race as a whole, that it is capable of knowing animals, plants and minerals as they are in themselves and valuing them for what they are in themselves.

The 'proper study of mankind' is not 'man', but being. This ontocentric conception of the human essence, while derived from Macmurray's own account of humankind as a rational animal, however, has consequences that cut against some of Macmurray's views. First, Macmurray is quite scathing about knowledge for its own sake and pure love of truth. Yet these are simply corollaries of our ontocentric nature. And second, he tries in some places to defend an anthropocentric conception of being. He tries to show, for instance, that the mechanical and the organic cannot exist without the personal (see *Interpreting the Universe*), although, even if his arguments worked, all they would prove is that the mechanical cannot exist without something not mechanical and that the organic cannot exist without something not organic: the symbiosis of the two would do the trick without postulating the personal. Of course, he is right that the personal is not reducible to the mechanical or the organic. But the mechanical and the organic existed millions of years before human persons. Then again, he gives an anthropocentric account of causality. A properly ontocentric world view would involve acknowledging that life comes later than inorganic matter and is unilaterally dependent on it, and that personhood comes later than organic life and is unilaterally dependent on it.

The profound implications of Macmurray's own conception of the rationality of human emotions would take us to a world view which, in its ontocentricity, its high regard for the work of the intellect and its valuation of knowledge as an end in itself, would be closer to Spinoza than to Macmurray's existentialism – although I think that Macmurray's theory of reason and the emotions is closer to Spinoza's than he realised. Not only is all knowledge objective, but objectivity as a human attitude is a virtue – even *the* virtue, of which more in the final section of this essay.

§5 Interlude: intentional and reflexive objectivity

I think it may help to make clear what is right and what is wrong about Macmurray's critique of objectivity and prepare the way for the discussion of Bultmann and Berdyaev, if we look at the distinction made by Samuel Alexander between 'enjoyment' and 'contemplation'. He writes:

> For convenience of description I am accustomed to say the mind enjoys itself and contemplates its objects. The act of mind is an enjoyment; the object is contemplated.
>
> *(Space, Time and Deity*, p. 12)

Both these terms are used in a rather peculiar sense, as is made clear by C.S. Lewis' account which, as we shall see, creatively misreads Alexander in one respect:

> I read in Alexander's *Space, Time and Deity* his theory of enjoyment and contemplation. These are technical terms in Alexander's philosophy; Enjoyment has nothing to do with pleasure, nor Contemplation with the contemplative life. When you see a table you enjoy the act of seeing and contemplate the table. Later, if you took up Optics and thought about Seeing itself, you would be contemplating the seeing and enjoying the thought. In bereavement you contemplate the beloved and the beloved's death and, in Alexander's sense, enjoy the loneliness and grief; but a psychologist, if he were considering you as a case of melancholia, would be contemplating your grief and enjoying psychology. We do not think a thought in the same sense in which we think that Herodotus is unreliable. When we think a thought, thought is a cognate accusative (like blow in strike a blow). We enjoy the thought (that Herodotus is unreliable) and, in so doing, contemplate the unreliability of Herodotus.
>
> *(Surprised by Joy*, p. 174)

Actually, Lewis' use of Alexander's distinction is different from Alexander's, for Alexander says that 'except in refinement and in purpose there is no difference in kind between the feeling expressed in the ejaculation of disgust and the reflective psychological analysis of that emotion' (*Space, Time and Deity*, p. 18). Both are enjoyments in which the disgusting object is contemplated. For Lewis, on the other hand, the psychological analysis contemplates the disgust that was enjoyed in the 'feeling expressed in the ejaculation of disgust'. Lewis is surely right here.

Now, in relation to this distinction, the common uses of the terms subjectivity and objectivity are systematically confused. Which is subjective and which is objective out of enjoyment and contemplation? Very often we are asked to attend to enjoyment in the name of objectivity: seeing the thought or feeling from the outside, seeing what it is, aside from what it claims (fallibly, of course) about something else. Yet this attention to enjoyment leaves aside the object of thought or feeling and attends to the subjective side of it. To take an example from university life, consider the relation between Departments of Theology and Departments of Religious Studies. Theology studies what is contemplated in religion: God or gods. Religious Studies, on the other hand, is concerned with what is enjoyed in religion: beliefs, religious experience, religious practices. Theology is concerned with the object of religion, Religious Studies with the subject of religion. In this sense, Theology is an objective study and Religious Studies a subjective one. But exactly the reverse is often claimed: Religious Studies claims objectivity because it takes religion as its object rather than 'getting inside' religion to contemplate *its* object, God or gods. Of course, it is a contentious question whether the object of Theology exists, whereas it is uncontentious that the object of Religious Studies exists: whether or not there are gods, there are certainly religious beliefs, etc. But this is not because Theology is subjective and Religious Studies objective, but exactly the opposite: religion is contentious because it makes objective claims; religious subjectivity is uncontentious.

It seems to me that 'bad objectivity' – better, reflexive objectivity – the objectivity that, according to so many existentialist accounts (in so far as those accounts do not rest on confusions, as I shall argue some of them do), impoverishes our view of the world, is the exclusive attention to enjoyment rather than contemplation. Actually, it is self-undermining to attend consistently to enjoyment, since every contemplation of an enjoyment is itself an enjoyment that could be contemplated. The psychologist studies the emotion, not its object, but it is in turn possible to study the psychologist's work in a way that ignores its relation to its object, as, for example, a sociologist of knowledge would do. The work of the sociologist of knowledge can in turn be studied in such a way that the object of its study drops out of the picture, and so on. Each mental act gains its interest and its validity where validity is applicable – for example, the status of a belief as knowledge or an emotion as appropriate – from its relation to the object contemplated. When attention is switched from what is contemplated to what is enjoyed, the issue of validity drops out of account. But this switch of attention can be made with respect to *every* mental act. So the mental act

B of contemplating the enjoyment of mental act A, which act (B) brackets off the question of A's validity, can itself be contemplated as an enjoyment by act C, bracketing off the question of B's validity in turn. So, while it is possible in any given case to switch attention from what is contemplated to what is enjoyed, if one tried to do this in all cases one would be unable to raise the question of the validity of the procedure. If, out of respect for reflexive objectivity, one were to declare only Religious Studies and not Theology as a respectable academic discipline, a sociologist of knowledge who made it their business to study Religious Studies Departments could, with as much justice, substitute their discipline for Religious Studies, only to be displaced in turn by a psychologist who studied sociologists of knowledge, and so on.

The kind of objectivity that attends to the object contemplated can be called intentional objectivity, since attention rests on the intentional object in Brentano's sense, on that which the thought or feeling is about. It can stand by itself; one could limit oneself to intentional objectivity and forget about reflexive objectivity without undermining intentional object-ivity in the way that reflexive objectivity undermines itself if it forgets about intentional objectivity. That is not to say that we ought to ignore reflexive objectivity in this way. It is useful in showing how intentional objectivity goes wrong – that is, how is it that our thoughts and feelings are sometimes merely subjective in the sense that they don't correspond to their objects and are to be explained by the nature of the subject rather than that of the object? But reflexive objectivity should always be the subordinate and dependent partner. Thus, as we shall see, sociological studies of science are very useful in exposing the motives of bad science. What reflexive objectivity can never be is the criterion of intentional objectivity. The sociologist of science cannot judge *whether* the science studied is bad science, only *why* it is when it is. Of course, the sociologist of science may also have a training in science and so be able to show where there is bad science, but as a sociologist of science he or she cannot do so. Sociology of science may give grounds for *suspicion* when it reveals grounds for believing that certain conclusions would have been reached, whether or not they were true. An obvious example would be a sociologist of science showing that the scientist had a financial interest in producing certain results, whether or not they were true. But we should be careful to get clear what such a 'hermeneutic of suspicion' does and does not do: it casts suspicion; it does not disprove. Probably any capitalist society would sooner or later have come up with a Darwinian theory of evolution, even if it were false; but that does not disprove Darwin.

This is why applied psychoanalysis is such a dodgy discipline. Because psychoanalysis deals in pathological processes, its accounts of cultural phenomena always look like debunkings. But one still needs to study a cultural phenomenon in its own terms and find whether it is justified or illusory in its own terms, even if a pathology exists that explains the illusion if there is one. As Marcuse says somewhere, an aeroplane may be a phallic symbol, but it will still get you from New York to San Francisco.

Whenever a plausible point can be made against objectivity, I think it is almost always a point against the intrusion of reflexive objectivity at the expense of intentional objectivity.

In conclusion, another observation may be apposite. We can be reflexive not only about thoughts and theories but about practices. It is a specific feature of human practice that we can always monitor what we are doing. It is another feature of human practice that we always do things worse when we do them reflexively. A monitored activity is a badly done activity. This has often been noticed:

> *The centipede was happy, quite,*
> *Until a toad in fun*
> *Said, 'Pray, which leg goes after which?'*
> *This worked his mind to such a pitch,*
> *He lay distracted in a ditch,*
> *Considering how to run.*
>   (Watts, *The Way of Zen*, p. 47)

Very often when people have been involved in an 'encounter group', where all the things that are said in the group are monitored, they become in-articulate and uncommunicative for some time afterwards. Fortunately, we can sometimes switch off our reflexivity even when our profession requires reflexivity, otherwise a psychologist who studied love could never be a good lover and a literary critic could never be a good writer. The same applies in the realm of theory. A sociologist of science may be a good scientist, but only by switching off the sociology; an adept at Religious Studies may be a good theologian, but only by switching off the Religious Studies.

§6 Bultmann: the theologian who cannot talk about God

I think the distinction between reflexive and intentional objectivity will help to clear some of the jungle of an existentialist text on theology – namely, Rudolf Bultmann's essay 'What Does it Mean to Speak of God?' (in *Faith and Understanding*). But first, a few remarks by way of situating Bultmann's position.

There is an extreme liberal position in theology – which is not Bultmann's – which is frankly non-realist about God. When we speak of God, it says, we are simply expressing some attitude of our own or engaging in meaningful fiction. There are many unclear statements of this position, but at least one clear one, namely that of R.B. Braithwaite in his paper 'An Empiricist's View of the Nature of Religious Belief' (in Mitchell (ed.), *The Philosophy of Religion*).

It is quite natural for an adherent of this position to deny that there are rational grounds for 'faith', whatever 'faith' means in this context. With the rejection of the objectivity of a putative fact (here, the existence of God) goes (as a rule) the rejection of rational grounds for or against believing in that fact. Thus subjectivism about the objects of science or about values leads to relativism about scientific judgements and non-cognitivism about moral judgements. We would expect the same about religion.

However much twentieth-century theology (this seems to me to include Barth as well as Bultmann) insists on God's independence of our judgements and experiences – his objectivity – yet at the same time it teaches that 'faith' has no rational grounds. I think this odd combination of views can only be understood as a reaction against an empiricist philosophy of religion that not only made religious experience the *grounds* for religious belief, but reduced theology to the study of religious experience, thus tacitly reducing God to a construction out of our experiences, rather as phenomenalism reduced material objects to sense data. Reacting against this reduction to subjective experience, these theologians also rejected the idea that experiences could be the ground for belief in an independently existing God who caused and was the object of these experiences, just as the material world causes and is the object of our perceptions. Hence, these theologians are left with a concept of revelation in which what is revealed is objective, but without a concept of criteria by which we might accept one putative revelation as true and reject another as illusory. It is left to 'faith' in the degenerate popular sense of the word: belief without grounds. Despite – or in a sense, because of – their defence of ontological objectivity, these theologians undermine epistemic objectivity.

But in addition to this irrationalism which is common to much twentieth-century Protestant theology, Bultmann is affected by existentialism. He was a close friend of Heidegger when *Being and Time* was being written and was also deeply influenced by Kierkegaard. The position he defends in the essay in question (which dates from 1925, two years before *Being and Time* was published) *could* have been expressed by saying: 'if we talk about God we make God our object [intentional object]; but God cannot be an object [an impersonal entity]'. However, he does not set it up in these terms, so something else is going on here than a mere sliding between two senses of 'object'. Other terms are needed to explain the paradoxical view he is defending: that we cannot talk about God without denying God. The paradox is forcefully presented in his opening words:

> If 'speaking of God' is understood as '*speaking about God*', then such speaking has no meaning whatever, for its subject, God, is lost in the very moment it takes place. Whenever the idea, God, comes to mind, it connotes that God is the Almighty; in other words, God is the reality determining all else. But this idea is not recognised at all when I speak *about* God, i.e. when I regard God as an object of thought, about which I can inform myself if I take a standpoint where I can be neutral on the question of God and can formulate propositions dealing with the reality and nature of God, which I can reject or, if they are enlightening, accept. . . . every 'speaking *about*' presupposes a standpoint external to that which is being talked about.
>
> (*Faith and Understanding* (hereafter *FU*), p. 53)

One red herring here is the idea of being neutral. If one talks about God, theists and atheists can both understand what is said, and in that sense the language is neutral. But it by no means follows that the speaker need be neutral; he or she may be speaking about God in order to convince an unbeliever.

Another red herring is the idea of an external standpoint. The speaker about God is certainly not identical with God and is not speaking about himself or herself. It looks here as if Bultmann is saying that the speaker *ought* to be speaking about himself or herself in order not to be 'external' to what is being said, but then the talk could really not be about God. Yet Bultmann is also saying that when we speak about God we are not speaking about ourselves, but about a being 'Wholly Other' (*FU*, p. 55). Indeed, Bultmann seems to have the same problem about speaking about ourselves as he does about speaking about God, for he extends the argument to speaking about love or about fatherhood and sonship:

> Actually, one cannot speak *about* love at all unless the speaking about it is itself an act of love. Any other talk about love does not speak about *love*, for it stands outside love.
>
> (*FU*, p. 53)

It would be easy to dismiss this as follows: if one talks about love from outside love it is still love that one is talking about and what one says may be true or false of love, just as, in order to talk about cricket, it is not necessary that one plays cricket. The fact that talking about cricket is not playing cricket does not make it false about cricket. However, Bultmann might be trying to say something that does have a point and is better expressed in the terms set out in the last section: in love, the loved one is contemplated and the love is enjoyed; in talking about love, the love is contemplated and the conversation enjoyed. In talking about love, reflexive objectivity has replaced intentional objectivity. But this is not so when the talk is part of the love: a declaration of love expresses the love rather than (or at least as well as) talking about it. But what is the equivalent to this in the case of talking about God? Surely, in talking about God, God is contemplated and religion enjoyed; in talking about religion, religion is contemplated and Religious Studies enjoyed. The real parallel to talking about God in the example of love would be talking about the loved one in a way that expressed the love but did not refer to the love. If we pursue this parallel, the conclusion should be not that talk about God is not about God, but that Religious Studies is not about God; but nobody ever thought it was.

Now we come to another red herring:

> speaking of God ... in general truths, means speaking in propositions the significance of which is their universal validity – a validity which is not related to the concrete situation of the speaker. But just because the speaker speaks in this manner, he puts himself outside the actual reality of his own existence, and therefore at the same time outside God. He therefore can speak only of what is not God.
>
> (*FU*, p. 54)

Now, in the first place, it is quite possible to speak of God in general truths, even if unrelated personally to God, and for those general truths to retain their meaning. A child may learn the Creed from jaded, cynical teachers and come to have a genuine belief in it. The words mean the same and are true or false, whatever the speaker's relation to them. But, more importantly, there is no necessity that we put ourselves outside something just because it is a general truth. We can be as passionate about what is universal as about what is particular. The person who has to substitute 'God loves me' for 'God loves the world' before they can relate to it is a selfish person.

Bultmann goes on to object to the notion of *reality* (FU, p. 58) because 'the picture of the world is conceived without reference to our own existence'. But this is not true. When we think of reality, we may also think of our own place in that reality. What we don't do is try to relate the whole show to ourselves or make ourselves the centre of it. And by taking this objective view of ourselves, we are not denying our subjectivity or our passion or our need to make decisions or anything else of the kind; we are simply being truthful about these things.

Bultmann seems to want God to be viewed egocentrically, as 'my God' rather than 'the God':

> The work of God cannot be seen as a universal process, as an activity which we can observe (as we can observe the workings of the laws of nature), apart from our own existence.
>
> (FU, p. 59)

Of course, if one regards something as the work of God, one will relate to it in a different way than if one thought of it as a natural event. But first we have to observe the process that is independent of us. To reduce the work of God to something that only goes on in our existential decisions is light years away from the New Testament view of Christ as the one in whom 'all things cohere'. It is close to the sorry view of Kierkegaard that only the truth that edifies is the truth for you. Against this, Nietzsche's protest is justified, that there are many unedifying truths; the glory of the human mind is to believe what is true, whether it edifies us or shatters us: it is called honesty.

We can summarise the points made in this essay of Bultmann's as follows:

1 The legitimate point that, when reflexive objectivity replaces intentional objectivity, the intentional object of the original experience drops out of account. Religion is about God, Religious Studies is about religion, Religious Studies is not about God.
2 The incorrect point that this has to happen as soon as language is used – as if to talk about God were to engage in Religious Studies.
3 The incorrect point that we cannot speak meaningfully or truthfully about something except when we are existentially related to it.
4 The incorrect point that when we talk *about* something, we cannot be existentially related to it.
5 The incorrect point that we cannot be existentially related to what is universal.

Although the concepts 'object' and 'objectivity' occur fairly rarely in the essay, it exemplifies the common existentialist error that what is objective in the sense of independent of us can have no concern for us.

Bultmann himself is obviously worried that the conclusions of the paper would seem to enjoin silence about God on us – an embarrassing injunction for a theologian. For if we talk about God externally it means nothing, and if we talk about him by talking about our own existence, we are not talking about him but about ourselves – and anyway we can't talk about ourselves without falsification through objectification. Bultmann modifies this conclusion by saying that we can talk about God when we 'must', the *must* indicating a divine command to do so. Yet even when we *must*, talking about God seems to be seen as sinful, although the Lutheran idea that we are at once sinners and righteous is used to imply that *everything* is sin, and also righteous. However, Bultmann concludes:

> even this lecture is a speaking about God and as such, if God is, it is sin, and if God is not, it is meaningless. Whether it has meaning and whether it is justified – none of us can judge.
>
> (*FU*, p. 65)

This seems to be an ironic admission that he has sawn off the branch he is sitting on, but, while if he has sinned he can be forgiven, if he has failed to communicate anything about God, his forgiveness makes us none the wiser.

There is a final point that I would like to make, although it is not raised directly by this essay. Bultmann is declaring information about God to be existentially irrelevant. From this essay one gets the impression that he means 'eternal truths' about God. And this coincides with Bultmann's rejection of the view of knowledge of God which makes it a matter of eternal truths that could have been discovered by anyone, rather than a historical self-revelation. But in the end, Bultmann's own view comes closer to the 'eternal truths' model than to the historical revelation model. For the *kerygma*, the proclamation of the fact of Jesus Christ, becomes severed from its historical basis, since it is not a vehicle for 'communication of historical information' ('The Historical Jesus and the Theology of Paul', *FU*, p. 241). It no longer has anything to do with the fact that Jesus was a friend of sinners or a teacher of unconditional love. If it really does not communicate historical information, it does not seem to have anything to do with the fact that he was crucified either, although Bultmann seems, inconsistently, to draw the line there. But even if we allow him this line, our response to Jesus' death would be different if it were shown (as some have tried to show) that he was a Zealot terrorist or an Essene 'Teacher of Righteousness' who taught hatred of the Sons of Darkness. Without the idea that Jesus revealed God *by what he did and taught*, there is very little of Christianity left. Why does Bultmann want to get rid of the objectivity of history as well as the objectivity of eternal truths? I think it is because, like everything objective, historical evidence is uncertain. Bultmann is all for objectivity in the sifting of historical evidence and his own conclusions in this area are very sceptical. He does not mind the sceptical conclusions because he thinks that whatever is historically objective can have no import for faith. For instance, he doubts that Jesus thought of himself as the Messiah, but claims that whether he did so or not has no bearing on whether we accept him as the Messiah. Most versions of Christian belief rest on historical foundations which are, of course, matters of probability. Bultmann cannot accept that uncertainty; faith has to rest on individual decision, which makes it unchallengeable and under each individual's control. He is not prepared to accept the riskiness of historical objectivity. There is a most unexistentialist craving for security under this existentialist conception of faith.

§7 Heidegger, realism and objectivity

Heidegger has what seems to be a knock-down transcendental argument against non-realism. He recognises that this puts him on the realist side in its historical dispute with idealism. But he is obviously unhappy about this placing of his thought, and it is instructive to enquire why.

One way into this idea is by contrasting a metaphor of Heidegger's with two of Popper's: Popper refers to bucket theories of the mind and search-light theories. According to bucket theories, mind is a container for bits of experience that we have collected; according to searchlight theories, it is directed on things, illuminating those on which it is directed. Heidegger has a third metaphor: a clearing in the forest. Only by virtue of the clearing are the trees visible, yet the clearing is nothing but the trees and the relations between them. We are not *in* the clearing, we *are* the clearing. This theory is obviously closer to the searchlight theory than to the bucket theory, but in many ways better than it: it catches the decentredness of the way the world is disclosed in us.

The theory is spelt out in terms of the relations between the entities in any person's world, organised around their projects. One of Heidegger's examples, to which I constantly return, is using a hammer to mend a shutter. The project of doing this generates a series of tools (and possibly obstacles) with a person (*Dasein*) at either end of it: you make a house weatherproof *for* someone, *by* mending a shutter, *with* a nail, put in *with* a hammer, hammered *by* someone. The totality of these series projected by any agent constitutes his or her world. But the world is not something external like the 'external world' of Cartesian and empiricist philosophy. We *are* our worlds. Whereas for Descartes what a person has apart from a body that makes them a person is a spiritual substance whose essence is to be conscious, for Heidegger he or she has a world and that is what it means to be a person, a '*Dasein*': to be in a world. As I have said, in place of Descartes' 'I think therefore I am', someone might summarise Heidegger's argument as 'I fix a shutter with a hammer, therefore I am in a world'.

One result of Heidegger's account of Being-in-the-world is that he is aggressively anti-non-realist. He says he is not a realist, but non-realism gets treated to a refutation which, as Sartre says of his similar dismissal of the 'problem of other minds', could be seen as 'cutting Gordian knots rather than untying them': that as 'Being-in-the-world' we are ourselves defined by our worlds. The idea that proofs of the 'external world' are needed wrongly assumes that we are worldless subjects, defined independently of our worlds. The world indeed is not 'external' in that sense at all: we are out in it. Hence, Heidegger admits that 'doxographically' – that is, in terms of placing his views on one side or the other in a historical controversy – he is a realist (*Being and Time*, p. 251). But, in the first place, he takes realism to have agreed with idealism that proofs of the external world are needed, but held that they are not lacking. I think most modern realists would agree with Heidegger that such proofs are not required, once a mistaken view of our place in the world is rejected.

But the matter does not end here. Heidegger goes on to claim greater affinities with idealism than with realism, despite his 'doxographical' alignment with the latter. For idealism 'expresses an understanding of the fact that Being cannot be explained through entities' (ibid., p. 251). This is a matter to which I will return.

It is possible that a part of Heidegger's grounds for dislike of the word 'realism' is that he interprets it etymologically, as is his custom: belief that being is just a collection of 'things', physical objects. In his own terminology, it is the idea that the 'present-at-hand' is exhaustive of what there is. This notion of an unstructured and one-level reality is not shared by all realists, certainly not those like myself known as 'critical realists'. Nevertheless, there is more than a verbal difference here. The difference is that Heidegger takes it for granted that any science-oriented realism can only be such a 'flattened' realism.

Here I must give a brief critical account of Heidegger's distinction between three fundamental kinds of being: *Dasein*, the ready-to-hand and the present-at-hand. *Dasein*, of course – etymologically 'being there' – is Heidegger's word for our presence in the world and more or less a synonym for 'person' or 'humankind'. The present-at-hand, of which more below, is much like the physical world of empirical realism. The ready-to-hand is the most distinctively Heideggerian concept of the three. It refers to the instrumental world encountered in our daily work; it is not a world of different things than the present-at-hand, but rather of the same things encountered differently. Our original encounter with things, Heidegger holds, is in their capacity as *pragmata*, gear that we use in our projects and that, in the manner in which they indicate and define each other in the light of our projects, form our world. Things so considered are understood by us, implicitly – for example, my understanding of the hammer is manifested by my banging in a nail with it. The organisation of our gear into a world is inconspicuous until some practical breakdown makes it conspicuous by its absence. I run out of nails, so the hammer becomes just a useless piece of wood with a metal end, the fence I was fixing becomes just a row of loose palings, and so on. They become merely present-at-hand, rather than ready-to-hand. My cognitive relation to them changes. Instead of the practically oriented looking, 'circum-spection' (*Umsicht*), by which I understand the ready-to-hand, I am left just staring at them (although this staring may not be useless, where the break-down in practice is due to something going wrong; it may have the function of finding out what is wrong).

Thus, to the two ways of being of things, as ready-to-hand and present-at-hand, there correspond two kinds of knowing: the understanding that is inherent in any practice and 'just looking', a purely contemplative stare. The sciences, although distinguished by their various rigorous methods, are seen as modes of 'just looking', of the purely contemplative knowledge that we have of things when they are no longer usable. This applies to theoretical knowledge generally.

Some disparate objections to this account present themselves, but first the following three points explain what Heidegger is right about:

1   That the world of our practical concern, composed of the ready-to-hand and understood implicitly by what Althusser would call 'knowledge in a practical state', is necessarily both historically and biographically prior to that given by theoretical knowledge, and remains closer to us even when we have theoretical knowledge.

2   That we nevertheless have a tendency (to which, at the philosophical level, Heidegger's writing is intended to be, and is, a corrective) to under-stand the world, and ourselves, in terms of the present-at-hand, the world as 'everything that is the case'. For instance, if asked what we mean by a 'thing', we would tend to answer 'a lump of lifeless matter', although we commonly use the word for any object of our concern, whether an activity, a relationship, a project or whatever; or again, we think of 'in' as denoting a relation of geometric containment: 'I am in a lecture room'. Yet I can also be in a lecture (not the same thing), in the Labour Party, in a quandary, in love.

3   That the original motivation of theoretical knowledge is given by break-downs in pre-theoretical practice. Incidentally, this gives rise to a useful methodological principle in the human sciences, which I have elsewhere dubbed 'the methodological primacy of the pathological'.

These points are summed up in a more Anglo-Saxon manner by John Macmurray – the Scottish Heidegger – in his idea that, while we commonly suppose that knowledge presupposes thought (in that knowledge is the result of thinking), actually thought presupposes knowledge, since it is only when the knowledge implicit in practice fails us that we stop the practice and start thinking, until we see our way to resolving the breakdown. Although Heidegger describes us as stopping and staring rather than stopping and thinking, he shares with Macmurray the view that the function of the stopping is to see our way to resolving the breakdown, so that practice can start again.

This way of putting it should immediately establish a conclusion that neither Heidegger nor Macmurray seem to draw consistently: that if theoretical knowledge is to have the role assigned to it by them, it must be able to *correct* practical knowledge, to have access to information that is not available to practice as such and perhaps contradicting the knowledge that is inherent in practice. And if theoretical knowledges can thus open up regions of being that would have been opaque without them, then, in some respects at least, they must enrich rather than impoverish our world view.

Yet it is a constant theme of Heidegger's that theoretical knowledge is not only secondary to, but an impoverishment relative to, practical understanding. There is one passage where the lines of Heidegger's romantic feeling for nature and his version of the primacy of practice in knowledge get crossed:

> In equipment that is used, 'Nature' is discovered along with it by that use – the 'Nature' we find in natural products.
>
> Here, however, 'Nature' is not to be understood as that which is just present-at-hand, nor as the *power of Nature.* The wood is a forest of timber, the mountain a quarry of rock; the river is water power, the wind is wind 'in the sails'. As the 'environment' is discovered, the 'Nature' thus encountered is discovered too. If its kind of being as ready-to-hand is disregarded, this 'Nature' itself can be discovered and defined simply in its pure presence-at-hand. But when this happens, the Nature which 'stirs and strives', which assails us and enthralls us as landscape, remains hidden. The botanist's plants are not the flowers of the hedgerow; the 'source' which the geographer establishes for a river is not the 'spring-head in the dale'.
>
> (*Being and Time*, p. 100)

At the end of this passage, the 'power of Nature' seems to be lost when we pass from the practical to the scientific relation to nature, yet it had already been said to be absent from the practical attitude, from nature as 'ready-to-hand'. Compare Marx:

> the dealer in minerals sees only the commercial value, and not the beauty and peculiar nature of the minerals; he lacks a mineralogical sense.
>
> (*Early Writings*, p. 353)

Of course, the practical relation to nature may not be that of the profit-conscious dealer, it may be that of the peasant or artisan working on nature who may or may not derive aesthetic inspiration from it, but anyway has a certain respect for his or her materials. But this may also be true of the scientist – the geographer who, far from just staring at the source of the river, has had to scramble up screes to find it; the mineralogist who, as a scientist, is precisely concerned with the peculiar nature of the minerals. Nor is one's appreciation of wild flowers impoverished by the knowledge of botany; one is much more likely to notice the variety of flowers if one has a smattering of botany. It is the difference between just saying 'Those are pretty purple flowers', and going on to say 'I don't think I've seen that sort before', taking a careful mental picture of them, checking them up in a book, discovering that they are early purple orchids, *Orchis masculus*, the double corms of which were once believed to have aphrodisiac properties, and thereafter being able to identify those flowers whenever one sees them. Where is the loss?

There is no exceptionless way of aligning the distinction between theoretical knowledge and practical understanding with that between richer and poorer views of the world. And the idea that *objectivity* necessarily aligns with either the poorer content or the contemplative attitude is unjustified.

Now it needs to be asked in what sense scientific knowledge, which is certainly the result of practice, can be called contemplative as opposed to practical knowledge. The case described by Heidegger in which the practical breakdown immediately motivates a 'just looking' kind of knowledge is certainly the exception. Suppose I want to know why a certain species of plant won't flourish in my garden. I don't just put my head in my hands and stare at the sorry specimen. I get a soil test kit, shake soil samples about with appropriate chemicals in a test tube, filter off the liquid and compare the colour with a chart. I find that the soil is too acid and add to it accordingly to correct this imbalance. The experiment is as much a practice as the gardening that preceded and followed it. But it is true that there is the point at which I just look at the liquid in the test tube and the colours on the paper to see, so to speak, what answer this little bit of nature has given to my question. This does distinguish such knowledge from that subliminally induced by practice. But work has to be done before the 'just looking' can get started. The main difference between scientific and practical knowledge is indeed that this work in science is *in order to* acquire knowledge.

Finally, theoretical knowledge is not necessarily knowledge of the present-at-hand. Economics is about the ready-to-hand (including *Dasein* considered as ready-to-hand). Human sciences are presumably about *Dasein* and not necessarily *Dasein* considered as present-at-hand (although, like human anatomy or physical anthropology, they can be).

Heidegger has been seen to argue for the priority of the world as everything that is ready-to-hand for a person over the world as everything that is present-at-hand. Hence his argument cuts two ways. On the one hand, we are Being-in-the-world and therefore cannot doubt the existence of the world. On the other hand, that world is not the world in the sense that the world is independent of us and the same for everyone. Heidegger is careful to distinguish different senses of 'world' (*Being and Time*, p. 93) and makes it clear that, in his special sense, world is always someone's world. This raises the question of whether he is not actually a kind of neutral monist – that is, someone who regards the ultimate reality as something neutral between mind and matter, out of which mind and matter are constructed by abstraction. The best known form of neutral monism is that once held by Russell, that the ultimate constituents of the universe are sense data, with minds being bundles of sense data – for example, all the sense data experienced by me – and matter being other bundles of sense data – for example all the sense data of the tree in the quad. This form of neutral monism is, in its atomism, light years away from Heidegger's. But Being-in-the-world could be seen as a holistic instance of the same neutrality: entities within the world can be abstracted from it, as can mind, but only Being-in-the-world concretely exists. This would explain why, after his doxographical alignment with realism, Heidegger not only rejects realism but gives credit to idealism, for, on the surface, the praise of idealism for its understanding that Being cannot be explained through entities looks purely negative, like the proverbial similarity of an elephant to a carrot (that neither of them can climb a tree). If it is to be more than this, it must indicate that what there is more to being than entities is that it is being for someone. This would support taking in its obvious sense Heidegger's remark that 'Of course [*sic*] only as long as *Dasein is* (that is, only as long as an understanding of Being is ontically possible) "is there" Being' (*Being and Time*, p. 255). Elsewhere Heidegger gives a different sense to this passage, but I have argued that this does not exculpate him from relativising Being to *Dasein* (see Heidegger's 'Letter on Humanism' in *Basic Writings*, and my discussion in *Being and Worth*, pp. 83–84). In other words, being does not seem to be objective for Heidegger, not only in the sense that 'objective' acquires in existentialist polemics – value-free, atomistic, mechanistic, quantitative – but also in the straightforward sense of being independent of human subjects. 'When Dasein does not exist, "independence" "is" not either, nor "is" the "in-itself"' (*Being and Time*, p. 255). However, for this sentence not to contradict what follows, 'is' has to be taken as meaning 'has Being' in a special Heideggerian sense, for he goes on to say:

> *In such a case* [that is, if *Dasein* no longer existed – A.C.] it cannot be said that entities are, nor can it be said that they are not. But *now*, as long as there is an understanding of Being and therefore an understanding of presence-at-hand, it can be said that *in this case* [when *Dasein* does not exist – A.C.] entities will still continue to be.
>
> (ibid., p. 255)

In other words, if no one existed no one could say that entities existed, but while people do exist we can truly say that entities would still exist even if we did not. So, entities seem to be independent of us, but their 'Being' seems to be dependent on us: realism about entities, idealism – or neutral monism – about Being.

This is a rather disappointing conclusion because much in Heidegger seems to suggest that there is more to Being than 'the world for us'. Perhaps something similar has happened here to what happened in the passage on nature. There are actually three concepts of nature there: a ready-to-hand one (forest of timber, quarry of rock); a present-at-hand one (brute matter); and a romantic one (nature which stirs and strives). The first is relative to us; neither the second nor the third seem to be. Yet, at the end of the passage, Heidegger only contrasts the third with the second, as if ready-to-hand nature were closer to romantic nature – possibly the latter also being relative to our projects (although perhaps poetic rather than industrial projects). Likewise with Being: it seems that he can see no way of saying there is more to Being than the present-at-hand without bringing us in. He has done more than anyone to liberate us from the spell of Descartes; but he has not freed us from the spell of Kant.

§8 Berdyaev: the problematic of objectification

To begin on a personal note: in my early twenties, I was more or less a disciple of Berdyaev. I still find much wisdom in his ideas, but it is all at the periphery of his thought, about ethics, politics and theology. In this essay I want to discuss something at the metaphysical centre of his thought, even the understanding of which I now find puzzling. But I think it is a puzzle which it is instructive to try to solve. It is instructive because it is an extreme version of the common existentialist polemic against objectivity.

The puzzle centres on the concept of objectification. Part of this is common existentialist heritage: the positivist identification of objective knowledge with knowledge of the mechanical, the atomistic, the quantifiable and the value-free is not so much challenged as inverted, so that 'the objective', with all these connotations, is seen as something bad and 'the subjective' is seen as something good. But there is more to it than this.

Berdyaev writes of good and bad senses of objectivity and subjectivity; the familiar senses in which objectivity is truth independent of the subject and subjectivity is personal bias are the good sense of objectivity and the bad sense of subjectivity; these might be called the epistemic senses. But Berdyaev uses the terms much more often in an ontological sense; 'objectivity', then, has all the positivistic connotations mentioned above and subjectivity means to do with 'subjects' – that is, persons. He claims that the objective (in the bad sense) world is ultimately unreal and is projected by us – that is, is subjective in the bad sense – while subjective knowledge (in the good sense) is knowledge of the real world behind the appearances (and so is objective in the good sense). Thus he writes of Kant:

> Critical philosophy is, of course, philosophy of the subject not of the object, and just for that reason it is not 'subjective' in the bad sense of the word and is 'objective' in the good sense.
>
> (*The Beginning and the End*, p. 10)

So one must never read Berdyaev's constant references to things as objective (in the bad sense) or subjective (in the good sense) as committing him to subjectivism in the sense of relativism about truth or values, which

relativisms he rejects. (He accepts the sociology of knowledge, as we shall
see, but only of 'objectifying' knowledge). Rather, he is inverting the usual
alignment of the 'inner' with the subjective (in the bad sense) and the 'outer'
with the objective (in the good sense).

In the book where he works out his metaphysics most systematically,
The Beginning and the End (hereafter *BE*), he takes Kant as his starting point:
'Kant . . . was a metaphysician of freedom, even, it may be, the only meta-
physician of freedom' (p. 8).

There is a world of appearance (the 'objective world' in the bad sense)
which is projected by our senses and intellect. In it, determinism reigns.
But behind it there is a real world of noumena, the world of freedom. So
far, so Kantian. But he departs from Kant in three ways, in holding (1) that
we have access to the noumenal world (the world of things-in-themselves,
independent of our perception and reason): 'Man is aware of himself not only
as a phenomenon' (p. 10) – that is to say, we are aware of ourselves also as
noumena, things-in-themselves; (2) that it is our fault that we are subjected
to the phenomenal world:

> This compulsorily perceptible world which is the only real world for
> prosaic workaday experience, the only 'objective' world is a creation of
> man, it expresses the direction in which his mind tends to move
>
> (*BE*, p. 6)

and (3) that the task of philosophy is to break through to the noumenal
world; his thought 'is concerned with a revolution in the mind . . . the
liberation of the mind from the power of objectification' (p. vii) and he tells
us that 'Philosophical knowledge is an act of self-liberation on the part of
the spirit from the exclusive claims of the world of phenomena to be reality'
(p. 6).

In the first of these points, he seems close to Schopenhauer whom he
mentions in this connection. But Schopenhauer's view, while much less
attractive than Berdyaev's, is also much clearer: we know ourselves as will
and thereby know that the noumenal reality of everything else is will too.
But for Schopenhauer, objectification is a necessary feature of all representation. It is not our fault. And the 'fallenness' of the world lies not in the
objectification of phenomena, but in the evil nature of the noumenon, will
itself. Finally, for Schopenhauer, if we see through the phenomena to the
noumena and draw the right moral conclusions, we find no rich world of
persons in communion, as Berdyaev does; instead, we find an undifferenti-
ated will, which is to be denied and the cessation of which is to be welcomed.

Objectification is, I think, seen as a process, due to our errors, by which
the noumenal world is degraded into the phenomenal world or comes to be
seen by us in terms of the phenomenal world; a metaphysical fall from
paradise, which is perhaps reversible if we learn a non-objectifying way of
relating to reality. This raises a number of questions:

1   How do we have access to the noumenal world?
2   What is the status of our knowledge of the phenomenal world – for instance, science?
3   What is it about our relation to the world that causes objectification?
4   Could we really kick the habit of objectification and, if so, what would the change wrought by this be like?

Objectification for Berdyaev is, among other things, something that (bad) philosophy can do:

> there are two paths, or two starting-points, in seeking a solution to the mystery of being. Either being is known and unriddled from the side of the object, taking the world as the starting-point, or it is known and unriddled from the side of the ego, that is from man.
>
> (*BE*, p. 5)

But this cannot be the fundamental thing because, in order to be taken as a starting point, the objective world of appearance has to be there; I take it that the point of the problematic of objectification is not just that there are two worlds, this world and the beyond, but that this world is unreal, that its appearance is down to us in that we guiltily objectify the noumenal world in experiencing it. Objectification is a process that is done to something. The noumenal world is objectified into the phenomenal world in the process or our knowing it, although we could and ought to have known it in a non-objectifying way. And this is not just done by philosophy but by 'workaday' experience. I think it will be useful before delving further into what Berdyaev says to look at four more familiar accounts of what could be called objectification, all of which are touched on in Berdyaev's account, yet none of which seems to be exactly what he is saying.

Reductionism

Some forms of knowledge focus on the mechanical to the exclusion of the personal, the quantitative to the exclusion of the qualitative, the atomic to the exclusion of the organic, the general to the exclusion of the particular, and the value-neutral to the exclusion of the valueful. I think it is true, and that Berdyaev would agree, that this is quite in order in some regions of knowledge (physics and chemistry, for instance), but out of order in others (the human world, for instance). It might look from what has been said so far that any such knowledge, since it is about the phenomenal/ 'objective' world, not the noumenal, is objectifying, but Berdyaev's view is that, given that the objectified world exists for us, we must know and control it so far as possible, and the natural sciences are the legitimate means of doing so:

If science is under the sway of determinism, if it is looking for causal links and does not discover primary creative movements in the life of the world, the blame for this does not lie with science but with the state of the world.

(*BE*, p. 45)

However, although there is a genuine error in attempts of the human sciences to be like the natural sciences in these respects (for instance, in behaviourist and physicalist psychologies or marginalist economics), these errors can hardly explain the all-pervasive objectification which, for Berdyaev, produces the world as we know it 'objectively'.

Expressing and being about

Language can be used to express an emotion or a value-judgement or it can be about that emotion or value-judgement. If you are asked your religion by a hospital receptionist or asked whether your are in love by a psychologist doing a statistical survey, your answer will be about your religion or your love, but not an expression of it. If you are praying or whispering loving words into your beloved's ear, you are expressing your religion or love. It could be thought that about-language is objectifying, while expressive language is not. However, expressiveness and aboutness are not mutually exclusive, in the first place because uses of language are usually expressive *and* about something, although not necessarily the same thing. A love poem, for instance, is typically expressive of the poet's love and is about the poet's beloved. Second, because in between the extreme cases given in my examples, there are many cases in which language is expressive of what it is about: for instance, a person holding forth enthusiastically or persuasively to a friend about their love or their religion. Indeed, in the cases of saying 'I love you' or saying the Creed, one is presumably doing both things by the same token; only a cynical lover expects his declaration to be taken as saying nothing about his emotions; and a Creed-sayer (and there are such) who claimed not to be saying anything about God but merely expressing their own faith would be one who had lost their faith. The distinction that is needed here is between intentional and reflexive objectivity, but both are about something – the beloved or the love.

The Heideggerian dimension

Despite the differences (Heidegger's intended, if not consistently accomplished, ontocentrism versus Berdyaev's anthropocentrism), Heidegger's account of inauthentic forms of knowledge is certainly echoed in Berdyaev's account of objectification. The interpretation of *Dasein* in terms of the present-at-hand, the dominance of the idle talk of the 'they', the quantification of the unquantifiable, all are there. However, for Heidegger the world of our concern in which we entangle ourselves is real enough; it is not a product of our inauthenticity. Nor is Being a noumenal reality. Everything is there before our eyes, but we miss the things that matter most. For Berdyaev, to live in the noumenal world would be totally different from living in the phenomenal world. It would be 'the end of the world': 'in every true act of knowing the end of the world comes, the end of enslaving objectivity' (*BE*, p. 50).

The Blakean dimension

The radical alienness of noumenal to phenomenal world, combined with the idea that we could break through to the noumenal world, suggests only one other writer – namely, William Blake. Blake asks 'How do we know but ev'ry Bird that cuts the airy way,/Is an immense world of delight, clos'd by our senses five?', and he tells us 'if the doors of perception were cleansed, everything would appear to man as it is, infinite' and that 'This will come about by the improvement of sensual enjoyment' ('The Marriage of Heaven and Hell', in *Complete Writings* (hereafter *CW*), pp. 150 and 154). If we all used our creative imaginations to see through the senses and not with them (see Blake's 'Vision of the Last Judgment', *CW*, p. 617), the last judgement would have come. I really think that Berdyaev's view is as radically uncommonsensical as Blake's here, but there are differences. The improvement of sensual enjoyment will not help, although creative acts of the spirit will. It is time to return to the words of Berdyaev to fill in the details of this idea as far as we can.

One thing that Berdyaev says which strikes me as a false start is:

> If intuitive knowledge is possible, it cannot be purely intellectual, it can only be integral, concrete, that is to say it must also be emotional and volitional. Thinking and knowing are always emotional, and the emotional is the deciding element.
>
> (*BE*, p. 14)

By 'intuition' here Berdyaev means (as the context shows) something which does the same trick as Kantian 'intellectual intuition' – that is to say, knowledge of the noumena – although Kant, of course, thinks that human beings cannot have such intellectual intuition. Berdyaev thinks that we can have intuition of the noumena, without sensory input, although not without emotion and volition. (He has just said 'It is a curious thing that in the denial of the possibility of intellectual contemplation without external sensations, in the recognition of such a possibility only for higher beings than man, Kant was akin to Thomas Aquinas.' This is meant as a criticism of Kant. Of course, for Kant 'intuition' meant any apprehension of external reality, the only form for us being sense-perception. 'Intuition' for him has none of the mysterious connotations that it has acquired in popular usage – although doubtless it does for Berdyaev.)

The odd thing that Berdyaev says here is 'the emotional is the deciding element'. He is quite right that 'Thinking and knowledge are always emotional'. Every thought carries with it an emotion, just as every emotion carries with it a thought. Thought and emotion can be distinguished analytically, like shape and colour, but they can never be experienced separately. However, when we are talking about the intuition of noumena, we are talking about knowing something that is independent of oneself. To say that in this intuition emotion is the decisive element is like saying that it is the fear, not the sight of a fierce dog, that tells us that there is a fierce dog. Of course, someone with a phobia of dogs may feel fear when they see a perfectly friendly pet dog, and the fear may evoke the judgement 'that is a fierce dog'. But here we are talking precisely about subjectivity in the bad sense. If intuition is cognition of noumena and is emotional as well as cognitive, it must surely be cognition by virtue of being cognitive, not by virtue of being emotive. In some places, Berdyaev says that what reveals the world of noumena to us is 'moral experience'. This sounds like an only slightly deviant Kantian: Kant thought that he could learn something about the noumenal world by asking how morality is possible; one might ask instead how moral experience is possible. But, for the Kantian, moral experience would be the experiences of reverence for the moral law and moral struggle against one's inclinations. I think that Berdyaev's moral experience is something much wider. It includes the struggle to make moral sense of the universe – the sort of moral experience expressed in the conversations of Ivan and Alyosha Karamazov in Dostoevsky's novel. Whether the universe does make moral sense is, of course, itself a moot point.

Now I turn to two longer passages in which Berdyaev lays out what he takes objectification (and its opposite) to be:

> There is a tendency in the reason to turn everything into an object from which the existentiality disappears. . . . The thing-in-itself is not an object or a 'non-I', it is a subject, or 'Thou'. . . . Objectification and the unauthentic character of the phenomenal world are by no means to be taken as meaning that the world of men and women, animals, plants, minerals, stars, seas, forests and so on is unreal and that behind it is something entirely unlike it – the things-in-themselves. It means rather that this world is in a spiritual and moral condition in which it ought not to be, it is in a state of servitude and loss of freedom, of enmity and alienation, of ejection into the external, of subjection to necessity.
>
> (*BE*, pp. 59–60)

What are the marks of objectification, and the rise of object relations in the world? The following signs may be taken as established: (1) the estrangement of the object from the subject; (2) the absorption of the unrepeatably individual and personal in what is common and impersonally universal; (3) the rule of necessity, of determination from without, the crushing of freedom and the concealment of it; and (4) adjustment to the grandiose mien of the world and of history, to the average man, and the socialization of man and his opinions, which destroys distinctive character. In opposition to all this stand communion in sympathy and love, and the overcoming of estrangement; personalism and the expression of the individual and personal character of each existence; a transition to the realm of freedom and determination from within, with victory over enslaving necessity; and the predominance of quality over quantity, of creativeness over adaptation. This is at the same time a definition of the distinction between the noumenal and the phenomenal world. Phenomenon and noumenon are settled by the process of objectification. The fight against the power of objectification is a spiritual revolt of noumena against phenomena, it is a spiritual revolution.

(*BE*, p. 62)

It seems from this that Berdyaev holds: (A) that the only reality consists of persons, 'Thous', yet (B) that the world of 'nature' is real too, and so presumably is, in its reality as opposed to its appearance, personal. In this connection it is worth quoting what Berdyaev says in another place, which even begins to take leave of metaphysics for frank superstition: 'nature is not a mechanism but a hierarchy of spirits' (*Freedom and the Spirit*, p. 298). Our moral or spiritual or existential fall (which is communal, not merely individual) makes us see nature and people in universal and deterministic terms rather than in particular and personalistic terms. It is rather like a Heideggerian critique of inauthentic '*mitsein*', combined with Blake's contrast between scientific and poetic ways of seeing nature:

Error, or Creation, will be Burned up, & then, & not till Then, Truth or Eternity will appear. It is Burned up the Moment Men cease to behold it. I assert for My Self that I do not behold the outward Creation & that to me it is hindrance & not Action; it is as the Dirt upon my feet, No part of Me. 'What,' it will be Question'd, 'When the Sun rises, do you not see a round disk of fire somewhat like a Guinea?' O no, no, I see an Innumerable company of the Heavenly host crying 'Holy, Holy, Holy is the Lord God Almighty.' I question not my Corporeal or Vegetative eye any more than I would question a Window concerning a Sight. I look thro' it & not with it.

('A Vision of the Last Judgment', in *CW*, p. 617)

Yet one cannot help feeling that two things are being conflated by Berdyaev here: the Blakean thing of appearance and reality affecting all knowledge, and the Heideggerian thing of authentic or inauthentic existence, referring to the way we live our lives and relate to our kind. His polemic against both the depersonalising of human relationships and the '*entzauberung*' of nature could be made within an entirely realist account of the phenomenal world, but instead he casts it in terms of two totally different worlds that we could exist in, according to whether we know noumena or phenomena. However, he is not only talking about knowledge:

> The fundamental question is this: does the conversion of 'things-in-them-selves' into 'appearances' take place in the process of knowledge and arise from it, or does it precede all cognition and occur within the actual 'things-in-themselves', in the primary reality itself, in existence itself, and is merely reflected in cognition? If the world is in a fallen state, the fault does not lie in men's apprehension of the world, as Shestov, for instance, would have it. The fault lies in the depths of the world's existence.
>
> (*BE*, p. 67)

> It is a mistake to think that objectification occurs only in the sphere of knowledge. It takes place above all in 'being', in reality itself. The subject introduces it, and does so not only as that which knows but also as that which exists.
>
> (*BE*, p. 78)

The fall is not at root a cognitive fall; it is tempting here to recall that Berdyaev was a Christian and to interpret fallenness as the fall of the creation away from the Creator who intended it to be a world of free persons in communion within a cosmos, not a world of alienation and slavery. But then we want to know why Berdyaev introduces it in terms of the appearance/reality opposition which belongs to epistemology and clearly treats some forms of cognition as guiltily implicated in the fall and others as conquests of it. For one can have a fully realist, non-Kantian theory of knowledge and still maintain the fallenness of humankind and creation generally, as all early and medieval Christian thought did. The answer perhaps comes in the next paragraph:

> When things-in-themselves have been turned into appearances, have they then ceased to exist, has the noumenal world finally gone away into the phenomenal world? Such an exhaustion of noumena in the disclosure of phenomena is not to be supposed. . . . We could more easily picture it as the passage of the noumenal subject-entities through a process of split-ting, division into two, alienation. This is a suggestion which implies a particular kind of cognition to correspond with it. Consciousness and cognition pass through the division into subject and object, but the primary reality does not on that account cease to exist and does not finally lose the possibility of a return to unity and relationship.
>
> (*BE*, pp. 67–68)

In other words, the fall splits the original world into two, a noumenal world that retains its original characteristics and a phenomenal world that re-duplicates it in an alienated form; we live for the most part in the latter and most forms of knowledge are knowledge of it. However, knowledge of the unfallen world is possible and liberates us from the fallen one. It is Platonism with the signs reversed: universality and necessity characterise the fallen phenomenal world, not the unfallen real one. What is still not quite clear is whether the phenomenal world exists anywhere but in our consciousness or knowledge. The idea that objectification takes place in being, not in knowledge, suggests that it does; but the use of the word 'phenomenal' suggests that it does not. Some light is thrown on the matter by the following paragraph:

> Different relations among men, a high degree of spiritual community among them and a lofty sense of their brotherhood would create a different world, another world would disclose itself to men. One single 'objective' world does not exist, it is nothing but social adjustment. Various worlds have already been revealed to various types of culture in the past and they have been revealed in various ways. The world presented itself in different ways to Hellenism, Judaism, to the Persians and the Indians. The criteria adopted by general consent for the establishment of truth, of which great use has been made by socialized religion and its armoury of theologies, are not criteria of truth, they are merely standards of what is useful for society.
>
> (*BE*, p. 71)

On the surface, this looks like a strong programme in the sociology of knowledge, and so it is so far as 'objectified' knowledge, knowledge of the phenomenal world, is concerned. Berdyaev avoids relativism only by saying that, in addition to, and in conflict with, all such knowledge, there is the noumenal knowledge provided by intuition, made possible by the fact that 'man is a microcosm', although 'only potentially and as a possibility, in a deep-lying stratum of his being which is in the case of the majority of people covered up and compressed' (p. 76). This knowledge is not relative. This explains the curious irony of Berdyaev's controversy with Lunacharsky and Bogdanov, when he was exiled with them to the far north of Russia for socialist agitation under the tsars. They were relativists in the sociology of knowledge and believed in 'class truth'; Berdyaev countered that there could be class untruth, as in the ideology of the exploiters, but no class truth. All three thought that this showed that Berdyaev was an idealist moving away from Marxism, while Bogdanov and Lunacharsky were materialists. Yet Marx shared Berdyaev's opinion here and Lenin was to attack Bogdanov and Lunacharsky virulently for this departure from Marxist materialism. However, Berdyaev's position is not that of Marx and Lenin either, for they believed that we could acquire truth by ordinary (for instance, scientific) knowledge.

But in the passage about different world views Berdyaev is suggesting that, just as different cultures live with different relative knowledges, there could be a culture with real noumenal knowledge, and that this would be achieved as a result of a different sort of human community. Even relative knowledges, though, have their valuable place within the objectified world which they did not constitute, and they partake in some degree of real truth:

> Knowledge takes two directions and has a twofold significance; it is on the one hand an active break-through towards meaning and truth, as it rises above the world, and on the other hand it is adjustment to the world as we are given it, to dull social routine. But even when it is of that second type, knowledge is a reflection of the Logos, it is a descent of the Logos into the world. In that fact the source of the high achievement of science, and of its independence is to be found.
>
> (*BE*, p. 73)

The view is summarised in the following paragraph which brings out the full eschatological ('Blakean') dimension to Berdyaev's thought, his idea that, given new human relations, the insights into things-in-themselves, which at present are rare and marginalised by socially constituted knowledge, could become available to all who would consequently live in a different world:

> A new aeon will come in which truth will be revealed to all, when all will pass through the experience of shock, not only the living, but still more those who have died. But in this era of ours, in this objectified, objective world, philosophy in a universal and healthy sense, discovers, not truth, but the socialization of truth, it discovers the necessary thing, that which is needful and useful for the life of society. The objectified world, the world of phenomena, is not conditioned by the individual reason, nor by divine reason, nor by individual, universal, general sensitiveness, but by socialized reason and socialized sensitiveness. The objectified world, which is regarded uncritically as the 'objective' world is conditioned by the transcendentally social.
>
> (*BE*, p. 72)

The allusion here is to Kant, and Berdyaev is among those who want to read social relativism into him: human understanding and sensibility, which impose their phenomenal form on all knowledge, are not universal but socially relative; however, a society that was built on free communion, not oppression, would not impose such a phenomenal form, but give us access to the noumenal world. Here a millennial religious theory of the end of history takes over from Kant, for even transience and death (as well as causal necessity) seem to be conquered in this noumenal world.

What are we to say about this theory of objectification? In the first place, I think it underestimates science. It does not, as we might expect, deprecate science, but it does depreciate it. It grants it the valuable role of giving us knowledge of the objectified world in which we live and thus enabling us to cope with that world. This project even participates in the 'Logos'. But Berdyaev does seem to deny the capacity of science to go beneath appearances, not indeed to noumena, but to underlying realities that we did not put there, but that can be known by us. And in underestimating science it also underestimates nature. Science can surprise us about nature, reveal unexpected depths to nature. The nature that science studies and the nature that romanticism loves are not two but one and the same. Much that is moving about nature would not have been known but for science, and nothing would be moving about nature were nature not something that existed in itself, independently of us, yet could be explored by us – the same characteristics that make it the proper subject of science. One could not be a Kantian and have a real feeling for nature.

Further, by underestimating nature's autonomy, Berdyaev commits himself to an unrealistic notion of human freedom. Freedom is not objectified into natural necessity, it is emergent from natural necessity. Every single instance of free human action shows that, for it takes into account known natural necessities and seeks its ends by or in spite of them. It is his failure to recognise this that makes possible his wild voluntarism, which a theologian would call Pelagian and a Marxist would call utopian, which projects a new world (of nature as well as society) as a result of changing human choices and attitudes and ways of relating. Even in a world that was communist enough for William Morris and Christian enough for St Francis, there would be old age and disease, transience and death, unrequited love and mental anguish. I should mention in passing here that this metaphysical overestimation of freedom links up with one of Berdyaev's most speculative and incredible doctrines – namely, the notion of 'meonic freedom' and the idea that freedom precedes being. Other existentialists too have argued that freedom involves the presence of nothingness or negative existence in the world, but Berdyaev links this with a primordial nothingness pre-existing creation, somehow incorporated into creation, as if nothingness were not an absence of being but some sort of substance, like anti-matter. And as to freedom preceding being, surely freedom has to be some being's freedom?

At the same time, there is much that can be salvaged from Berdyaev's metaphysics. He is right to combine a relativist account of historical world views with an anti-relativist account of truth; he is right to object to the sway of quantitative, mechanical and atomistic thinking; he is right to see in the sociology of knowledge a potential critique of social conformism; the ethical commitment to human emancipation and recognition of the irreplaceable individuality in the natural as well as the human world which underlies his metaphysics is admirable.

His chief failing seems to me to be an inability to value one thing over another without making claims that the valued thing is prior to or more real than the less valued thing. Of course, the whole Judaeo-Christian tradition holds that the highest good, God, is prior to and more real than all lower beings. But that is quite compatible with recognising the regional priority of the lower goods. St Thomas Aquinas had no problems recognising that our knowledge of material things precedes our knowledge of God.

It is basically this lack of a reality-principle that explains why someone as insightful in ethical matters as Berdyaev could go so far wrong in metaphysics.

§9 Sartre: the other as subject and as object

The initial quote from Marx suggests that, for a certain anti-objective outlook, all relations between people are degrading, because to make the other an object in the sense of an intentional (or even grammatical) object is to treat them as if they were an object in the sense of a non-conscious, mechanically determined entity. In *The Transcendence of the Ego* Sartre seems to have bypassed this pitfall, for he recommends that 'the subject–object duality, which is purely logical, definitively disappear from philosophical preoccupations' (p. 105). By 'purely logical' he may mean grammatical or concerned with intentional objecthood; at any rate he means not ontological. But in *Being and Nothingness* (hereafter *BN*) subject and object are again ontological categories and mutually exclusive ones. One of the things going on in the part of that book called 'Being for Others' is a conflation of intentional objects with ontological objects. And the pessimistic conclusions of the chapter 'Concrete Relations with Others' could, perhaps, have been avoided if Sartre had recognised, as Marx does, the possibility of a 'good objectification' – that is, making another person an intentional object and causally affecting them without degrading them by treating them as a subhuman being. Let us consider how the argument of that chapter works.

Section II of Sartre's chapter 'Concrete Relations with Others' concludes with a footnote:

> These considerations do not exclude the possibility of an ethics of deliverance and salvation. But this can be achieved only after a radical conversion which we can not discuss here.
>
> (*BN*, p. 412)

This footnote highlights a problem about the whole chapter in which it appears. If authentic relations with others are possible, why can't Sartre discuss them here? After all, *BN* is supposed to be an ontological enquiry into the structures of the for-itself (i.e. free, conscious agents – people). Sartre has just described a number of kinds of relation between people that are doomed to failure. If people can relate to each other in ways that are not doomed to failure, we would like to hear about it. The reader suspects that

Sartre cannot talk about such relations because he has presented a general account of human relations that makes authentic, non-doomed ones a priori impossible. In this section I am asking whether he has, in fact, done so or not.

In 'Concrete Relations with Others', Sartre seems to give two sorts of reason why relations with people fail. First, there is an a priori reason, which seems to admit no exceptions. 'The Other holds a secret – the secret of what I am' (*BN*, p. 364). Relations between people are a series of attempts to wrest that secret from the other. One's identity is always at a distance from one, since it is necessarily conferred by the other and the other's consciousness is always opaque to one. It is opaque, not because of the traditional Cartesian problem of other minds, but because the other is always free and so can transform one's identity in unpredictable ways at any moment. To wrest this secret, one has to reduce the other to a predictable object of knowledge. But if one could do so, the other as subject, who alone could confer identity on one, disappears. Sometimes it appears that Sartre is simply conflating two senses of 'object' here; that he is assuming that, in making the other one's intentional object, by perceiving, knowing, loving, hating or desiring the other, one also reduces them to an object in the sense of something less than a free human agent. But there is more to it than this.

Sartre shares with many analytical philosophers of mind the idea that there is an essential difference between predicting and deciding – that one cannot normally (Sartre would say not ever) predict one's own future actions. This is brought out by a contrast with Schopenhauer, one of the few philosophers who thought that intending to do something really is nothing but predicting that one will do it. Schopenhauer mentions a murderer who begged the court to sentence him to death because he knew that if he were ever released he would kill again. Schopenhauer sees this as an insightful recognition of his own unchangeable essence. Sartre would see it as bad faith. The murderer could choose not to kill again, but is deciding against that choice by 'predicting' that he will remain a murderer. The bad faith lies in the pretence that the decision is a prediction.

However, Sartre goes further along this road. Not only is predicting one's own future in bad faith, even describing one's own present is, for we freely intend what we are as well as what we will do. One can, of course, without bad faith describe one's facticity – one's appearance, social standing, state of physical health, and so on, but not one's emotions, thoughts, etc. Sartre – himself no mean diarist – tells us in *The Transcendence of the Ego* that: 'Doubts, remorse, the so-called 'mental crises of consciousness', etc. – in short, all the content of intimate diaries – become sheer *performance*' (p. 94). The surrealist who describes his or her innermost fantasies in order afterwards to act them out is in bad faith; they are choosing those fantasies in the act of 'describing' them.

We can, however, predict the future actions and describe the present emotions of others, but in doing so we degrade the other's possibilities to probabilities. A possibility for Sartre is always something that can be freely laid hold of. But our relation to others' possibilities is not, of course, that we can lay hold of them, but that we can know them. Since they are free possibilities we cannot know them with certainty, but we can calculate with them as probabilities. But this attitude of knowledge towards the other person is incompatible with another experience we can have of the other. This is described in the famous passage on being caught looking through the keyhole of a hotel room (*BN*, p. 259). One does not have knowledge of the other person who catches one; rather, they are experienced in the collapse of one's own project of seeing what is going on in the bedroom and the sudden sense of one's own visibility. One experiences oneself as an object for the other. But if one were to turn on the other and look at them in turn, their objectifying look would collapse; one cannot see the look, one can see 'only eyes'. One experiences the other, not in knowledge of their probabilities, but in the collapse of one's own possibilities. Hence, Sartre sees the subject and object roles as mutually exclusive. I am reminded of some advice I read once on how to stop your boss telling you off: stare at his bald patch. As he goes into object position, his subjectness collapses and he can no longer make one an object.

Hence, Sartre tells us that relations with others are in large part a set of ruses to make the other remain an object. These manipulative relations with others are not however, the relations that Sartre discusses in 'Concrete Relations with Others', for in that chapter he is talking about relations that precisely depend on the other's subject role. They depend on it to constitute one's own identity, but at the same time they violate it in grasping that constituting freedom as object. Hence, their doom to failure. All this looks a priori and inescapable. So does that failure of the second attitude to others discussed in the following quote (which is the first attitude to be discussed by Sartre at length in the text):

> the profound meaning of my being is outside of me, imprisoned in an absence. The Other has an advantage over me. . . . I can attempt to deny that being which is conferred on me from outside; that is, I can turn back upon the Other so as to make an object of him since the Other's object-ness destroys my object-ness for him. But, on the other hand, in so far as the Other as freedom is the foundation of my being-in-itself, I can seek to recover that freedom and possess it without removing from it its character as freedom. In fact if I could identify myself with that freedom which is the foundation of my being-in-itself, I should be to myself my own foundation.
>
> (*BN*, p. 363)

Being one's own foundation is what one is after in both these attitudes, and of course it is impossible. The former attitude is, I think, slightly misdescribed by Sartre in this passage. The aim is not to destroy my own objectness, but to determine it. To do this, one must determine the conscious-ness of the other at the same time as that consciousness remains free. In the latter case, the aim is to let one's own consciousness be determined by the other – yet that letting remains a free act. For Sartre, freedom and deter-minedness are incompatible – hence both forms of attitude to others are impossible to realise a priori.

But when Sartre comes to discuss particular instances of these relations – sadism and masochism and love and hate and sexual desire – he gives different reasons why they fail and in each case contingent ones. The sadist can never completely control the victim's consciousness, it always escapes him or her; hate issues in murder, which leaves the other with no consciousness with which to confer being on one; masochism generates a contradiction between the active role needed to satisfy the desire and the passivity of the satisfaction: one is reminded of the scene in the film *Belle de Jour* in which the inexperienced part-time prostitute does not know how to satisfy the masochist who eventually complains angrily to the madame that this stupid whore cannot humiliate him properly. But, while there is at least a paradox in this case, there seems to be no a priori reason why a masochist should not find satisfaction without 'objectifying' their partner in a happy story of sadist meets masochist. In the case of love, the grounds of its necessary failure are more complex. At the end of the discussion, Sartre sums up the 'triple destructibility of love', the first point being that to love is to wish the other to love oneself and this is implausibly deemed to generate a regress; the second point is that the other may always 'awake' and make me appear as an object, whereas what I want to be is the other's whole world. This, however, looks like a danger rather than an impossibility. The same goes for the third point – that there are people other than the two lovers who may always intrude. Earlier he makes the more psychologically insightful claims that we always want to see our love as at once fated and free, and the other's commitment as at once pledged for all time and free. Here, however, he uncharacteristically gives us a form of love that would not be in bad faith to compare it with, while pointing out that we would find it unsatisfactory:

> Who would be content with a love given as pure loyalty to a sworn oath? Who would be satisfied with the words 'I love you because I have freely engaged myself to love you and because I do not wish to go back on my word'. Thus the lover demands a pledge, yet is irritated by the pledge. He wants to be loved by a freedom but demands that this freedom as freedom should no longer be free.
>
> (BN, p. 367)

At the same time Sartre calls this unsatisfying pledge 'that superior form of freedom which is a free and voluntary engagement'. And Sartre does not consider the possibility that what may be unsatisfactory about the avowal of the pledge is not the pledge that it avows, but the fact that stating the pledge in this form strongly suggests that it is now renewed only as an unwelcome duty.

As to sexual desire, Sartre thinks that this necessarily fails for a reason that has nothing to do with bad faith: because it comes to an end when satisfied, yet what had been desired was not satisfaction in the sense of detumescence, but the couple's becoming wholly flesh. But this is not failure, merely transitoriness.

Only the accounts of sadism and the ambivalence about the pledge in love look like instances of the a priori reason for failure in human relationships, as opposed to examples of contingent failure. And in the case of love, the reference to a superior form of engagement suggests a form of love which, if unsatisfactory to unregenerate humanity, is nevertheless possible and escapes inevitable failure. After all, the form of love described in the text does have some odd features. It is regarded as usual for the woman in love to demand 'that the beloved in his acts should sacrifice traditional morality for her, and is anxious to know whether the beloved would betray his friends for her, "would steal for her", "would kill for her", etc.' (*BN*, p. 369). One wonders which women Sartre knew who made such demands: not Simone de Beauvoir, that's for sure. And in the case of sadism, it may be that the kind that Sartre discusses is not typical; a sadist might not care that the victim is having free thoughts about him, just so long as that victim is suffering.

And indeed, if failure is a priori necessary, Sartre has argued himself into a blind alley, for pursuit of inevitable failure is for him a form of bad faith or 'vice' and, if we are to avoid bad faith, as Sartre clearly thinks we should, such an assumption would lead to the conclusion that we should all become either hermits or the sort of 'practical solipsist' that is purely manipulative in relation to others (see the account of indifference as an attitude to others, pp. 380–82).

I think we may be able to take the question further by looking at Sartre's play *Huis clos*. (I use the French title, not out of pretentiousness, but because there are three English translations, all with different titles. I quote from the translation titled *In Camera*.) *Huis clos* takes place in hell where, due to the rationalisation of demonic resources, people are no longer tortured but selected to torture each other mentally by the way that they interact. Three people are placed in a room together, furnished in Second Empire style, with no mirrors and with the central heating turned up too high. Their stories come out slowly in the course of the play. Inez (actually Inès, in French) was a lesbian who had had an affair with a married woman. The husband was run over and killed by a tram, and Inez's lover turned the gas on one night and gassed both of them. Estelle was a married woman who had had an affair with another man, had his baby and murdered it. Her lover committed suicide. Garcin had been the editor of a pacifist newspaper. When war came, he enlisted, then deserted. He was caught at the frontier and shot. He says he is in hell because of the lousy way he treated his wife, but he is obsessed with the question of whether he acted on principle or out of cowardice. Inez wants to make love to Estelle, but she also rather relishes the role of torturer that they have been assigned. She despises Garcin. Estelle despises Inez, partly because Inez is working class and Estelle is a snob. She wants Garcin's love, not because she loves him, but so that he can confer on her a different identity than that of child-killer. Garcin wants confirmation that he is not a coward. At one time he thinks he can get this from Estelle if he makes love to her, but it becomes clear that she will say anything she thinks he wants to hear and he loses interest. It is the intelligent and hard-bitten Inez that he must convince – all an excellent recipe for mutual mental torture.

However, the question arises whether *any* three people placed in a room would create such a hell. Sartre has been accused of adapting to convention by placing in hell people whom the popular imagination would place there, when in fact any three people would do. Take a hero of the resistance who has been shot for refusing to betray his comrades, a mother who has died saving her child's life, and a nun who has stayed in a plague-ridden town to nurse the victims and has herself died of the plague. Place them together in a room, even with a palatable alternative to Second Empire furniture and with the need of each to wrest from the others the secret of what each is, combined with the fact that any relation between any two of them will be under the eyes of the third, they will make their own hell. If the a priori account is correct, this would work, and indeed constitute a transcendental argument for the impossibility of heaven, since God himself could not make free beings abstain from mutual torture.

However, there are clues in the play that this criticism does not strike home. When Inez is trying to seduce Estelle, she says twice of Garcin 'he doesn't count'; when Estelle is trying to seduce Garcin, she says of Inez 'she doesn't count, she's a woman' and again 'Don't listen to her. She has no eyes, no ears. She's – nothing.' Later Garcin says of Estelle to Inez 'she doesn't count. It's you who matter; you who hate me. If you'll have faith in me I'm saved.' Of course, each is trying to neutralise the third so as to win over the other. To that extent this is simply an effect of there being three in the room. However, one should not place too much weight on the conventional wisdom of 'two's company, three's a crowd', here. Even from the point of view of sexual relations, there is no a priori necessity that these involve precisely two people; there are such things as threesomes. Aside from this, it would be possible, given goodwill, for one to go and stare into the corner to give the other two a time of privacy. Rather, the claim that someone does not count typifies an attitude of indifference to the others' possibilities on the part of each of them. Even the one to whom each is trying to relate is treated with complete disregard for what possibilities they themselves are projecting. And this inability to allow the others to have their possibilities means that each, to an extent, loses their own possibilities for there are for them no free beings to engage with. Hence, each remains obsessed with what they were, rather than with what they still could be. Of course, this could be seen as a feature of their situation as dead. As Inez puts it: 'One always dies too soon – or too late. And yet one's whole life is complete at that moment, with a line drawn neatly under it, ready for the summing up. You are – your life, and nothing else' (*In Camera*, p. 189). This is indeed Sartre's own account of death. As long as one is alive, one has no essence for one always has an open future. With death the future is closed and one acquires an essence. But this is part of Sartre's philosophy which precludes life after death; in the fictional context, these characters' futures are not closed, since they are conscious and make free choices. Yet by these choices they treat their futures as closed. Garcin's question is '*Was* I a coward or not?'; it does not occur to him that it is open to him *now* to act in a cowardly or a courageous fashion. Inez says 'I'm cruel . . . I can't get on without making people suffer'. She is describing herself as cruel 'as an inkwell is an inkwell'. But no one is cruel like that. They are cruel by repeatedly making cruel choices – as Inez continues to do throughout the play. But she makes cruel choices in bad faith, by continually acting as though there were no choice but cruelty, since that is her essence. Estelle wants to be what she was before she killed her baby. She reminisces about her youthful admirer who called her his glancing stream, his crystal girl. She sees him on Earth being told by her erstwhile friend what she has done, having his illusions shattered, and she hates it. She has no thought that she can become something else now. It is this closing of their own futures, a free act in bad faith, that creates hell for the trio.

The play is often said to end with the conclusion: 'Hell is other people' (*l'enfer, c'est les Autres*). Actually, that is not quite the end – there is a brief half-page of action after it. Estelle stabs Inez with a paper-knife. Inez responds: 'What do you think you're doing? You know quite well I'm dead' (*In Camera*, p. 191). They all laugh as their post-mortality dawns on them. Then Garcin concludes: 'Well, well, let's get on with it . . .' (*Eh bien, continuons . . .*). An ambiguous ending, I think. Does he mean: 'Let's go on torturing each other like we've been doing' or does he mean: 'We've got all eternity to make a different life of it'? If the laughter signifies a sudden realisation of their freedom and of the bad faith that was wasting their freedom, the room might cease to be hell, even with Second Empire furniture and the central heating turned up too high.

And here the question of what would have come of the other trio, the three heroes, in a similar plight, can perhaps be answered. In so far as their heroic choices on Earth showed a freedom from bad faith, a recognition of their freedom for an open future, their threesome need not be hell. Of course, if they were as obsessed with their past good deeds as Sartre's trio were with their past bad deeds, if they took those deeds to constitute their essence, then they would doubtless create just a different kind of hell – a self-righteous hell. The conclusion should be, not 'hell is other people' but 'hell is a closed future'.

Now to return to *Being and Nothingness*: reading between the lines, I think it is obvious what sort of ethic 'of deliverance and salvation' Sartre wants to get out of his ontology. He would like to show that we can only realise our own freedom through the freedom of others, so that the freedom of others is not an obstacle to but a condition of our own. How does recognising our own and others' open futures help here? Perhaps it enables us to take the identity conferred by the others whatever it is – recognising on the one hand that the other is always free to change that identity, and on the other that I am always escaping from it through my own free projection of possibilities. The identity conferred by others, in so far as it is welcome, is then accepted as a grace rather than pursued as a goal. But it is also recognised as transient. Meanwhile, one confers their identity on others in the same spirit. Mutual 'objectification' or the conferring of identities still goes on, but it is no longer self-referential, no longer motivated by the identity we expect to receive back; it is no longer a relationship of purchase, but of the exchange of gifts. One confers identity and has identity conferred on one, but one does not confer identity in order to have identity conferred on one. And what if the identity the other confers is an unwelcome one? Sartre recounts how, after his exposure of the Soviet labour camps in his journal, the French Communist Party, to which he was in many ways quite friendly, began to vilify him: 'Their insults didn't bother me in the least: rat, hyena, viper, polecat – I rather liked this bestiary. It took me out of myself' (*Situations*, p. 270). That is the attitude of one who does not allow his future to be closed by the identities conferred on him by others.

§10 Laing: appearance, objectivity and liberation

To many of us who read Laing's works in the 1960s, they came as a revelation, and a liberating revelation. They explained much that had seemed inexplicable and they were liberating quite simply by virtue of their explanations. How is it that explanation can be liberating?

If knowledge or understanding replaced simple ignorance, we would not describe it as liberating. It might enable us to do something we could not do before, but that is not what we mean by 'liberation'. It might assist us in some struggle for liberation from oppression, but in that case the understanding is a means to a liberation that is yet to be won. We only say that understanding is of itself liberating when it replaces some *misunderstanding* that was enslaving us.

In fact, most increments of knowledge are like that, as has long been recognised by those who linked the project of science to that of human liberation. Thus Bacon:

> On waxen tablets you cannot write anything new until you rub out the old. With the mind it is not so; there you cannot rub out the old till you have written in the new.
>
> (From 'The Masculine Birth of Time',
> in Farrington (ed.), *The Philosophy of*
> *Francis Bacon*, p. 72)

And thus Marx:

> Scientific truth is always paradox, if judged by everyday experience, which catches only the delusive appearance of things.
>
> (From 'Wages, Price and Profit', in
> *Selected Works in One Volume*, p. 209)

If we ask: how is it possible that an increment of understanding should itself be liberating, the answer must be that this is so because appearances are deceptive and the deception is enslaving. The possibility of liberating knowledge depends on the distinction between appearance and reality, and the possibility that we can go beyond, explain and correct the data of appearance. The knowledge or understanding that liberates is necessarily that which is *counter-phenomenal*, contrary to appearances.

This brings us to a paradox in Laing's thought. For his chosen philosophical method is *phenomenology*: etymologically, 'the science of appearances'. Of course, phenomenology as a philosophical movement has often meant more and often less than that, but it has never lost touch with this meaning. Can a study that restricts itself to appearances be liberating? It can certainly be useful, even an essential preliminary to a liberating science: we need to know what the appearances are before looking beneath them. Furthermore, phenomenology has made a valuable contribution by directing attention to intentional objectivity in an age when reflexive objectivity has been the fashion: it speaks of things as experienced by us, rather than our experiences of things. But liberation starts, not with the phenomenological preliminary, but with the counter-phenomenal investigation.

Philosophers in the phenomenological movement have sometimes limited themselves to such a modest preliminary task. Often, however, they have practised what might be called militant phenomenology – refusing to admit that science can find anything beneath the appearances and providing purely phenomenological explanations as an *alternative* to scientific ones that might have been counter-phenomenal.

One might expect such phenomenology to be inherently conservative, imprisoning us in the world of appearances. In fact, however, phenomenologists have been radically critical of the 'common-sense' view of the world.

In Heidegger's account of phenomenology in the introduction to *Being and Time*, he distinguishes 'phenomenon' in the sense he uses it – 'that which shows itself' – from 'appearance' in senses in which there is a contrast with something that does not appear – that is, first, from *semblance*; second, from cases where something that does not appear 'announces itself' in something that does (for instance, disease in a symptom); and third, from the Kantian sense, in which an appearance is of something that can never appear (the 'thing in itself' or noumenon). Yet 'phenomenon' does contrast with something:

> 'Behind' the phenomena of phenomenology there is essentially nothing else; on the other hand, what is to become a phenomenon can be hidden. And just because the phenomena are proximally and for the most part *not* given, there is a need for phenomenology. Covered-up-ness is the counter-concept to 'phenomenon'.
>
> (*Being and Time*, p. 60)

Phenomenology, then, has the task of making things show themselves that were previously covered up. That looks like the sort of understanding that can liberate, in just the way that science, as counter-phenomenal, can do so. Yet Heidegger is reluctant to allow *science* its appearance/reality distinction.

Indeed, he tends to invert the relation as usually conceived between scientific and pre-scientific knowledge, treating scientific results, despite – or perhaps because of – the fact that they are the product of a laborious work of uncovering, as merely subjective, and as tending to cover up Being, to which the knowledge that is implicit in everyday practice gives us genuine access.

Despite analysing what is closest to us, Heidegger, in fact, sees his analysis of Being-in-the-world as running against the difficulty that our world has been preinterpreted to us in terms of something that is existentially further from us – the world of mechanically related objects. In the world that is closest to us – the work-world that we inhabit prior to theoretical explanations – the hammer is encountered as that with which we fix the shutter, which in turn is that with which we make the dwelling weatherproof. This world is a whole composed of the gear we use and structured by its reference back to some projected being of ours. Only when the head flies off the hammer are we forced to consider it as an entity with properties other than being-hammerable-with. So begins 'objective' theoretical inquiry, of which the sciences are instances. And we habitually misread our lived world as being like the 'objective' reality thus discovered. (I put 'objective' in quotes not because I don't think it is objective, but because I think the work-world that Heidegger describes is objective too.) Heidegger has done valuable work in correcting such misreadings, which have abounded in the empiricist tradition of philosophy (sense data, knowledge of other minds as inferential, action as intentional muscular contractions, and so on).

But since, on Heidegger's own account, the function of theoretical inquiry is to put to rights some upset that has occurred in the everyday work-world, that inquiry must, in some respects at least, produce more adequate ideas than the phenomenological understanding implicit in the work-world did. The work-world understanding of the hammer as 'ready-to-hand' is indeed an appearance, not in the sense of being false, but of being partial. The understanding of the hammer in its construction out of iron and wood (which the theoretical inquiry gives us) is also true and needs to be brought into account if the hammer is going to get mended and the shutter-fixing restarted. So, what is it that is mistaken about our interpretation of the work-world along the lines of the 'objective' world of science?

Well, the 'objective' interpretation really does fall into error if it treats 'Being-in-the-world', the work-world and the human world generally, as related to the world of wood and iron and skin and bone and muscle and blood as *an appearance to its reality*. For the human world too has its structures – that of the work-world described by Heidegger, that of families described by Laing, that of societies described by Marx, and many others – which structures do not necessarily appear, and which explain appearances. In other words, the appearance/reality distinction is not the same as the human world/natural world distinction, but rather cuts across it. There are breakdowns in the human world that, like the headless hammer, motivate objective inquiry – not, however, into the natural world (in the sense of the non-humanly-structured world, including human physiology), but into the underlying structures of the human world itself.

The writings of Laing and his collaborators on social phenomenology are among the best places to study the openings that such a phenomenology can give to objective inquiry into the human world – inquiry that will not explain it away as an appearance of the natural world, but open up its own deep structures that explain its appearances. (I am thinking in particular of the books *The Self and Others*; *Sanity, Madness and the Family*; *Interpersonal Perception*; and *The Politics of the Family*.)

For Laing's phenomenology is *social* phenomenology – for the most part, the study of people's appearances to each other. And since people appear differently to others than to themselves, and differently again to different others, there is here no seamless web of incorrigible appearances, but *contradictions*, that in this instance, if no other, are contradictions both in the dialectical sense (antagonisms between mutually dependent elements of a structure that at once make the structure the one that it is and disrupt it), and in the logical sense (beliefs – or emotions and perceptions presupposing beliefs – that make incompatible claims about the real world).

Here – in these contradictions – there is both the motive and the opportunity for enquiries that will liberate the participants (or at least the victims) of the group, by supplanting the various appearances with a more adequate – more objective – understanding of the group's structure. And such an enquiry is the only liberatory option here. The relativist exit – saying 'there is no objective truth, everyone's view is equally valid' – simply misdescribes the contradictions, for we do not understand what anyone is doing in believing something unless we recognise that they are making a claim about the world and implying the denial of all incompatible claims. To grant that a belief is 'valid' while granting equal 'validity' to incompatible claims, is simply to refuse to take it seriously as a belief – a supercilious insult, like whistling through an unwelcome contribution to a conversation. Micro-social contradictions can be resolved only by an understanding that disproves at least some of the beliefs it starts by describing. It is a matter of moving from appearances to the counter-phenomenal realities underlying them.

I think that the liberating understanding present in Laing's works of the 1960s was of the kind I have just described. Even in those works, militant phenomenology had a presence as a metatheory, which I have criticised elsewhere. In *The Voice of Experience* (1982) (hereafter *VE*) this tendency is more pronounced. In the following section I shall comment on the second chapter of that book, 'The Objective Look'.

In 'The Objective Look', Laing is attacking scientific understanding in the human world from the standpoint of militant phenomenology. I suggest that, if that attack were accepted, understanding would be restricted to appearances in such a way that it could never be the liberating kind of understanding. For he is attacking their 'objective look', the look that goes beyond appearances and uncovers the counter-phenomenal reality behind them. What he ought to be attacking is their identification of the human world with appearance and the natural world with objective reality. Instead, he works within the terms of that identification and defends the inviolability of appearance in the course of defending the irreducibility of the human world.

The problem emerges at the beginning of the chapter, in Laing's unclarity about what he means by 'object' and 'objective'. It is the by now familiar shifting between the older and philosophical sense of 'object' as intentional object and the popular sense of 'object' as a manipulable, less-than-human particular. The adjective 'objective' gets pulled into this equivocation.

Thus, when Laing says:

> To the purely objective point of view, everything is an object and the only real relations and correlations are objective ones
>
> (*VE*, p. 15)

– which sense does he mean? If 'object' means 'object of knowledge or experience', well, either everything can be made the object of knowledge or experience, or some things cannot. If everything can, then what are the objective lookers accused of missing? If some things cannot, then we may express ignorance or perhaps wonder at their 'mystery', but we cannot say anything about them, for we cannot substitute some other kind of awareness of them which does not 'objectify' them since, as soon as they are known or experienced, they would, by definition, be the 'objects' of that knowledge or experience. But if object is used in the other sense, then of course knowing objects is not knowing people, but no reason is given why we cannot also know people in a way that is objective in the usual sense – that is, independent of the knower's subjectivity. One could, of course, have knowledge of people considered purely as objects – their weight and spatial location, for instance. But there is no reason why equally objective facts, such as whether they love each other, should not be known as well.

Laing seems to deny this when he says 'objectively, there are no intentions' (*VE*, p. 28). This is playing his opponents' game. The behaviourist may study behaviour as if there were no intentions and the physicalist may relegate intentions to the world of appearance and regard brain-states as the underlying reality. But we are not obliged to accept such programmes by virtue of commitment to objectivity. We may wish, like Freud, to study intention objectively, to go beyond the apparent intention to the hidden intention underlying it, but perhaps contradicting it. We need the appearance/reality distinction *within* the human world. Laing is writing as though the only way to be objective about the human world is to reduce it to the world of natural science.

A word here about Laing's attitude in this text to natural science itself: at times he only seems to be saying that a cobbler should stick to his last, that the methods of natural science are fine so long as they don't encroach on the human world; but at times he seems to be saying that natural science itself is implicated in an objectionable attitude. He takes up Bacon on his metaphor of experiment as like judicial torture, forcing nature to give us information. Of course, Bacon as Lord Chancellor was no stranger to judicial torture, so the metaphor is bound to leave a nasty taste. Nevertheless, we should not extend the metaphor; Bacon only means that we have to set up situations that are not themselves natural (experiments) to find out how nature works. Nature cannot literally be tortured since it is not a sentient being. To us in the late twentieth and early twenty-first centuries, the metaphor suggests another meaning: the commercial abuse of nature, marring its beauty, reducing its fecundity and variety, and threatening its biogenic powers. But this flows not from the experiments of scientists but from the irresponsibility of commerce, combined with an ignorance of nature that only more and better science can overcome.

Of course, Laing is quite right that science does not of itself preclude its own abuse and that 'an experiment may be scientifically impeccable and spiritually foul' (*VE*, p. 22). But there is nothing peculiar about science that renders it especially liable to such callous abuse. Art fares no better: it is not so long ago that boys were castrated in the interests of music; the painter David sat sketching the last writhings of the victims of the September Massacres; animals have been killed and mutilated in the making of films; many great artists have been willing to sacrifice others as well as themselves to their art; envy and snobbery often poison the personal relations of artistic communities. Not that art, any more than science, fares particularly badly; the histories of religion, industry, politics, sport, sex, gastronomy, cosmetics, are full of cruelty and lies. Yet we should not reject them on that account, but try to purge them of the cruelty and lies. Likewise with science.

To return to the main argument: the chapter concludes with a list of emotions, values and purposes, and tells us: 'The natural scientist finds none of these things. Of course not! You cannot buy a camel in a donkey market' (*VE*, p. 34). But natural science makes no great issue of excluding these things; the donkey market has no taboos or sinister designs against camels; it is just that the camel market is down the road and round the corner; go there, and you will find camels. So what is Laing's complaint here?

I think it is that some methods in the human sciences imitate what are taken to be the methods of the natural sciences and, as a result, miss certain phenomena that are then claimed not to exist. Behaviourism is an obvious example and one that Laing uses. But the problem with behaviourism is not that it is objective in the sense of excluding subjectivity from the determinants of its work, but that it excludes subjectivity from the subject matter of its enquiry which, since subjectivity is there, makes behaviourism *less* objective than phenomenology or psychoanalysis that have no taboos when talking about 'subjectivity' in the sense of the first-person view. But militant phenomenology (which seems to be Laing's metatheory, although not Laing's social phenomenology which is his working theory) tends to limit itself to the first-person view, precluding the counter-phenomenality of psychoanalysis (or social phenomenology). The whole purpose of this section has been to defend the capacity of the human sciences to be counter-phenomenal without being reductive of the specifically human to the natural. The need to do so stems from Laing's tendency to slide between different senses of object and objectivity.

Instances of objectivity

§11 The objectivity of everyday knowledge

To defend objectivity in any area of knowledge is to defend a realist reading of that area. In the third part of this essay I will be defending realist readings of a variety of areas of knowledge. I start with the sort of knowledge which is prior to others, at least in time, for all of us: lay or everyday knowledge. There are scientific realists who are non-realists about everyday knowledge, who deny its objectivity. I think Althusser was one. Conversely, there are those who assert the objectivity of lay knowledge and deny that of science. Heidegger can be read that way. I do not address either of these contrasts directly, but argue separately for the objectivity of each of these two areas. The transcendental arguments for scientific realism are familiar from several texts of the critical realist philosophy to which I adhere; those for the objectivity of lay knowledge are perhaps less so.

I hope in this section to contribute to the opening up of this neglected area of critical realism. The theory of scientific knowledge has been well explored by critical realists, but critical realism does not, as some philosophies do, assimilate scientific and lay knowledge, or denigrate either of them. There is a place for a theory of lay knowledge in critical realism; Roy Bhaskar has said to me that transcendental arguments to realism need not be from the possibility of scientific experiment – they could be from the possibility of losing and finding the teabags. Yet this place for a theory of lay knowledge is still largely unoccupied. By 'lay knowledge' I mean, in the first place, all non-scientific knowledge, although a central place in this knowledge is held by the knowledge acquired by, and implicit in, our practical interaction with our environment.

Empiricism from the seventeenth to the nineteenth centuries typically assimilated the two sorts of knowledge. Its concentration on perception, of the 'just looking' kind, left out both the knowledge that was tacitly acquired by work, and the knowledge that is the intended product of cognitively oriented work. The significance of training and experiment in science was missed: in this way science was falsified by being assimilated to lay knowledge; and yet causes were understood from Hume on as constant conjunctions – 'whenever A happens, B happens' – although, in fact, constant conjunctions are rare outside situations set up by us for the purposes of scientific experiment. In this way, the lay knowledge of causes was misrepresented. Thus the 'actualism' that is characteristic of empiricism is a result of a theory which 'does the splits', keeping one foot in science and one in lay knowledge, misunderstanding both in the attempt to deny the difference.

Twentieth-century philosophy has begun to put this right as a result of two philosophical movements, largely independent of each other and sometimes mutually antagonistic. On the one hand, the philosophy of science has grown up as a separate discipline, stressing the distinctive nature of science and trying to develop an epistemology adequate to it. Popper, Bachelard, Kuhn, Lakatos and Harré (one might add Althusser) are not epistemologists in the general sense but philosophers of science, and in academic philosophy departments their works are unlikely to figure in the reading list of courses called 'epistemology', even though their works have been far more fruitful than those of epistemologists plodding on in the empiricist tradition. The founding works of critical realism belong in this tradition of philosophy of science.

But, on the other hand, there are philosophers who have pointed out how lay knowledge has been both misinterpreted by assimilating it to science and undervalued by comparison with science. Three names are enough to identify this tradition: John Macmurray in the UK, Heidegger in Germany and Merleau-Ponty in France. If we need a label for this kind of philosophy, 'existential phenomenology' will have to do. That these two traditions have had little contact should perhaps not matter: they are fighting on different ground, one to liberate scientific knowledge and one to liberate lay knowledge from the empiricist straitjacket. They could be seen as topographically separated allies, like the Scottish National Party and Plaid Cymru, engaged in a sort of pincer movement. And they have in common that both have foregrounded the notion of knowledge as the outcome of work; the intended product of scientific work or the tacit concomitant of everyday work. But unfortunately they have often misunderstood and despised each other.

In the next part of this section, I shall discuss both what is right about the existential phenomenologists' position and where they tend to go wrong, straying into anti-scientific and non-realist positions that do not follow from their essential insights. This will lead me to a discussion of hearsay and the means of testing and correcting it; this seems to me to be the central issue in the theory of knowledge. I shall show how this account necessitates realism.

On two issues the existential phenomenologists are absolutely right. First, in shifting attention from the perception to work, or rather situating perception in the context of work. We may sympathise with the sentiments:

What is this life if full of care
We have no time to stand and stare?
(W.H. Davies)

– yet most of our perceptual knowledge is generated by caring, not staring. Because the empiricists foregrounded 'looking at' and neglected 'looking for', 'looking after' and 'looking into', they analysed experience as a succession of images. Yet the perception involved in riding a bike or fixing a shutter cannot be so analysed without falsification. If Hume had given a true analysis of such activities, he could not have said that we have no experience of causality. Indeed, Roy Bhaskar's account of the 'transitive verb model' of causation gives some indication of how causes figure in lay knowledge – in a way that generates far fewer problems both for the theory of science and for that of human action than Hume's account does: Tania pushes the door open; we can all see that happen; and if it happens, the door is necessarily open at the end of the action and Tania's pushing it is the cause of its being open (see *A Realist Theory of Science*, p. 121).

Second, the existential phenomenologists are quite right to insist that scientific knowledge presupposes lay knowledge in a number of ways. Obviously, it presupposes it in time. Both the human race and each human individual has to accumulate a great deal of lay knowledge before they can start doing science. But this lay knowledge is not mere 'prescientific' knowledge if that is taken to mean a ladder that science climbs and can then throw away. We cannot learn geography unless we have learnt in the countryside what a river and a mountain are; we cannot learn physics unless we know what pushes and pulls, what heat, light and sound are – from pushing wheelbarrows and lighting fires and banging drums, and so on. Furthermore, we don't know how to respond to sciences, why we should be interested in them or what to do with their results unless we understand the relation of the entities and mechanisms that they uncover to those that we are used to operating and being affected by.

Much of this lay knowledge is tacit; we can use it without spelling it out. And while one may sometimes be able to improve one's practice by spelling out the knowledge implicit in it, one will certainly make one's practice much worse if one relies only on such knowledge as one has been able to spell out and ignores one's own tacit knowledge. The current fashion in management for spelling out or ignoring all grounds for decision-making is extremely destructive.

Now I come to another point that both Heidegger and Macmurray make in slightly different ways: their accounts of why we do not simply make do with the vast store of tacit knowledge that is implicit in our everyday work and ignore theoretical knowledge. This option might well be preferable to the opposite error of contemporary management with its mania for stated and preferably measurable criteria for everything; I think it has had its advocates in Daoism and certain versions of romanticism and English conservatism. Heidegger and Macmurray go along with this position some way, I think – at least to the extent of applying to tacit knowledge the excellent maxim 'If it ain't broke, don't fix it.' But sometimes it is broke. The origin of theoretical knowledge, according to both of them, is, as we have seen, in practical breakdowns. For instance, while I was crossing a busy road on my bike one day on the way home from work, the bike suddenly jammed still in the middle of the road and would not move. I got off and dragged it to the edge of the road in time to avoid sudden death and started looking at it to see what was wrong. The knowledge implicit in practice – knowledge of how to ride a bike – was no longer enough. I needed explanatory knowledge. Although both Macmurray and Heidegger think that theoretical knowledge originates in such breakdowns, they have got slightly different accounts of our initial response to them. As I have mentioned earlier, according to Macmurray, we stop and think; according to Heidegger, we stop and stare. I certainly did both, but I also fiddled with the back wheel, which it soon became clear had slipped in its sockets and jammed against the brake blocks. The importance of breakdowns as a ground of theory I have long accepted and discussed under the heading of 'the methodological primacy of the pathological' in connection with Freud's claim that neurotic mental functioning is much more psychologically instructive than normal functioning. But – and here is my first criticism of Macmurray and Heidegger – what breakdowns give rise to is not pure comtemplation, whether perceptual or intellectual, but a new kind of work with cognitive aims. This is important because both Macmurray and Heidegger seem to think that, while the contemplative attitude generated by breakdowns has its uses – to get the bike back on the road – it necessarily yields a sort of knowledge that is impoverished relative to the great store of tacit knowledge implicit in work. Macmurray even says that science can do nothing but spell out knowledge that we already have. Heidegger thinks that contemplation gives us knowledge only of the 'present at hand'; that is, brute matter, as distinct both from the 'ready to hand' – the world as the system of things that are our way of doing things – and from the 'power of nature' as understood in romanticism, as I have discussed in Section 7 of this part of the book.

But we saw there that theoretical knowledge need be neither passive, nor impoverished, nor unemotive. The geographer as much as the romantic poet has to scramble up screes to get to the source of the river. More generally, science requires experimental work by trained workers if it is to get anywhere. And the theoretically mediated knowledge, 'this little spring is the source of the great River Severn', may itself evoke wonder. More generally, while certain kinds of scientific knowledge (the more abstract kinds) may be impoverished in *some* ways relative to lay knowledge, they will be enriched in others, and this enrichment may evoke emotions of its own: on discovering the life cycle of an insect that one would previously have brushed away indifferently, one may come to have a real concern for its survival as a species. Indeed, if theoretical knowledge did not add something new to the stock of knowledge, it is hard to see how it could correct practical breakdowns, as both Macmurray and Heidegger think it is purpose-built to do. Tacit knowledge may be prior in a hundred and one ways; nevertheless, theory is the *growing tip* of knowledge. Without it, tacit knowledge stagnates. Any attempt to downgrade theory relative to tacit knowledge is necessarily conservative. So, while we should accept realism about the knowledge implicit in work, we should not treat that familiar reality as exclusive of the reality that science opens up to us.

But there is another reservation that needs to be made about the primacy of tacit or practical knowledge. Much – though by no means all – knowledge that is now tacit and implicit in some practical skill, was once learnt by being spelt out and communicated in words by someone else. When I cook, I usually prefer to rely on my tacit knowledge and not measure ingredients or follow recipes, but I learnt to cook almost entirely from books. Riding a bike is a sort of know-how that is quite difficult to 'put into words' – yet I remember as a child being told to 'turn the way you're tipping' and learning not to fall off by following that instruction. In short, we don't just pass from tacit to spelt-out knowledge by means of breakdowns; we pass from spelt-out to tacit knowledge by means of familiarisation. Only when the explicit instruction has been, for practical purposes, 'forgotten' has one acquired the skill.

Indeed, much of what is now tacit, or at most 'commonsensical' knowledge for us was once hard-won theoretical discovery, just as many everyday words were once technical neologisms. When we look at the sky and 'see' infinite depth of space, we are seeing in a science-informed way; our ancestors saw a solid vault. Everyday words like 'matter', 'form' and 'quality' were once the technical terms of Aristotelian philosophy. If Aristotelianism sometimes appears to be 'common sense', that is not because there is an enduring stock of lay knowledge called 'common sense' and Aristotle gave it philosophical expression; it is because Aristotle's thought has so pervaded culture in the Islamic, Jewish, Christian and Marxist worlds that it has become 'common sense'. Maybe in 2,300 years' time, pub banter and garden-wall gossip will be couched in the language of Roy Bhaskar's *Dialectic*.

The role of teaching in knowledge – and of course in this teaching informal teaching predominates over formal as much as tacit knowledge does over theoretical – has been neglected (one might even say repressed) since the Enlightenment for entirely understandable historical reasons (although both Spinoza and Heidegger see the power of hearsay). I shall suggest that the issue of hearsay and how to correct it ought to be the central question of epistemology. The enlighteners rightly took up a critical stance to the authority of hearsay-based knowledge, but they thought this could be done by bypassing 'second-hand' knowledge altogether and returning to 'first-hand' knowledge. And on the face of it, it sounds plausible that second-hand knowledge must have been first-hand knowledge once, and so can be ignored by the epistemologist. The answer to this can be seen from Spinoza's analogy:

For in order to work iron, a hammer is needed, and in order to have a hammer it must be made, for which another hammer and other instruments are needed, for the making of which others again are needed, and so on to infinity; and in this manner anyone might vainly endeavour to prove that men had no power of working iron. But in the same way as men in the beginning were able with great labour and imperfection to make the most simple things from the instruments already supplied by nature, and when these were completed with their aid made harder and more complex things with more facility and perfection, and thus gradually proceeding from the most simple works to instruments, and from instruments to other harder pieces of work, they at last succeeded in constructing and perfecting so many and such difficult instruments with very little labour, so also the understanding by its native strength makes for itself intellectual instruments wherewith it acquires further strength for other intellectual works, and with these makes others again and the power of investigating still further, and so gradually proceeds until it attains the summit of wisdom.

('On the Correction of the Understanding', paras 30–31)

If knowledge is produced by means of knowledge, we must acquire second-hand knowledge before we have the wherewithal to produce first-hand knowledge. That this applies to lay as well as scientific knowledge is suggested by three facts:

1   The huge bulk of our knowledge is and remains pure hearsay: all knowledge of times before we were born and places we have never been to, and most knowledge about our own time and place, as well as all lay reception of scientific knowledge.
2   Hearsay precedes other knowledge. First we are told about things, then we discover them. We are largely taught through language how to 'see for ourselves'. We rarely notice things that we have not been told about.
3   When we do see for ourselves, we do so in ways made possible by what we have been told. While it is possible to learn by experience that what we have been told is false, it is not easy. And when we do so, the message 'what you learnt by hearsay was wrong' is still couched in terms of that hearsay. This is the same issue, at the level of lay knowledge, as that of the theory dependence of observations. Observations are theory dependent, but that does not mean that the theory cannot be refuted by observations. Observations only answer questions put by the theory, but the answer may be 'your theory is false'. The difficulty of seeing what would refute the received opinion is not something that could be avoided by coming to experience without received opinions. We have to learn from others how to refute what we learn from others, and we do learn it.

For, of course, massively predominant as hearsay is in our knowledge, it can be false and often is. There is a difference between something's being true and its being generally believed to be true – difficult as it is to persuade arts-side academics outside the philosophy department of this.

The deliverances of hearsay can be false and can sometimes be shown to be false, and if this were not so, dissent would be pointless and the growth of knowledge impossible. I think that there are three grounds on which one can criticise hearsay and show it to be false or likely to be false:

1   Logic: two deliverances of hearsay can be shown to contradict.
2   Experience: we can try out a deliverance of hearsay in practice and find it wanting.
3   Suspicion: we can have reasons to doubt the well-informedness or truthfulness of our informants.

Two points are worth noticing about these three means.

First, historically, each of them has been taken by some philosophy in isolation from the others and from the hearsay that they presuppose and made the foundation of knowledge. Rationalism does this with logic, empiricism with experience and 'universal symptomology' – the modern and postmodern tendency to treat ideas only as symptoms, not as either true or false – does it with suspicion.

But each of these philosophies falsifies the nature of its own preferred tool in doing so. Logic cannot generate knowledge as the rationalists thought it could: it can only show that two inconsistent propositions cannot both be true. The empiricists (if one excepts Bacon who got it right on this matter) were wrong about experience: it is not the imprinting of an image on a blank wax tablet; it is the correction of information on that tablet in response to the outcome of actions based on the information that was previously there. And suspicion is not just the belief that people always have motives for their beliefs, as much relativist use of it seems to suppose, but that they sometimes have motives for believing what is not true.

Second, we have to assume realism in order to make sense of any of these tools of knowledge. Logic shows that some propositions contradict others; that is to say, that some groups of propositions cannot all be true. Nothing is more absurd than the sort of non-realist position that rejects the notion of truth and then thinks that you can go on criticising theories rationally by showing them to be inconsistent. If there is no truth, what is inconsistency anyway and why does it matter?

Experience in the relevant sense also presupposes realism. Experience is always experience *of* something, it is always referential and makes sense only in terms of the independent reality to which it refers. In the psychoanalytical phrase, it is 'reality-testing'. If it were not, it could not correct hearsay. It can do so because it provides access to the reference of concepts, of which hearsay only teaches us the sense. Referenceless hearsay is what Heidegger means by *Gerede*, 'idle talk'. Postmodernists, on this as on so many issues, have taken Heidegger's account of a phenomenon of inauthentic existence and made it into the norm: discourse that refers us only to other discourse, never to what it is about. But the point for Heidegger, who was no fool, is to get out of this self-enclosedness of discourse, to achieve 'aboutness'.

Finally, we come to suspicion; I mean suspicion in cognitive contexts, where we have reason for saying 'They would say that, wouldn't they?', and therefore doubting the truth of what they say. However, this is not always, and not most interestingly, a question of motives for lying, but of explanations why people might believe and pass on ideas that are false and that they could have known to be false. If suspicion becomes universal, it becomes uninteresting. What is interesting is why *some* people in *some* respects in *some* situations tend to misunderstand what they are doing or what is happening. Suspicion – in the sense that Marx, Nietzsche and Freud were masters of suspicion – is not a reason for treating all ideas as equally unreliable, but for treating some ideas as more unreliable than others. Otherwise it does not help and we might as well forget about it. To give an analogy: suppose you were given good reason to believe that some food for sale in a given supermarket was contaminated by dangerous bacteria. You would try to find out which food and avoid it; if you were politically active, you might also try to bring reprisals against the firm which, for the sake of profits and disregarding public health, sold that food. But if someone came along and said 'But *any* food *might* be contaminated; and all food is produced for profit. So you should treat all food as equally suspect', then you would either have to starve to death or say 'Well, there's nothing we can do about it then' and buy whatever food you could. The second view looks more radical, but it is actually a conservative response to radicalism – and one that has been cleverly used by recent endangerers of public health to get themselves off the hook. Universal symptomology, which sees suspicion not as a means of getting to the truth but as an alternative to it, is in a similar case. Suspicion as a useful tool in assessing information presupposes realism, as is shown by Eric Millstone's excellent work on the misinformation propagated by governments and commerce on the basis of bad science (of which more in the next section).

My conclusion, at the epistemological level, is that an account of lay knowledge should put in the foreground hearsay and its correction by logic, experience and suspicion (where 'experience' means not a succession of images, but work, causal interaction with one's environment). All these means of correction are possible only if realism is true.

How does this affect the practical conclusions that can be drawn from accounts of that particular aspect of lay knowledge which is the knowledge implicit in practice, usually tacit and impossible to incorporate into organised bodies of public knowledge? The argument is now familiar that the importance of this kind of knowledge for decision-making is so crucial that any kind of central planning is bound to be inept since it cannot tap it. Hayek used this argument against socialism, but while it can reasonably be used against large-scale command-economy planning such as the Soviet

Union attempted, it has also been turned against the market economy in which decisions can be taken even further from the people with the requisite practical knowledge by multinational corporations or world financial institutions. The type of economy indicated by the view that practical knowledge is essential to rational decision-making is a tightly planned economy, covering no greater a geographical area than can be walked across in an afternoon.

Now my foregrounding of hearsay may seem to marginalise practical knowledge and so undermine this anti-centralist case, but in fact it strengthens it. For while the part of the world with which one is practically familiar is only a small proportion of the part one knows about by hearsay, it is both the part that one is least likely to be deceived about and the part that one knows about concretely rather than abstractly – and, as I have argued elsewhere with reference to applied science, only concrete knowledge has rational practical implications. (See my 'Value, Rationality and the Environment' and 'Unhewn Demonstrations', both reprinted in this volume.) The effect of the preponderance of hearsay in lay knowledge can best be seen if we ask about the effect of the great increase in the amount of hearsay available to us in the modern world relative to earlier times. If, for instance, you lived in a kingdom which, in accordance with the Daoist ideal, was so small that you could hear the cock crow in the next kingdom, yet never be tempted to go there – or, one might add, read a newspaper from there – then there are certain facts about the next kingdom that one would be likely to guess right. You would know that your own king lived by exploiting the peasants and assume, no doubt correctly, that the king of the next kingdom did the same. If, on the other hand, you took heed of the next kingdom's mass media, you would think: 'Over there the kings and queens mind the swine and the poor have all the money. So there can't be anything wrong with monarchy, it's just that we're unlucky in the king we've got.' A voter in the United Kingdom is asked to decide between nationwide parties when 99 per cent of his or her information about them is derived from particularly tainted sources of hearsay. So it is very easy for a voter in Yorkshire to think 'I'm not voting Labour – look at all those loony left councils in London', while a voter in London might be thinking 'I'm not voting Labour – look at all those striking miners in Yorkshire.'

In order to prevent the epistemic predominance of hearsay leading to the political dominance of misinformation, massive decentralisation is needed. But the market cannot supply that decentralisation since it removes decision-making power even further from those who are in a position to know what they are doing.

§12 The objectivity of scientific knowledge

In everyday knowledge we encounter the independence of the objective world by, so to speak, bumping our heads on it in the course of activities that do not themselves aim at knowledge. Science is different. Here we are setting out to find knowledge, that is the whole purpose of the operation. As we have seen, this may be motivated by the breakdowns that occur in practices, due to their being based on inaccurate information. So we might expect science to be more objective than everyday knowledge in order to correct it. Many philosophers and most scientists do assume science to be more objective and, provided that science is not identified with any particular science or any particular model of science (for instance, atomism), I think that this is correct. However, one sometimes encounters the view that the reverse is the case: that everyday practical knowledge is more objective than science. Sometimes this is based on particular examples where scientists have been shown to know less about some particular bit of reality than people who are practically engaged with it. I am told that Ministry of Agriculture specialists have sometimes got it wrong about what is good for sheep, while shepherds have got it right, and I find that quite plausible. Certainly, generations of academic psychologists have now been shown (for instance, by the work of Colwyn Trevarthan) to have been in error about aspects of child psychology about which mothers have usually got it right. But what we are dealing with here is either shoddy science (of which more later) or (what can be regarded as a particular and rather common instance of shoddy science) the assumption that abstract knowledge can be used to explain concrete particulars without passing through the stage of concrete analysis, to bring in all sorts of factors that do not figure in a particular abstract science (see my essay 'Unhewn Demonstrations', pp. 37–45, this volume).

But there is another reason why science is sometimes regarded as less objective than everyday knowledge: it is much more our work. Before it tests anything, it constructs theories and the theories determine what tests are considered significant. The tests themselves – experiments – are activities of ours in which nature is made to do things that it would not have done naturally. If nature did naturally what we can make it do in experiments, we would not need experiments. Yet experiments are designed to tell us what nature does, not what we do. Ancient and medieval cultures might quite easily have regarded modern experiments, had they seen them, as so artificial as to be irrelevant to the knowledge of nature. Indeed, early scientific experiments were often mistaken for magic. Is science, then, just something we do and its discoveries just human products? It is indeed something we do and its results are our products, but, I shall argue, not *just* our products. For it is the essence of a good experiment that it sets things up so that the outcome of the artificial process will be one thing if some hypothesised law of nature holds and another thing if another law holds. This is the sense in which it is a question put to nature: things are so set up that nature, not us, will determine the answer. It is the willingness to listen to the answer that nature gives that constitutes the attitude of scientific objectivity, without which making the experiment would be pointless. There is, so to speak, an ethic involved in scientific experiment: an ethic of care to ensure that it is really nature that speaks in the outcome. If the outcome is predetermined by us independently of what nature says or is determined by factors that are random relative to the natural mechanism that is being tested, then the experiment fails the test of scientific ethics.

We now turn to evidence for the objectivity of science from just those cases where that objectivity is lacking. As will be the case with one of my arguments about the objectivity of values, my starting point will be one that is often misconceived as throwing doubt on objectivity. I refer to the growing number of instances of exposure of the abuses of science, an exposure often motivated by environmental concerns. Science can be abused in (at least) three ways, only one of which I am concerned about here:

1   Science can carry out experiments which are perfectly adequate to their scientific purpose of discovering the objective truth about something, but which are for some other reason morally wrong. The most horrific examples of these are the cruel and often fatal experiments carried out on human beings in Nazi Germany and by their Japanese allies at Harbin. Examples for liberal democracies are not in the same league, but they do occur: nuclear testing, with resulting radioactive fallout; cruel experiments on animals; many behaviourist experiments on children. These examples raise issues about social responsibility in science, but not about the objectivity of science.

2   Scientific discoveries can be applied in ways that are destructive to the environment or in some other way immoral. Thus electricity can be used to make electric chairs and electric batons, the internal combustion engine can be overused until it destroys the environment, amniocentesis can be used (in misogynist cultures) to discover the sex of a foetus and abort it if it is a girl, and knowledge of nuclear fission and fusion and of bacteriology can be used to make weapons that could never be used in a just war. These examples raise issues about the commercial and military uses of the findings of science, but not about science itself.

3   Scientists are mainly employed by military or commercial institutions and are paid to get results that are profitable to these instutions. Where one finding would damage the profits of a company, scientists may be encouraged to come up with other findings. Examples are the alleged results of research at tobacco companies about the safety of smoking (which are now publicly discredited) and that of research by companies with an interest in the burning of fossil fuels, regarding the supposed unseriousness of the dangers of global warming (which is regrettably still widely believed).

These cases do raise issues about the objectivity of science. They certainly impugn the objectivity (as an attitude) of many *scientists*. Whether this throws doubt on the objectivity of science or, on the contrary, presupposes it, is what I shall discuss in the rest of this section.

Some of the examples of commercially motivated impairment of scientific objectivity are quite clearly just that, and their description equally indicts the commercial impairment and illustrates the need for scientific objectivity. Thus a report from a United States pharmaceutical company on the safety of one of its products was returned to the company by the Food and Drugs Administration (FDA) because the summary with which the document opened did not fit the data contained in the document. The summary is presumably presented as the basis on which policy decisions can be made. But if the data do not support it, the objective grounds for these decisions are removed, since it is the data that are the evidence of how the world stands objectively. But:

> the report was returned to [the company] in the expectation that it would change the summary to fit the data. [The FDA researcher] was surprised when a fresh submission arrived with some of the data altered to fit the summary.
>
> (Millstone, 'Sweet and Sour', p. 71)

It is clear that what is wrong with this is precisely the overriding of objective for expedient considerations. Other examples from the same company relate to the testing of DKP, a decomposition product of Aspartame (Nutrasweet), by feeding it to rats and mice. The FDA found that it was:

> impossible to identify from the laboratory records exactly when a particular animal had died. . . . Observation records indicated that animal A232M was alive at week 88, dead from week 92 through week 104, alive at week 108, and dead at week 112.
>
> (ibid., p. 72)

It was further impossible to find out how much DKP the rats had eaten, whether it was properly mixed with their food or could have been avoided by them, and so on. This is simply shoddy science – that is, science whose results will not be determined by how the world objectively is, whatever conclusions it is used to support. If the aim of science were not to discover how some aspect of the world objectively is, it would be impossible to say what was shoddy about this science.

However, there are also more directly socio-political facts about the way that scientific findings gain authority. For instance, both the US and the UK have a framework of legislation and a set of institutions monitoring the use of potentially dangerous chemicals as pesticides, fungicides and herbicides. A paper by Zwanenberg and Millstone of SPRU (The Science and Technology Policy Research Unit at Sussex University) compares the work of the US Environmental Protection Agency (EPA) and the UK Ministry of Agriculture, Fishery and Food's Advisory Committee on Pesticides (ACP). They conclude that the American practice is better than the British – there is more investigation of commercial companies' own researches, results are made more public, there is more opportunity for elected authorities or members of the public to challenge findings, and so on. But what is it that is preferable about American practice? Why are public inspection and accountability desirable? They are not good things in themselves, independently of subject matter. They would be very bad things in marriage guidance or the work of creative artists. They are good with reference to commercial uses of science because science aims at objective knowledge and good public policy requires such knowledge, but commercial interests give a strong motive for impaired objectivity in the interests of public relations.

Hence, Zwanenberg and Millstone conclude that:

> Analyses based on realist sociological deconstructions of competing knowledge claims can make a positive and critical contribution to science, sociology and policy.
>
> ('Beyond Skeptical Relativism: Evaluating
> the Social Constructions of Expert Risk
> Assessments', p. 277)

This benefit, however, 'can only accrue from the adoption of a realist framework' (ibid., p. 278); a framework, that is, that recognises criteria that are internal to science for its success, criteria aimed at objectivity, and that studies these alongside the sociological determinants that may reinforce or deflect and impair that objectivity.

The conclusion is significant because many sociologists of science think that the socially determined plurality of views in applied science only makes sense on relativist, non-objectivist assumptions. But, whereas these assumptions could account for the plurality, they could not account for some practices being worse than others: they are worse because they are less objective. It makes no sense to criticise shoddy science as an inadequate basis for policy-making unless one has a notion of objectivity by the impairment of which it becomes shoddy. Both the practice of science and the politics of science make sense only on the assumption that the attitude of objectivity is essential to science, and that the achievement of objective knowledge is the criterion of its success.

§13 Objectivity, moral diversity and moral change

While I think many people are likely to agree with my defence of objectivity in the knowledge of facts, whether everyday or scientific, most people take it for granted that ethics and value judgements generally are not objective. Some hold that they are up to each individual to decide (the position known as subjectivism); some hold that, within any given community, there will be agreed norms that are binding on its members, but that communities differ in their norms and there are no objective grounds for preferring one to another (the position known as relativism). I think it would be true to say that the large majority of people in the UK, if confronted by the issue of whether morality is objective or not, would opt for either subjectivism or relativism. This is certainly true of first-year philosophy students. But at the same time, when they are *making* moral judgements rather than talking about them, they would talk as if these judgements were objective. They would not treat differences over abortion or racism or foxhunting like differences over one's preferred brand of beer or cheese. They would not say things like 'I disapprove of rape', but things like 'A man who commits rape is a bastard.' Why, then, are they so convinced that morality cannot be objective?

Until about two hundred years ago, almost everyone agreed that morality was objective. There are no doubt ideological reasons why this has changed, to do with the increasing pervasiveness of commerce, but I think there are also two reasons that need to be taken seriously philosophically. Two phenomena that have become more widely known which have led people to accept some form of relativism or subjectivism, namely: moral diversity, the plurality of mutually contradictory moral judgements in different cultures and even in different subcultures of the same culture; and moral change, the fact that some acts and character traits that were previously condemned come to be approved, and some that were previously approved come to be condemned. Although these two phenomena are equally appealed to by first-year philosophy students as grounds for doubting the objectivity of morals, there is, in fact, a big difference between them. Moral diversity really is a problem which the onus is on the moral objectivist to explain away; on the face of it, it looks like an argument for relativism. Moral change, on the other hand, is the best possible argument *for* the objectivity of morals. Let us deal with diversity first.

There are three possible ways of explaining the fact of moral diversity. The first is to say that, while there are indeed objective values, such that if people's moral judgements were true they would all be agreed, people sometimes make false moral judgements, just as they sometimes make false judgements about matters of fact. When two people make conflicting judgements about a moral issue, at least one of them must have got it wrong, just as, if one person says that Scotland is to the north of England and one says it is to the south of England, one has got it wrong. If one says that Scotland is to the south of England and one says that it is to the east of England, both have got it wrong. Likewise (one might argue), if one person says that killing is always wrong and one says that it is right when it is for 'reasons of state', both have got it wrong. Either way, diversity is explained by error, exactly as with factual beliefs. This view, of course, is a straightforwardly objectivist one, making no concessions either to relativism or to subjectivism. It should be noted that there is nothing intrinsically paradoxical about it, since it is exactly parallel with what most sane people hold about factual beliefs. The only thing that might be claimed to differentiate the two cases is that there is more agreement about facts than about values. I doubt whether this is the case. Certainly, in explaining political differences, differences about facts are much more important than differences about values. I would guess that, in general, outside the scientific community in well-established sciences, differences about facts are more common than differences about values.

The second explanation of moral diversity is that, while some act may be right in one society and wrong in another, or some human quality a virtue in one society and not in another, there are reasons in the different environments or social structures in those societies why these different judgements hold. If we analyse these reasons we will find that there are some underlying values which, combined with certain social circumstances, lead to one judgement but, combined with different social circumstances, lead to another judgement. Just as it is right to feed meat to dogs but wrong to feed meat to cows, not because we have different values when we feed dogs and when we feed cows, but precisely because we have the same values – the health and welfare of the animals – and know that cows need grass while dogs need meat. This second explanation is sometimes put forward by people who think they are defending relativism, but it is not actually a relativist position. The idea that there are underlying objective values which, however, generate different concrete duties when combined with different circumstances is no more paradoxical for an objectivist than the injunction: give an aspirin to a person with a headache, but not if they are an asthmatic. Once again there is a parallel in science: asked what sort of thing water is, someone might say 'It is a liquid', and then when told that below 0° Celsius it is a solid and above 100° Celsius it is a gas, they might conclude 'Then it doesn't really have any common properties.' But this would be incorrect: it has a common molecular structure as H_2O which *explains* its different phenom-enal properties under different circumstances.

Now we come to the third explanation of moral diversity, the one that, one the face of it, looks a relativist one. This is the view that different societies have different but equally good sets of customs, each being right for its own society just because they are the customs of that society, and not, as in the second case, because of any objective feature of that society outside the list of its customs. According to the relativist account, these are objectively valid for anyone in a given society, but there is no reason to prefer those of any one society to those of any other.

Now let us look at some examples to see which of these accounts fits them most plausibly. What we will find, I think, is that some examples fit plaus-ibly into each of the three explanations. But when we come to look for examples of the third, the plausible instances break down into three groups, none of which requires a relativist account of morality.

First some examples about which the first account – that some things are just wrong, but some societies get it wrong and think they are right (or vice versa) – is the most plausible one. Some societies accept torture, some societies accept slavery, others do not. One does not want to say that slavery was right in the ante-bellum South of the United States but is wrong in the United Kingdom in the twenty-first century. One wants to say rather that they got it wrong in the South. Likewise with torture, which was accepted in medieval and early modern society, and has revived in many parts of the world in the twentieth century. Whatever relativists say in their studies, they are gener-ally in practice objectivists about these issues: they say that societies that accept torture are wrong and ought to be changed.

There are also examples in which the second theory is plausible, where there are good reasons to believe that something is a virtue in one society and not in another. Take thrift, for instance, the tendency to save money. There are real reasons why this is a prudent quality to have in a capitalist society, and, if one has responsibilities to other people, a morally good quality to have in such a society. It is not just that capitalist society judges it to be right and prudent; given the institutions of capitalist society, it is right and prudent; yet in a feudal or socialist society, it would be simply an aberration of a miser, someone who keeps their money under the bed instead of using it. So there are good reasons for regarding it as a virtue in one society and a vice in another. One cannot look after one's children as well in a capitalist society if one is not thrifty as one can if one is; but in a feudal or socialist society, the reverse is the case. The value of looking after one's children is common to all societies and underlies these different virtues.

Now we come to the third case: are there plausible examples of differing but equally good customs in different societies, each right for its own society just because it is the custom of that society? When we look for examples, we find that they fall into three categories. The first is where it is a matter of differing customs that really have no grounds other than custom. For example, in England people don't eat horseflesh, whereas in France they do. We can here bracket off the genuine moral issue of vegetarianism, for that equally forbids eating sheep and cows; English meat-eaters are, for the most part, as reluctant to eat horse as vegetarians are, so there must be some reason other than that moral principle. Yet the reason seems to be quite simply 'custom'. There are, of course, historical reasons for the custom. I am told that, for our pagan ancestors, the horse was a sacred animal which was sometimes ritually eaten, so when the Angles and Saxons became Christians, they gave up their horse feasts which became taboo as a sign of paganism; whereas the pagan Gauls had no such ritual, so there was no reason to give up horseflesh when they became Christians. But clearly no modern Englishman avoids horseflesh for fear of lapsing into paganism. This is a historical cause, but not a contemporary reason for the taboo.

It looks as though the relativist account holds in this case, except for one thing: that, as most people would agree, it is not a moral issue at all. No one who accepts meat eating at all, I take it, *condemns* the French for eating horses, or indeed would condemn an Englishman for breaking his national custom and doing so. So we may have here an example of some sort of relativism being true in certain instances, but not of moral relativism.

The second case that looks on the surface like a relativist one is the case in which something may actually be right or wrong in a country just because of local customs. We have seen that this is not the case in the horseflesh example: it is not wrong to eat horseflesh in England, even though it is not the custom. But there are cases in which something not intrinsically wrong would be wrong in a given country because of the customs of that country. A good example would be questions of decency in dress. There is nothing intrinsically good or bad about showing your face or your torso or your whole body in public places, but different cultures have different rules about it. But breaking those rules is, I think, genuinely wrong. In the UK (bad weather aside) we hide only our erogenous zones, but some societies cover up everything but the eyes, while others accept complete nakedness. Indecent exposure is genuinely wrong in the UK, but there is nothing wrong with a society that accepts nakedness. So the issue is indifferent as between cultures, but not within cultures, which is exactly what relativism teaches. However, if we ask why indecent exposure is wrong in the UK, the answer is that it is offensive to people. The offensiveness makes the transition from custom to morality; the breach of custom is offensive, the offensiveness is morally wrong. But this means that here we are back with the second explanation of moral difference: there is an underlying value, that of avoiding unnecessarily offending people; and there is a difference of circumstance (itself not a moral issue) – namely, a difference of custom and, hence, of what does in fact offend people. Together they generate different prescriptions for conduct in different societies; but there is no difference in values. This, then, is not a genuinely relativist case.

Finally, there are things about which there must be some rule in society, although it is a matter of moral indifference which of several is adopted. A clear, if rather trivial example is the rule about which side of the road to drive on; left and right are equally good, but it would be wrong, not to say extremely imprudent, to drive on the right in the UK or on the left in continental Europe. But there are also instances which cut deeper into the moral fabric of society. When I was a child, I was extremely puzzled by the story in the Gospels where the disciples are plucking corn and eating it as they walk through farmers' fields. They do this on the Sabbath and get into trouble because it is an offence to work on the Sabbath; the whole issue between the disciples and the Pharisees is that it was done on the Sabbath. But it struck me that surely they were stealing the farmer's corn; why were they not condemned for this? It was explained to me that Hebrew laws allowed them to do this, so it was not stealing, although it would be in the United Kingdom today. What counts as stealing depends on the way the laws of the land define property rights. There are many different ways. But there has to be some way, otherwise no one will know what they can use and what they must leave for someone else; and if the laws are just ones, they will apply equally to everybody. To allow, as I believe the law did in pre-revolutionary France, an aristocrat to hunt over a peasant's land, but not a peasant to hunt over an aristocrat's land, is unjust (I am leaving aside the further question of the justice or otherwise of the unequal distribution of land). A minimum condition of a just law is that it enforces the same rights for everyone. But that leaves it open which things it allows and which it forbids. One could have rectified the injustice of the pre-revolutionary hunting law either by letting everyone hunt over everyone's land, or forbidding anyone to hunt over anyone else's land. In some cases at least it may be morally indifferent which law one adopts; it is decided by pragmatic considerations. But that there must be a law and that it ought to be the same for everyone are principles that apply to all cultures and countries and are therefore not relativist. In that way, examples like this seem, like the last group discussed, to fall into the category of varying applications of an underlying principle, and not to belong after all to a separate relativist class.

So we have in the end broken down the examples into those that fall into the first and second categories and are therefore accounted for most plausibly in objectivist rather than relativist terms, and those that are not moral issues at all. And indeed it looks likely that any argument to prove that, in a given instance, there is no cross-cultural principle enjoining observing a given custom, will also prove that it is not a moral principle at all.

This argument from how to give plausible accounts of different examples does not conclusively refute relativism; but I think it does show that the phenomena that were thought to make relativism plausible can actually be accounted for more plausibly on objectivist assumptions. So much for moral diversity. Now we come to moral change, of which more can be claimed:

it is not just that it does not disprove objectivism; it only makes sense on the assumption of objectivism.

First, the theory about scientific change with which my argument here is an analogy. It is paradoxical that scientific change, which is the proof of the intransitive dimension of science, the essential relation of science to a reality independent of it, has also been the occasion of views of science as non-objective. At one level it is understandable enough: people thought that existing scientific theories were the final word; those theories were overturned by new theories; people came to think 'No theories are true, they are just different theories of ours.' It is as psychologically understandable as a disappointed lover turning misogynist. But a moment's reflection should show that it is not the rational response. If we have abandoned one theory for another, we must have had grounds for doing so. In what way is the new theory better? Attempts to explain it by fashion or political correctness only discredit the new theory. There are only three answers with even initial plausibility: that the new theory is closer to the truth than the old, as shown by its ability to account for more of the phenomena; that it is more internally consistent; or that it works better in practice. Consistency quickly refers us back to the first account, for if we ask what is wrong with an inconsistent theory, the answer can only be that it cannot be true. In a given case an inconsistent theory may be better than a consistent alternative. But it cannot all be true because if some of its statements are true, those that are inconsistent with them are false – that is just what it is for them to be inconsistent.

For a theory to work better in practice than another theory means this: that if we base our actions on the assumption that the theory is true, we get better results than if we base them on the assumption that the alternative theory is true. Truth in a non-pragmatically defined sense is tacitly presupposed in every use of the test of practice.

The philosophical use of scientific change to justify relativism about the object of science works like this: first the epistemic fallacy is assumed – that is, it is assumed that questions about what *is* can be reduced to questions about what *we can know*. This assumption is only plausible on a static, snapshot view of knowledge: if I am staring at the horizon, how can I distinguish between the horizon and my image of it? If I consider a scientific theory at a given time, how can I distinguish the theory from the realities that are known only through it? But as soon as I start walking or the theory starts developing, everything is changed: we must then distinguish between what does not change in the world and what does change in our knowledge of it. Because the terrain remains the same, I can change my perspective on it by, and only by, moving about it; because water was always H_2O, we could discover its previously unknown feature that it could be separated into oxygen and hydrogen by electrolysis. Hence, the fact of cognitive change requires the abandonment of the epistemic fallacy. But if one sticks to the epistemic fallacy, recognition of cognitive change imposes the paradoxical result that changes in our theories change the world as well – or, as this is more usually formulated, that there is no world independent of our theories. It then becomes impossible to explain why we change our theories at all. But we do so, regularly, expensively and irreversibly. There is something other than irrational leaping going on here.

Now how does moral change compare with this? Once again it is easy enough to see how, as a psychological fact, rapid moral change generates scepticism about the objectivity of morals. Someone who would not have doubted that objectivity, if a general consensus prevailed, may see the diversity that exists in any morally changing community as a sign that one opinion is as good as another. Some people think that homosexuality is sinful and others do not; some people think battery farming is sinful and others do not – you pays your money and you takes your choice. However, the seriousness with which moral convictions are held belies this relativism. In practice, people only extend the belief that morality is a private matter to sexual morality – in which area there are, anyway, good reasons for holding that objectively it is a private matter. No one thinks that it is a private matter whether we let old people die of cold when they cannot pay their fuel bills or whether it is acceptable to execute personally innocent hostages.

In short, if we cannot simply accept the moral code we were brought up with, but must think for ourselves in this matter, this cannot be because we have the right to arbitrary private judgement about morals any more than about science; when we change it is because our inquiry into the nature of things compels us to change. For example, I was brought up to believe that homosexuality is wrong, but as a result of what I have learnt I could no more choose to regard it as wrong now than I could choose to believe in phlogiston or a flat Earth, or to believe that battery farming is right. It is precisely the fact that, despite the personal anxiety and social dissonance caused by changing one's moral views, one is constrained to abandon old views and adopt new ones, that indicates that there must be an intransitive dimension to morality: a reality that exists independently of our moral judgements, about which our moral judgements might be wrong, but which they seek to match, and which is the ground of the possibility of their refutation or of their rationality.

Roy Bhaskar says with regard to knowledge that we must accept judgemental rationality within epistemic relativity within ontological realism. That is to say (working backwards), that the world is what it is independently of us; nevertheless, our knowledge of it is always limited and varies from time to time and from place to place; nevertheless judgements within that knowledge are not arbitrary, but can be rational or irrational. This last point is rooted in the first: it is because of the independent reality of the world that our theory, as a serious attempt to map it, can be rational or irrational: if the world were not independent, any judgement would do. Likewise, I am arguing that there are real values existing whether we recognise them or not, that our moral codes are varied and more or less erroneous attempts to match that independent order of values, and that judgement within and between those codes can be rational or irrational because it seeks to match that order.

Now, whereas scientific diversity is almost entirely a consequence of scientific change, moral diversity also exists synchronically, as difference between different cultures. This has made the relativist case easier to make, as we have seen, for the diversity suggests the question 'If there is an objective order of values, why isn't it recognised?', yet does not, as moral change does, suggest the question 'If there is no objective order of values, why change the one we've got?' The first question is not unanswerable, though, as we have also seen. If there really is an analogy with science, it should not surprise us that whole communities and epochs can be radically mistaken; they have often been mistaken about the explanation of natural events. It is more difficult for the relativist to escape the second question. As Lévi-Strauss says:

> While often inclined to subversion among his own people and in revolt against traditional behaviour, the anthropologist appears respectful to the point of conservatism as soon as he is dealing with a society different from his own. This is more than just a bias. In fact, it is something quite different: I know some anthropologists who are conformists. But they are so in a derivative way, by virtue of a kind of secondary assimilation of their society to the foreign ones they study. Their allegiance is always given to the latter, and the reason why they have abandoned their own initial revolt against their own, is that they make the additional concession to foreign societies of approaching their own as they would like all societies to be approached.
>
> (*Tristes Tropiques*, p. 502)

Thus the typical anthropologist may start as a moral rebel in their own society; constant study of moral variety without moral change makes a relativist of them (relativism is surely more typical of anthropologists than of any other profession); and relativism makes nonsense of moral change; applied at home, it makes them conservatives. To take moral change at home as seriously as the anthropologist takes moral variety abroad would commit one to the objectivity of values.

One alternative account of moral diversity and change needs to be considered, though, because there are no serious parallels to it in the case of scientific change.

Just as someone might explain moral difference as the superstructural effect of different substructures of technology, economic organisation and politics, so one might explain moral change as the effect of substructural changes. This view is often Marxist, and in that case involves some sort of ranking of different substructures and hence their attendant moralities: socialist morality is superior to capitalist morality, and so on. Hence, although this view may be relativist in so far as it says that in a capitalist society capitalist morality has objective validity, it does make a place for the moral dissenter as potentially the harbinger of a coming, better society.

This view is often presented as relativist because at a superficial level it is so, like the second position discussed above with regard to moral diversity; it can grant feudal society its honour and capitalist society its enterprise – it can admire Alfred the Great and Dick Whittington – yet can advocate a society in which neither virtue would have a place. Yet, in so far as it recognises objective differences in technology and organisation as the ground of objective differences in morality, it is at a deeper level non-relativist. It allows for the possibility of universal values which, when combined with different particular social realities, yield different sets of virtues and duties. The fact that I, as a socialist dissident in a capitalist society, can admire King Alfred, indicates that at some level there are common values; that I am saying 'in that sort of society, King Alfred's virtues were just what were needed' – needed, that is, to realise values that are mine too. It is certainly not a matter of admiring those who succeeded by the standards of their own society; I do not admire William the Bastard (alias the Conqueror).

I am claiming, then, that, although there is a possible account of moral change that takes as paradigmatic changes unlike scientific change (that is, Marxism), it does not deny an intransitive dimension to morality. It might still be said that the Marxist account renders my comparison of moral with scientific change unnecessary, since moral change is carried by substructural change. However, there is nothing in the Marxist account to show that *all* moral change is carried by substructural change and I think there are historical examples of moral change where this is not so; it is arguable that the dissident morality of socialists within capitalism is not entirely explained by our class position within capitalism. Along with the oppressor/oppressed axis of dissidence, there is also the market relations/internal relations one. In a formula, socialists resist the assimilation in capitalist ideology of all relationships to contractual ones, of all work to production for sale, of all enjoyment to consumption, of all qualities to quantities, of all ends to external ends. These aspects of socialist ethics are of particular importance from an environmentalist point of view. Furthermore, the idea that moral change as between successive modes of production from slavery on is characteristically progress requires the recognition of transhistorical moral truths; it is not itself just a judgement belonging to the morality of a particular society.

The emergence of environmental concerns into a major part of many people's ethical outlook today is an excellent example of moral change presupposing values that existed before that moral change gave them recognition. Concern for the diversity and prolificity of nature, the integrity of ecosystems and the letting be of parts of nature unaltered by human actions, is not an explicit part of most older moral traditions, if indeed it is of any. It is implicit in some; in Daoism, I think, and in the Augustinian tradition that holds that being as being is good. Its emergence as an explicit part of ethics is due partly to social and technological changes that have made it necessary to defend what might earlier have been taken for granted; it is partly due also to new scientific knowledge that shows that nature can be wounded in ways that will not heal. It is paradoxical that ecological concerns are sometimes thought to be antagonistic to natural science, for no aspect of ethics is more dependent on the findings of natural science than they are.

But what these social and scientific changes have prompted is a *discovery* of values that were always there to be discovered, not an *invention* of new values. The facts that this discovery was prompted on the one hand by a new threat to those (previously unrecognised) values and on the other by new knowledge about the world that had been true of the world before it was known to us, bear witness to its character as discovery, not invention.

I think, then, that the model of (some) moral change as analogous to scientific change stands and can accommodate the truth of the Marxist account of history.

§14 The objectivity of worth and the worth of objectivity

If there are objective values, entities with intrinsic worth independent of what judgements we may make about them, then what sort of things are they? I think there are six possible candidates that have been suggested historically. I shall begin with the one that I regard as least plausible, and work through ones with increasing plausibility until I reach the one that I want to defend. My criticisms of each, after the first one, will tend to show that whatever is true and plausible in each depends on its pointing towards the sixth view, the view that I will defend. The fifth view indeed implies the sixth and passes over into it.

The first suggestion is that values are a distinct kind of entity, as objective as physical objects but independent of them, belonging to what can metaphorically be called a realm of values. If this is true, how can we know these values? Not, presumably, through our knowledge of the world of people and things. It presupposes some kind of intuition or moral sense, which just tells us what is good and what is bad, as our eyesight, if we are not colour-blind, tells us what is red and what is green.

Now it seems to me that the diversity of moral judgements, while not an insuperable obstacle to objectivism as such, is an insuperable obstacle to this version of it. If there were a standard view of values and those who differed from it were very few or all manifestly defective in some way, then one might use the analogy of colour-blindness to understand moral diversity. But if, on the one hand, morality is based on complex knowledge and arguments it would not be surprising that, for instance, Kant should regard lying as in every case wrong, while Aristotle should regard the virtue in this matter as being a mean between pathological lying and pathological truth-telling, or that Moses should regard homosexuality as an abomination while Plato regarded it as a higher form of love. But if we just *see* what is right and wrong, these differences would show that the moral sense is simply different in different people and we would be back with subjectivism rather than objectivism; unless of course we argued, as a Calvinist might, that only a minority of people had an accurate moral sense, the rest being colour-blind in their various ways. But such a Calvinist would have a hard job convincing the rest of us that they were right. I am not, of course, denying that we can rationally decide between incompatible moral views – any objectivist must claim that in principle we can. But it is a matter of complex evidence and arguments, where there is plenty of scope for going astray and arriving at various wrong conclusions; it is nothing like the reporting of the data of a sense.

The second view is that what is good in itself is some human experience, usually pleasure or self-realisation. Let us take pleasure first. Utilitarians hold that pleasure is quantifiable, which could only be so if one pleasure was essentially the same as another, only caused differently. One case of pleasure is caused by listening to music, another by playing tennis, another by conversation, another by killing animals, another by watching scenes of violence on television, and so on. Which is best depends not on the cause but on the quantity. Pleasure being equal, watching scenes of torture is as good as going to the pub with a friend. Now this account – quite apart from its moral degeneracy – is just phenomenologically false. A pleasure is not related to that which gives pleasure only as effect to cause, but intrinsically. A pleasure has an intentional object and is defined by what its intentional object is. It is a pleasure in walking, singing or eating, and so on. The fact that 'pleasure' is a noun is as misleading as the fact that 'experience' is a noun. It is better to use the transitive verb 'to enjoy something'. We never *have* a pleasure, we enjoy something. (NB: this has nothing to do with enjoyment in Alexander's sense. When you enjoy a pint of beer in my sense, you contemplate it in Alexander's.) Enjoying one thing is not substitutable saving the pleasure for enjoying something else. When Bentham says that, pleasure being equal, push-pin is as good as poetry, one should reply 'As good *what* as poetry; as good push-pin yes – better, rather; but not as good poetry.'

A comparison of enjoyment with belief may be instructive here. It is tempting to say that enjoyment, like belief, involves a claim: just as to believe in fairies means to claim that fairies exist, so to enjoy The Rolling Stones' music means to claim that The Rolling Stones' music is good. This is not quite true, however, for while it is possible to say 'I believe in fairies but I may be mistaken', it is not possible to say 'I believe in fairies but I think I am mistaken.' Whereas it is possible to say 'I enjoy The Rolling Stones' music, but I think I am mistaken.' Like belief, there is a mistake if the enjoyed object is not in fact good; but unlike belief, one can admit the mistake but continue to enjoy the object. I think the difference is that, while belief and enjoyment do involve claims, they also involve a sort of buzz of feeling; and one would ascribe enjoyment to oneself on the basis of the buzz even if the claim was subtracted from it, although the enjoyment would be an impaired enjoyment with the claim, which is normally part of it, subtracted; on the other hand, one would not ascribe belief to oneself on the basis of the buzz, when the truth claim had been subtracted. Perhaps there are some who would: I sometimes think that some liberal theologians are people from whose faith the truth claims have been subtracted, but the buzz remains like the Cheshire cat's smile after the cat has gone; they then make it their life's work to find a world view that will justify the buzz without the claims. But these theologians aside, belief is no longer belief at all without its truth claims, while enjoyment is some sort of enjoyment even with the goodness-claims subtracted, just as a man without legs is still a man, but a man without a head is not. Nevertheless, the goodness-claims are a natural part of enjoyment; it is normal for enjoyment to involve the ascription of value to something outside itself. Enjoyment is not itself the value, but a particular way of experiencing the value. And it can be right or wrong about the value it ascribes. It is appropriate to enjoy one's friends and lover, good music and beautiful landscapes; it is not appropriate to enjoy scenes of torture or murder.

In addition to pleasure, I mentioned self-realisation as a good according to certain philosophers. This is typical of idealist philosophy, so making allowances for the limited accuracy of all national stereotypes, one could retort to Nietzsche's quip 'Men do not seek happiness – only Englishmen do' with 'Men do not seek self-realisation, only Germans do.' For self-realisation, like happiness, is surely not achieved by pursuing it, but by pursuing other things. Sibelius realised himself by composing his seven symphonies, but his aim, I assume, was not self-realisation but the symphonies.

The third view is this: in modern (as opposed to ancient and recently revived) moral philosophy, the main alternative to pleasure and self-realisation as the repository of intrinsic worth is *actions*. Actions are usually contrasted with consequences, in opposition to the utilitarians, who say that it is one class of the consequences of an act – those that are cases of pleasure or pain – that make the act good or bad. Against this utilitarian view, it is said that actions are intrinsically good or bad, without reference to the consequences. Murder is intrinsically bad, even if the murdered man would have done great evil had he lived; giving money to a beggar is intrinsically good, even if the beggar uses it to get drunk. But the whole terms of this debate seem to me to be confused. One cannot say what any given act is (murder, giving to a beggar) without taking in some of the consequences. An act may be an act of killing an enemy soldier. But that description takes in the consequence of pulling the trigger – namely, that the enemy soldier died. But it excludes the further consequences that the battle was won and the invasion of the country averted. The pacifist thinks we only need to know that it was an act of killing to know that it was wrong; the patriot says we need to know that it was an act of saving the country to know that it was right; the 'revolutionary defeatist' (like Lenin in the First World War) says we also need to know that the consequence of national victory would be the perpetuation of oppression; whereas the Amish say we only need to know that it was an act of using a gun. The question then cannot be whether consequences count, but how many consequences are essential to the morally relevant description of the act. This draws attention to an obvious enough feature of acts: with a few exceptions such as solitary dancing, they are done so that the world shall be *thus* and not *thus*. They refer, in other words, to values that are inherent in the world and not in the action, and are done for the sake of those values. Just as one must see through enjoyment to the values enjoyed, so we must see through actions to the state of the world brought about. But this need not lead to a utilitarian focus on pleasures and pains.

The fourth view is this: the locus of moral judgement for ancient and medieval philosophy, and for an increasing body of ethics today, is neither experiences nor actions but virtues. According to this view, the fundamental question of ethics is not 'What ought I to do?' but 'What sort of person should I be?' This 'virtue ethics' has issued in very much better work than utilitarian and 'intrinsicalist' views have. But I have two reservations about it.

First, it suggests that we should act in such a way as to cultivate our virtues, and it does not seem to me that the best actions are self-referential in this or any other way. Take Sartre's example of going to help Pierre, motivated by the awareness of Pierre-needing-to-be-helped. If instead it is motivated by me-finding-an-opportunity-to-cultivate-my-virtue-of-helpfulness, it is of lesser worth. That surely is right. The person who pursues their own virtue becomes a Pharisee, not a saint. When St Francis kissed lepers, I am sure he felt 'That leper must feel unloved; he could do with a good kiss', rather than 'Won't I be virtuous if I go up and kiss that disgusting leper?' If he thought the second, he would have been a great prig, not a great saint. And although Aristotle (the inspirer of virtue-ethics) is the greatest philosopher of all time, it has to be said that he was a bit of a prig too, with his remark that one would not sympathise with a sufferer if the suffering were the result of self-indulgence, and his ideal of the 'great-souled man' (big-headed man, as one of my ex-students has aptly translated it), who resembles nothing so much as the man most likely to get the Tory candidature for parliament.

Second, as in the case of pleasure-ethics and act-ethics, virtue-ethics suffers from the vice of reflexivity: of focusing not on what the pleasure or the act or the virtue is about, but on the pleasure or act or virtue itself. For virtues too are about something. Kindness is about people's well-being, courage is about threatened evils being defeated, justice (as a virtue) is about justice (as a state of society). To value virtue rather than what it is about is like looking at a window rather than through it.

The fifth candidate for intrinsic value leads us straight to the sixth (and in my view correct) one; so that the fifth is not, like the first four, mistaken, but rather needs only to be analysed to take us to the sixth. It is that what has intrinsic worth or unworth is *emotions*. On one reading, this is Spinoza's view. It also seems to me to be that of the New Testament, where the emotion on centre stage is love: if one loves God and one's neighbour, morality will look after itself. 'Love and do what you will' as Augustine says (*dilige et quod vis fac*).

I say that this leads us into the next theory, because it is transparently the case that love is not reflexive, that in love worth is ascribed to the beloved rather than to the love itself. The temptation of reflexivity that led the second, third and fourth views astray does not exist here. To love for the sake of love is not to love at all; only to love for the sake of the beloved is love. This may be the point of Augustine's remark in his *Confessions* in which he refers to the time of his lustful youth in Carthage: 'I loved not yet, yet I loved to love' (Bk III, Ch. 1). What he found valuable in love, was the love not the loved one, so it was not yet love. Hence the morality of emotions, if love is seen as the central emotion, is necessarily the morality of the intrinsic worth of the beings that we can love. This takes us to the sixth view.

The final view, then, is the doctrine of the intrinsic worth of beings and the consequent debt of love we owe them. This view is characteristic of St Augustine and after him of those medieval philosophers who took up this strain, notably Aquinas. For Augustine, all beings have worth, but some more than others (God most of all, then people, and so on) and should be loved in due order. But everything has some intrinsic worth, even a rock. The world of objective values is identical with the world of objective beings. This view I have defended in a whole book (*Being and Worth*), so I will say no more about it now. But my claim here is that it is 'the truth of' all the other theories: we enjoy, act, have virtues in order that beings might be cherished in accordance with their worth.

This is the doctrine of the objectivity of worth that I hold, but there is also the question of the worth of objectivity – objectivity, that is, as a human characteristic, the project of and tendency towards being objective in one's judgements and emotions. I want to argue that this objectivity is not only a virtue, but in a sense the core of all the virtues.

This is easily argued with regard to two clusters of virtues. The first is the cluster around truthfulness, sincerity and intellectual honesty. First, there is truthfulness in the obvious sense of truth-telling rather than lie-telling. It is rarely said that the disparagement of objectivity can be a cover for telling lies, no doubt because it seems too simplistic and too insulting to sceptics about objectivity. Nevertheless, one does sometimes encounter instances of liars defending their lies theoretically with the claim that there is no such thing as objectivity. I have heard an eminent writer admit on television to writing lies in a newspaper and defending himself with the claim that there is no such thing as objective journalism. I have also written elsewhere criticising a view in social work theory, according to which most of the evils in the world come from a belief in objective truth and that it is therefore acceptable to lie to clients (see my essay 'The Language of Objectivity and the Ethics of Reframing'[1]). But what is much more common than using scepticism about objectivity to justify barefaced lying is to use it for ignoring evidence for unwelcome conclusions. Firms exposed for their abuses of science have been known to appeal to 'postmodern' scepticism about objective truth to justify ignoring the exposure. Regrettably, the left is not immune to this sort of manoeuvre. Rejection of the findings of psychology on the grounds that they are 'reactionary', without troubling to investigate whether they are true or false, is often excused on the grounds of such fatuous slogans as 'Objectivity is just male subjectivity.' We have also already seen in relation to Kierkegaard and Bultmann that, in the philosophy of religion, scepticism about objectivity is used to defend 'blind faith' – that is, belief without, or contrary to, the evidence. In all these cases we have, I would argue, breaches of intellectual honesty – oddly in some instances, given the great devotion of thinkers like Bultmann, for example, to that virtue as he conceives it in arguments about demythologisation.

Sincerity likewise, although a difficult virtue to define (see Sartre's critique of 'good faith'), involves being objective about oneself, not in any way that involves alienation from oneself, as existentialist polemic alleges, but in avoiding self-deception and the deception of others about oneself.

Second, there is a cluster of virtues around humility (in the best sense, for there are certainly types of humility which are vices rather than virtues), open-mindedness and tolerance. First of all in the avoidance of that sort of pride in the bad sense, of hubris, involved in Kantian, pragmatist and post-modernist views of nature. There would be no point (apart from pragmatic, technological ones) in *investigating* nature if it were somehow our product; no point in cosmological science or zoology, but no point either in gazing at the night sky, out in the country where it is free from light pollution; no point in being amid trees and hills and waterfalls rather than watching cartoons on television. For these things involve an appreciation of what we did not make and what is independent of us, partly *for* its independence and strangeness. They involve humility about the limits of our own works compared with those of nature. Humility in the ordinary sense, humility in interpersonal relations also consists in a kind of objectivity. It is not *under-valuing* oneself – that is a vice not a virtue – but having an objective understanding of one's own limits and seeing others for what they are, not how they fit into our world.

Openmindedness is closely related to humility before what is outside us, and it is also impossible for a sceptic about objectivity, for if the world is not independent of us, what is there to be open to? The subjectivist is trapped inside their own certainties. Indeed, it was the perverse Cartesian quest for certainty that led to the classical form of subjectivism, the phenomenalism of empiricist philosophers from Berkeley to Ayer. Sense data were regarded as the foundation of knowledge because they were regarded as indubitable, while the 'external world' was open to doubt. Modern non-realism is in no better a case, for if there is nothing outside discourse, then there is nothing to judge and criticise discourse by, and we are trapped inside the certainty of our own discourse. But if the world is objective, then there are no certainties; everything is open to challenge by new encounters with and discoveries about the objective world.

Openmindedness, then, is a corollary of objectivism, but this does not, of course, mean that the objectivist is a sceptic, one who is never convinced about anything; an open mind is by definition open to being convinced. But we can never have the indubitable certainty that Descartes and the phenomenalists claimed and we can never have certainty simply by choosing to have it – there must always be an input from the objective world.

Tolerance of the right sort – the tolerance defended by John Stuart Mill – also depends on the attitude of objectivity. Because we want to know the truth and we know that our own ideas are vulnerable to contradictory input from the objective world, we will want to hear all sides to a question. There is also a false tolerance that stems from relativism: the tolerance of 'You hold to your truth and I'll hold to mine.' This is false because it fails to put one's own 'truth' at stake and because it insults the other person by treating them as one would treat a deluded paranoiac or a spoilt child, instead of taking their beliefs seriously as claims about the world and giving reasons for or against them. Relativism does not always issue even in this sort of tolerance, though. Mussolini was a relativist and drew the conclusion that, since there were no objective grounds to be reasoned about, each believer had the right to try to impose their view on the other by force.

The dependence of these two clusters of virtues on the objective attitude may be fairly obvious. But I would claim that it has a more central role in ethics than this, for all the other-regarding virtues depend on, and are largely constituted by, having a clear perception of other people. It is no doubt *logically* possible to have a clear perception of others and yet to disregard their good. But I doubt if any case of mistreating others occurs without some blindness to or misconception of who and what they really are. And it is certainly not possible to treat people well without objective awareness of them, even with 'the best will in the world'. It is therefore quite appropriate that we call kind actions by the cognitive terms 'thoughtful', 'considerate' and 'sensitive', and callous actions 'thoughtless', 'inconsiderate' and 'insensitive'. What is at stake is recognition of other people's being. The objective attitude seeks that recognition, while the subjective attitude – the attitude of being comfortable with projection, wishful thinking, assigning other people places in the world based solely on one's own desires – incapacitates a person for such recognition. In large measure, virtue is objectivity as defined by Macmurray in his account of rationality: relating to other beings as they are in themselves.

By contrast, it could be argued that many of the vices involve reflexivity in the sense of self-referentiality: valuing pleasure rather than the beings that we take pleasure in, valuing our love rather than the beings whom we love, valuing our own moral goodness rather than the good that we do.

This reflexivity has manifestly evil and apparently moral forms. The manifestly evil one is the attitude advocated by those economists who argue that friendship and family love are and ought to be based on investment in another for one's own future benefit. In the words of that wonderful satire on early capitalism, John Gay's *The Beggar's Opera*:

The Modes of the Court so common are grown,
That a true Friend can hardly be met,
Friendship for Interest is but a Loan,
Which they let out for what they can get.
'Tis true, you find
Some Friends so kind,
Who will give you good Counsel themselves to defend,
In sorrowful Ditty,
They promise, they pity,
But shift you for Money, from Friend to Friend.

(This should be sung to the tune of *Lilliburlero*.)

The economists normalise these corrupt 'modes of the court'. When economists leave behind their 'dismal science' of why low wages, high prices and unemployment are much to be desired and trespass on the land of personal relationships, their discipline becomes not just a dismal science but a satanic science.

However, there is also a moralistic, sometimes religious, version of self-referentiality. Consider the words of the hymn:

The trivial round, the common task,
Will furnish all we need to ask,
Room to deny ourselves, a road
To bring us daily nearer God.
(J. Keble, 'New every morning is the love',
in *Hymns Ancient and Modern*, no. 4)

Self-denial is not here seen as necessary for the sake of doing good to someone else, but as something to be desired independently of any good it does to others, for the sake of one's own salvation. Martin Luther would have regarded such self-referentiality as highly displeasing to God. Secular moralists have also criticised this attitude, for instance Bertrand Russell:

Conscious self-denial leaves a man self-absorbed and vividly aware of what he has sacrificed. . . . What is needed is not self-denial, but that kind of direction of interest outward which will lead spontaneously and naturally to the same acts that a person absorbed in the pursuit of his own virtue could only perform by means of conscious self-denial.
(*The Conquest of Happiness*, p. 158)

However, there is perhaps a certain irony that this wise advice should occur in a book with a title so suggestive of self-referentiality.

I am not claiming that *all* the vices involve reflexivity in this sense. Indeed, the very worst ones involve precisely absorption with the object of one's project in a way that is inordinate and idolatrous, such as the devotion to their nation-states of Bismarck or Stalin. But those vices which are called 'selfish' are better described as reflexive. If 'selfishness' is defined as wanting to get what one wants, it is easy (though incorrect) to present it as tautologically universal, and it is surprising how often one hears the view that everyone does everything out of selfishness, presented as though it were a tautology. But the point is not whether you try to satisfy your wants, but whether your wants are self-referential or not – that is, whether or not they can only be fully specified by including a 'for me' in their description. The selfish person is not the person who pursues their wants, but the person who has mainly self-referential wants (at worst, like our satanic economists, only self-referential wants). Unselfishness is not the denial of one's wants, but having wants that value their objects for what they are rather than for their effects on oneself.

But as the nationalist examples show, unselfishness is not a sufficient condition for virtue, only a necessary condition. Does this also apply to objectivity? The state-worshippers may exhibit objectivity as an attitude, but they are objectively wrong in their valuations. For different beings have different worths. Inordinate or idolatrous devotion to an object consists in a greater devotion to object A than to object B, when B has objectively more worth. The six million peasants deported by Stalin to Siberia had objectively more worth than the status of the Soviet Union as a world power.

It looks at this point as if we have arrived at two principles of ethics: objectivity as unself-referentiality and objectivity as rightly ordering the worth of beings. Actually, the former can be subsumed under the latter, since reflexive or self-referential desires value the lesser good, the pleasure or love, more than the greater, the being that is enjoyed or loved. One could then extend the ancient maxim 'Virtue is knowledge' into 'Virtue is objectivity.' I say extend, not paraphrase, since objectivity is a property, not just of knowledge, but of emotions.

Note

1   In Walrond-Skinner and Watson, *Ethical Issues in Family Therapy.*

References

Alexander, Samuel, *Space, Time and Deity*, Macmillan, London, 1920.
Anscombe, Elizabeth, *Collected Philosophical Papers*, vol. 2, Blackwell, Oxford, 1981.
Augustine, Aurelius, *Confessions*, Penguin, Harmondsworth, 1961.
Berdyaev, Nicholas, *The Beginning and the End*, Geoffrey Bles, London, 1952.
——, *Freedom and the Spirit*, Bles, London.
Bhaskar, Roy, *A Realist Theory of Science*, Leeds Books, Leeds, 1975.
——, *Scientific Realism and Human Emancipation*, Verso, London, 1986.
Blake, William, *Complete Writings*, Oxford University Press, London, 1966.
Bultmann, Rudolf, *Faith and Understanding*, SCM, London, 1969.
Collier, Andrew, *Being and Worth*, Routledge, London, 1999.

Farrington, Benjamin (ed.), *The Philosophy of Francis Bacon*, University of Chicago Press, Chicago, 1966.

Gay, John, *The Beggar's Opera* (lyrics from sleeve notes of EMI LP).

Heidegger, Martin, *Being and Time*, trans J. Macquarrie and E. Robinson, Blackwell, Oxford, 1967.

——— , *Basic Writings*, Routledge, London, 1978.

Kierkegaard, Soren, *The Present Age*, Oxford University Press, London, 1940.

——— , *Concluding Unscientific Postscript*, Princeton University Press, Princeton, 1941.

Kolnai, Aurel, *Ethics, Value and Reality*, The Athlone Press, London, 1977.

Laing, R.D., *The Self and Others*, Tavistock, London, 1961.

——— (with Aaron Esterson), *Sanity, Madness and the Family*, Tavistock, London, 1964.

——— (with H. Phillipson and A.R. Lee), *Interpersonal Perception*, Tavistock, London, 1966.

——— , *The Politics of the Family*, Tavistock, London, 1971.

——— , *The Voice of Experience*, Penguin, Harmondsworth, 1983.

Lévi-Strauss, Claude, *Tristes Tropiques*, Penguin, Harmondsworth, 1976.

Lewis, C.S., *Surprised by Joy*, Fount, London, 1977.

——— , *The Last Battle*, HarperCollins, London, 1980.

Macmurray, John, *The Philosophy of Communism*, Faber & Faber, London, 1933.

——— , *Reason and Emotion*, Faber & Faber, London, 1935.

——— , *Interpreting the Universe*, Faber & Faber, London, 1936.

——— , *Persons in Relation*, Faber & Faber, London, 1961.

Marx, Karl, *Early Texts*, ed. D. McLellan, Blackwell, Oxford, 1971.

Marx, Karl and Engels, Frederick, *Selected Works in One Volume*, Lawrence & Wishart, London, 1968.

——— , *Early Writings*, Penguin, Harmondsworth, 1975.

Millstone, Erik, 'Sweet and Sour', in *The Ecologist*, spring 1994; (see also Zwanenberg).

Mitchell, B. (ed.), *The Philosophy of Religion*, Oxford University Press, Oxford, 1971.

Plato, *Gorgias*, Bobbs Merrill, Indianapolis, 1952.

Russell, Bertrand, *The Conquest of Happiness*, Unwin, London, 1961.

Sartre, Jean-Paul, *Being and Nothingness*, Methuen, London, 1957.

——— , *The Transcendence of the Ego*, Noonday, New York, 1957.

——— , *In Camera* in *Three European Plays*, ed. E.M. Brown, Penguin, Harmondsworth, 1958.

——— , *Situations*, Hamish Hamilton, London, 1965.

Spinoza, Baruch (Benedict), 'On the Correction of the Understanding', in *Ethics*, trans. A. Boyle, Dent, London, 1910.

Walrond-Skinner, Sue and Watson, David (eds), *Ethical Issues in Family Therapy*, Routledge, London, 1987.

Watts, Alan, *The Way of Zen*, Penguin, Harmondsworth, 1962.

Zwanenberg, P. van and Millstone, E., 'Beyond Skeptical Relativism: Evaluating the Social Constructions of Expert Risk Assessments', in *Science, Technology and Human Values*, vol. 25, no. 3, 2000.

Index

Lightning Source UK Ltd.
Milton Keynes UK
UKOW06f0605010316

269363UK00005B/120/P

9 780415 436694